PRAISE FOR MASTERS OF TRUE CRIME

"A fascinating, must-read compendium of true crime by some of the genre's leading authors."

—Gary C. King
Bestselling author of *Blood Lust*

"[Readers] will quickly be caught up in each bizarre tale as the writers masterfully guide them through those dark places known only to homicide investigators and others closely connected to the world of murder."

—Kevin M. Sullivan
Author of *The Bundy Murders*

"A chilling selection of recent writing . . . in a dazzling array of the sinister, the absurd, and the just purely evil."

—Peter Vronsky
Author of *Serial Killers: The Method and Madness of Monsters*

"Striking, well-written tales sparkle in this ocean of murder."

—Diane Fanning
Author of *Mommy's Little Girl*

Friday
Jan 24, 2014

✓

MASTERS OF TRUE CRIME
CHILLING STORIES OF MURDER AND THE MACABRE
EDITED BY R. BARRI FLOWERS

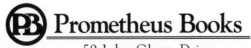

Prometheus Books

59 John Glenn Drive
Amherst, New York 14228-2119

Published 2012 by Prometheus Books

Cover image © 2012 Getty Images/Photo Alto Agency
Cover design by Nicole Sommer-Lecht

Inquiries should be addressed to
Prometheus Books
59 John Glenn Drive
Amherst, New York 14228–2119
VOICE: 716–691–0133
FAX: 716–691–0137
WWW.PROMETHEUSBOOKS.COM

16 15 14 13 12   5 4 3 2 1

Library of Congress Cataloging-in-Publication Data

Masters of true crime : chilling stories of murder and the macabre / edited by R. Barri Flowers.
       p. cm.
    ISBN 978–1–61614–567–5 (pbk.)
    ISBN 978–1–61614–568–2 (ebook)
    1. Murder—Case studies. 2. Murderers—Case studies. 3. Crime—Case studies. I. Flowers, R. Barri (Ronald Barri)

HV6515.M32 2012
364.152'3—dc23

                                                                    2012013318

Printed in the United States of America

To my loving wife, H. Loraine, for her undying support.
And to "Big D," my little brother, a budding screenwriter.

Also to my alma mater, Michigan State University, and its great
School of Criminal Justice, as well as to fans of gripping true-crime tales.

CONTENTS

A NOTE FROM
THE EDITOR

I conceived the idea for this anthology as a means to gather a group of veteran true-crime authors, journalists, and others with impressive credentials in the world of true crime and criminals to lend their diverse voices to a collection of true-crime tales. The result is seventeen gripping stories that explore historical and modern-day true crimes involving murder, mayhem, madness, and some truly terrifying and often cunning perpetrators and hapless victims.

I commend the contributors to this anthology for taking time out of their busy schedules to share their stories, making this book worthy of the title *Masters of True Crime*.

Readers will undoubtedly find the collection to be a winning one and will want to look for other true-crime material by the contributors or search out more in-depth material on the subject.

The truth is always more absorbing than fiction, and, unlike invented stories, each tale in this collection really happened.

So sit back and read each terrific account for yourself!

—R. Barri Flowers

Foreword

THE SEDUCTION OF WHY

by Katherine Ramsland

I have been reading true crime for several decades and writing it for over fifteen years. For me, it all started with a serial killer dumping the bodies of young women in fields around my hometown when I was a kid. I read the newspapers as each new picture was posted of a smiling girl, who was now dead, and as more puzzle pieces were added from crime scene behavior. An unknown menace confronted us, and it was scary . . . and exciting. Enthralling, actually. A map showed me just how close to my home each murder had been.

This unknown killer was stalking two adjacent college campuses and the countryside in between. He even taunted a renowned psychic who arrived to assist the police. He went to a funeral home to look at a mutilated victim and stood outside a building that police were searching, eluding them in broad daylight. He seemed like a phantom they'd never catch. Everyone was tense, their hearts pounding. But then he was caught, and we held our collective breath to see who he was. It turned out to be a handsome college boy studying to be an elementary school teacher, who was close to graduation. He had traveled, too, so he might have been gone in a flash, never caught.

A few years later, I read the true-crime book that was published about him and thought the investigative procedure had been lacking. Assumptions about guilt were rampant, triggering plenty of confirmation bias. Just one of the seven dead girls could be linked to the killer.

So, I started reading more. I went to graduate school to acquire more forensic education and wrote articles for Court TV's (now TruTV) *Crime Library*. I continued to believe that procedures for that case had relied on faulty assumptions and junk science, but the draw to follow a true-crime story never diminished.

I generally post a true-crime news story each day on my Facebook® page. One of the more interesting tales from the past year featured "the Perfumer," a multilingual Russian historian who searched cemeteries for the bodies of young women to bring home to his apartment. He had desecrated over 150 graves to grab enough corpses to create twenty-nine "dolls," which he dressed in clothing stolen from the cemetery. *Why?* That's the question that calls me to true crime. It probably draws the majority of writers in this anthology, and most of our readers.

So, when I was invited to submit a story, I looked for a unique case—a middle-aged Italian woman who had killed and dismembered three friends, baking their blood into cakes in a misguided effort to save her son. She told the court her reasons, but this still didn't fully address why she would—*could*—do this. Friends don't cut up friends with cleavers and saws.

As I read the other contributions, I observed that my anthology mates also looked for something out of the ordinary. Carol Anne Davis, a long-time true-crime author whom I admire, brings us a little-known child arsonist with a low IQ who found revenge for abuse and bullying in the form of flames that engulfed other people. He's among the youngest serial killers in the world, and was stunningly prolific.

From the same era, the 1970s, R. Barri Flowers tells the story of a Bundy-esque serial killer, Donald Miller, who once had been a clean-cut youth minister. An angry narcissist rejected by a woman, he killed several more women pretty much in his own backyard. But like most narcissists, his madding sense of immunity was his weakness.

Harold Schechter needs no introduction to readers of true crime, having covered some of the most sensational offenders in American history. In his unerring sense of time and place, he re-creates one of Manhattan's most intensive murder investigations from the 1930s. The wife of an NBC executive is found dead in her home in an exclusive neighborhood, a place where she herself believed that "nothing could ever happen to anyone." A character in this tragic tale is the renowned biochemist Alexander O. Gettler, a "modern Merlin," who pushed the trace evidence toward an unexpected suspect.

But no one had to investigate James Ruppert, who turned himself in after slaughtering his entire family in Ohio on Easter Day. Former detective turned writer Lee Lofland moves us through this bloody rampage as if we'd been there.

In this book, attorneys, reporters, professors, cops, and true-crime writers describe exploding bombs, missing persons, cold cases, domestic homicides, organized crime, escaped convicts, kids gone wrong, a dead Girl Scout, and even a psychopathic Russian countess. There is truly something for everyone, and it's easy to move from one story to another without stopping.

Many people believe that the lure of a crime story like those you'll find in these pages is its core mystery. We all love a good challenge. But then again, we're not just sitting around doing thousand-piece jigsaw puzzles of sunsets, so the lure of true crime is not just about a mental challenge. I recall too well the chill I felt when another dead girl turned up in my hometown, reminding us we were not safe. So, I think we also like being scared.

Danger is strangely attractive. It's arousing, and this makes us feel alive. When we read true-crime accounts, we can experience this shivering dread within a protective frame. The stories fascinate us, but we also know we can put the book down and walk away. We can feel the energy without being overwhelmed by anxiety. We get close to the bodies without having to do the autopsy, or see through a killer's eyes without concern over being arrested. We're voyeurs. We step through a massacre to satisfy our morbid curiosity but also to raise our sense of anger: we want good to prevail, limping along though it may be, and the perp to go down. The investigation that probes closer and closer provides tension and relief, and the court case with a final just verdict is cathartic. If the story is well told, we feel for the victims, the investigators, and the families who must suffer through it. With the exception of crimes not solved or bodies never found, these stories feel right. They restore our sense of safety and hope.

Fans of true crime are always looking for new and unique stories, and here we have seventeen tales by some of the best writers in the genre today.

Chapter 1

TERROR IN EAST LANSING

The Michigan State University Serial Killer

by R. Barri Flowers

In the latter part of the 1970s, Michigan's Big Ten school Michigan State University (MSU) in East Lansing was the place to be for higher education, athletics, sexual experimentation, keggers, smoking pot, and expressing oneself. The school had a well-deserved reputation for partying. And MSU in the 1970s also turned out to be the place and time for a brutal serial killer to emerge, one who would take aim at young women, sexually assaulting them before violently ending their lives.

Donald Miller was not just another serial killer. The twenty-four-year-old graduate of MSU's renowned School of Criminal Justice once seemed to be on track for a totally different connection with the criminal justice system. But at some point, destiny took a deadly turn, and Miller achieved the distinction of becoming East Lansing's and MSU's only known serial killer—a distinction the community would prefer to forget. But Miller left a mark that seemingly makes such a thing impossible in the halls of academia and the surrounding area.

Michigan State University's School of Criminal Justice, founded in 1935, is the country's oldest continuous program for granting degrees in criminal justice. Originally known as the School of Public Administration and Public Safety, it followed the "land-grant philosophy" established by Michigan State Agricultural College. This philosophy is derived from the Morrill Act, signed in 1862 by President Abraham Lincoln to provide a generous "grant of land to each state, the revenue of which was to be used for the development and support of agriculture schools."

Within this context, the land-grant institution became the first college in the nation to offer a bachelor of science degree in police administration, the intent being to use scientific education and training to properly prepare students for careers in law enforcement, in private investigation, and in other areas of criminal justice.

By 1977, MSU's School of Criminal Justice had presented undergraduate and graduate degrees to thousands of students under the direction and tutelage of such criminal justice and criminology legends as Donald Bremer, Arthur Brandstatter, Ralph Turner, Robert Scott, Louis Radelet, Zolton Ferency, Leon Weaver, Vincent Hoffman, and Robert Trojanowicz, among others.

Donald Miller was among those graduates to receive a degree in criminal justice from Michigan State. But rather than use it to pursue a career in law enforcement, government, or perhaps teaching, he took a decidedly different and dark path, turning into a psychopath, rapist, and serial killer.

Born on December 28, 1954, Donald Gene Miller was described as the "quintessential boy-next-door." Having grown up in a peaceful, middle-class area in the college town of East Lansing, Michigan, during the rebellious 1970s, it would have been quite easy for him to have gotten caught up in the type of crowd among which long hair, drug use, and sowing one's oats was fairly common. Instead, by all accounts, Miller walked the straight and narrow, respected his elders, kept his hair short, and was a youth minister at the local church. He attended Michigan State University, majoring in criminal justice. It seemed like he was well on his way toward finding a successful career in law enforcement or some other impressive occupation within the world of law and order.

Adding to this picture of apparent perfection, Miller had started dating a girl from his church, Martha Sue Young, who lived down the street and was friends with Miller's older sister. By the winter of 1976, Miller, twenty-one, and nineteen-year-old Young, who also attended Michigan State, were engaged. The couple seemed to be headed toward matrimony and a good life as two bright students in love with life and each other.

But that all changed rather abruptly. Just before New Year's Eve 1976, Young called off the engagement. According to her mother, Sue Young, there were a number of reasons her daughter did not go through with the marriage, such as "the fact that Don was twenty[-two] years old and never had a job," apart from a brief stint working in a resort community the previous summer.

The two also differed in their attitudes about education. Whereas Young loved college and was serious about studying and getting good grades, Miller felt just the opposite. "Don never studies, and his grades aren't good," Martha told her mother. Sue Young noted that her daughter enjoyed athletics and socializing in college but complained that "it's not only that [Don] doesn't, but he doesn't want me to either."

Whatever the reasons, or combination thereof, for breaking off their engagement, an embittered Miller had no intention of fading into the woodwork as Young sought greener pastures. Miller was able to convince her that they should remain friends at the very least, insisting that she keep the engagement ring, no strings attached with regard to the promise of future romance.

Young, who may have been wary of such an offer, chose to give her ex-fiancé the benefit of the doubt and maintain the friendship. Based on Miller's clean record with the law, on their being members of the same church, and on the strong camaraderie between their families, it seemed there was no harm in giving Miller at least this much.

But Young could not read Miller's devious mind. Nor did she realize that he was anything but a safe bet—not until it was too late to change the dark destiny in store for her.

New Year's Day 1977 marked the start of the winter term at Michigan State University, with students streaming back on to the campus from Christmas break, prepared to resume their march toward fulfilling necessary requirements for degrees. Then, of course, there was catching up with old friends, making new ones, and partying—both to welcome in the New Year and simply for the sake of keeping up with campus traditions.

It was on that cold day that Martha Sue Young went missing. East Lansing police officer Kenneth Ouellette had just begun his shift when the call came in. It was from Gene Miller, Donald's father. Ouellette knew the Millers because he and Donald had sometimes gone to a local sportsman and rifle club together.

Gene Miller was calling the station at the request of Sue Young, Martha's mother. The young woman was missing after allegedly being dropped off at her home by Donald a few hours earlier, having gone out with him as friends.

Ouellette went to Young's house, initially believing there was probably nothing to worry about. "Typically, most of these things turn out to be that they stayed at a friend's house or their date's house," the officer suggested. "It's that college-town type of thing you associate with it."

But Ouellette changed his tune once he got to the house. Martha Sue Young's disappearance suddenly struck him as anything but normal. As he homed in on some of the things about her and Donald, such as that they did not drink, that neither were known to be active in the party scene, that both still lived at home, and that both attended church regularly and held religious views that were conservative, the officer grew increasingly concerned about Martha's unexplained absence.

In 1985, Michigan State University's School of Criminal Justice celebrated its fiftieth anniversary. With a rich history of producing graduates who went into fields across the criminal justice spectrum and around the world, there was reason to celebrate.

When the new program began in 1935, there were a mere twenty-three freshman and eleven sophomore and junior enrollees. By 1985, enrollment in the school had soared to six hundred undergraduate students, one hundred and fifteen students seeking master's degrees, and twenty PhD candidates.

Among the school's accomplishments was the first annual Institute on Police Community Relations in 1955 and a designation by the Law Enforcement Assistance Administration in 1973 as a national center of excellence. According to a 1979 article in the *Journal of Criminal Justice*, "Michigan State University ha[d] the highest known reputation among the almost 1,200 criminal justice programs in the country." Moreover, the Joint Commission of Criminology and Criminal Justice Education and Standards had consistently rated the School of Criminal Justice as one of the top two such programs in the nation.

In all, nearly six thousand students had graduated from the School of Criminal Justice in the program's first fifty years, many going on to distinguished careers in law enforcement, government, criminology, and other related fields.

A few days before Martha Young's disappearance, the coed had expressed relief that Donald Miller had seemingly accepted the end of their engagement with no hard feelings. As a result, she even agreed to attend Miller's birthday party at the home of a friend of his grandmother the following evening as previously planned, if only to keep up appearances for his family.

On Friday afternoon, New Year's Eve 1976, Young stopped by the Great Steak Restaurant in East Lansing, where her mother was having lunch with a friend, to show the two women the shoes she had purchased for a party she planned to attend on New Year's Day. It seemed as though 1977 was destined to get off to a great start for the college student.

That evening, Sue Young was in the kitchen when Martha came in to give her a kiss good-bye before leaving for what was supposed to be a fun night that she and Donald Miller were sure to enjoy.

It would be the last time Sue Young would ever see her daughter alive.

Police officer Kenneth Ouellette was worried about the missing Martha Sue Young. And there was plenty to consider when it came to her health and safety. "We started to focus in on the fact that Donald was not a drinker or a partier," Ouellette said. "Martha Sue was not a partier, they both lived at home, they both had conservative religious views, they were active in the church. As I would eliminate some of these things, the concern grew."

As a result of the officer's alarm over Martha Young's inexplicable and uncharacteristic absence, he focused his investigation on the last known person believed to have seen her alive: Donald Miller.

At midnight on January 1, 1977, Peter Houk took his place as Ingham County's new prosecuting attorney. His very first case turned out to be one of the most important and publicized of his career. It also laid the groundwork in forever changing the facade of innocence and safety that had seemed a given across the beautiful campus of Michigan State and the surrounding community. A killer was on the loose and hidden in plain sight.

The spotlight was squarely on Donald Miller, whose alibi would be discredited over the coming months. Evidence indicated that Miller had not told police everywhere he had been on the day Martha Sue Young disappeared. He took two polygraph tests and failed both. The lack of emotion shown by the suspect about his ex-fiancée's disappearance gave the authorities and family members of the missing young woman further cause for suspicion.

Houk and the lead investigator, East Lansing police detective Rick Westgate, had little doubt that Martha Young was the victim of foul play and that Miller was behind it. Unfortunately, there was no solid evidence to build a case. Without such, Miller was able to remain free, which would cost other young women their lives. For the time being, there wasn't anything the authorities could do about it.

The suspect lived with his parents, who staunchly supported his innocence, much to the chagrin of the police, who were convinced otherwise. Westgate would later say, "If the parents hadn't been so stubborn and they had listened to all of the information we had regarding where he had been, if they wouldn't have blocked us, there wouldn't have been three other homicides."

Miller found work as a security guard after graduating from Michigan State University with a degree in criminal justice. To law enforcement and prosecutors, this was surely a slap in the face. Miller, who should have been on the road to becoming one of their own, had instead thumbed his nose at them, almost daring them to prove what they knew before he killed again.

Almost a year passed before the authorities finally got a break in the case that had gone nowhere. A high priority had been given to the case in an effort to reassure coeds that the college campus was safe with a normally low rate of violent crime in East Lansing, in spite of the unsolved mystery of Martha Sue Young's disappearance.

In October 1977, clothing belonging to Young was found in Bath Township, just north of East Lansing. According to police, it had been "systematically placed as if she'd levitated out of her clothes."

"That's when our office, in particular, and East Lansing knew we were dealing with something out of the normal," Houk recalled. "We were convinced we were dealing with some type of psychopath."

Unfortunately, this crime took place in the pre-DNA-technology era, making it difficult to cull any useful evidence from the clothing and crime scene. Minus the solid physical evidence needed, authorities were unable to charge Miller with anything. Once again, the case was stalled, and the killer continued to plot his strategy for more victims right under the noses of the police.

On June 15, 1978, twenty-eight-year-old Marita Choquette went missing from her apartment in Grand Ledge, Michigan, a city west of downtown Lansing, the state's capital, and popular with rock climbers because of its ancient sandstone and quartzite rock ledges. Choquette worked for WKAR, a television station in East Lansing.

Twelve days after Choquette's disappearance, her mutilated remains were found in Holt, southeast of Lansing. The same day, June 28, 1978, Wendy Bush, a twenty-one-year-old student at MSU, disappeared. She was last seen alive on campus outside of Case Hall, home to James Madison College in the South Complex.

It was obvious to authorities, students, and East Lansing residents alike that a killer was on the loose, targeting young women and almost daring the police to stop him in his tracks. But before they could do so, another life was claimed.

On August 14, 1978, Kristine Rose Stuart, a thirty-year-old middle-school teacher who happened to live just blocks from Donald Miller's house, vanished. This, in addition to the other cases of murdered and missing women, caused hysteria on and off campus, with the local media feeding the flames, fury, and fear of a serial killer at large.

"It was very unnerving," Detective Westgate recalled. "You just don't have things like that go on in the community."

For the thousands of coeds and other women in the normally tranquil college town, that fact was small consolation, as a murderer had obviously made his presence felt and intended to strike fear into the hearts of those most vulnerable.

As with most serial killers, overconfidence and a brazen, reckless nature proved to be this one's undoing. On August 15, 1978, with the disappearance of Kristine Stuart still very fresh, Donald Miller randomly picked a house in East Lansing where he sexually assaulted and attempted to murder fourteen-year-old Lisa Gilbert. Her younger brother Randy came home during the attack, and Miller went after him.

Lisa managed to escape from the house and go for help. A local fireman spotted Miller's car leaving the scene and called the East Lansing Police Department.

With several eyewitnesses, the police were finally able to get what they needed to arrest Donald Miller. Having worked the case for many months and coming up empty, a relieved Westgate took the suspect into custody.

Former prosecuting attorney Houk was especially pleased that Miller had been apprehended. "I had a wife, I had a young daughter, and I used to be terrified at night when Donald Miller was on the loose because I was certain he was a serial killer," he recalled. "I used to take to sleeping down on my couch in the living room."

In 1979, after a trial by jury in Eaton County, Donald Gene Miller was convicted of "two counts of assault with intent to commit murder and one count of first-degree criminal sexual conduct" in the attacks on Lisa Gilbert and Randy Gilbert. Miller was sentenced to three concurrent terms of thirty to fifty years behind bars.

Miller's imprisonment notwithstanding, the police still did not know the whereabouts of the four young women they were convinced he had murdered. In an attempt to put closure to the cases for families of the victims, the decision was made to offer Miller a plea deal, with the cooperation of Sue Young, Martha's mother, and Ernie Stuart, the husband of Kristine Stuart.

In addition to his earlier convictions, Donald Miller pleaded guilty in 1979 to two counts of manslaughter in the deaths of Young and Stuart, and he assisted authorities in locating the remains of the murdered, missing women.

With the help of psychiatrists and the "truth serum" drug sodium amytal, Miller confessed to killing all four women. In July 1979, he led authorities to the skeletal remains of his ex-fiancée, Martha Sue Young, and of schoolteacher Kristine Stuart.

"He knew exactly where he was taking us," Westgate indicated. "He didn't even get out of the car. He just pointed to where [they were]."

Miller's defense attorney, Thomas Bengston, tried to explain his client's murderous actions. He suggested that Miller had "severe mental illness," which caused him to "lose control of his conduct."

Law enforcement officials saw Miller as merely another serial killer who found sexual and sadistic satisfaction in murdering his victims and burying them where they couldn't be found without his help.

Incredibly, the plea bargain to which Donald Miller agreed did not add any time to the thirty to fifty years behind bars to which he had already been sentenced. Regardless, the higher end of that term would have been enough to keep him incarcerated for a good while, had it not been for issues within the Michigan prison system that allowed Miller's sentence to be reduced.

In 1999, at age forty-four, after spending twenty years in prison with time off for good behavior, Miller was eligible for parole. That wasn't exactly what the family members of his victims had envisioned when the plea bargain had been approved.

"You talk about a guy who had unbelievable luck," Houk griped. "Michigan enters into a real crisis in prisons, and we start whopping all sorts of prison time off of prison sentences, so [Miller's] forty-year prison sentence in the Eaton County case gets reduced by almost half, and he became eligible for parole."

There was little reason to believe that Donald Miller had been adequately rehabilitated while serving time. Studies show that few violent offenders have been able to successfully rehabilitate within the difficult environment of the prison system. Indeed, according to Dr. Frank Ochberg, former director of the Michigan Department of Mental Health, "These guys don't get better. After they pass such a certain threshold, none of them can be treated or reformed. They are ruthless predators."

With this in mind, and with the clock ticking until the day Miller walked out of prison a free man, concerned members of the community, including Ochberg, Houk, Sue Young, and Donna Irish (stepmother of Lisa and Randy Gilbert), banded together to try to find a way to keep Donald Miller locked up. At the very least, they were determined to keep an eye on him and keep the city of East Lansing safe should he be released.

It took months before Eaton County Prosecutor Jeffrey Sauter uncovered information that would prevent Miller from being released anytime soon. It turned out that, in 1994, a weapon was confiscated from Miller's three-person cell by prison officials. The weapon, found in a footlocker inside a box with velvet lining, was a "heavy, six-foot shoelace with two large wooden buttons attached that had been tied with a large knot." This was considered a tool that could be used to strangle someone.

Sauter, with help from Chippewa County and Ingham County prosecutors, went to court with this information in 1998. Felony charges of harboring a concealed weapon were filed against Miller. If the jury found him guilty, Miller would have four convictions of felonies, which could lead to a life sentence without the possibility of parole.

Donald Miller; his parents, Gene and Elaine Miller; and his attorney battled back, claiming that the shoelace hardly constituted a weapon and that Miller was being "railroaded." During the trial, his attorney was successfully able to suppress evidence of Miller's previous crimes, meaning the case had to be decided without the jury's knowledge of the murders he had committed.

That didn't help Miller. He was convicted of intending to use the shoelace as a weapon and received an additional sentence of twenty to forty years in prison.

Needless to say, the East Lansing community was relieved that Miller would have to remain behind bars for years to come. "That means, in my lifetime, he's never going to get out of prison," Ochberg remarked. "It really was a wonderful thing."

Lisa Gilbert, who survived an attack by Miller, concurred. "Life without parole sounds better," she said, "but I'll take twenty to forty."

Since Martha Sue Young's death, her mother, Sue Young, has campaigned for antiviolence and longer sentencing for violent criminals. "We need to start looking at the things we tolerate," Young said. "We're naive in thinking that there isn't real evil in the world."

As proof of this, Young never saw her daughter's murder coming. Donald Miller was perhaps the last person she would have suspected as her daughter's killer. As she put it, "He was normal, everybody thought. He was the guy next door."

Unfortunately, when it comes to serial killers, it is often the unassuming neighbor who may become a target's worst nightmare. Many serial killers also go after intimates and family, putting them at greater risk than strangers.

In the case of Donald Miller, this proved all too true for Martha Sue Young.

In 2010, Michigan State University's School of Criminal Justice celebrated its seventy-fifth anniversary with much pomp and ceremony and events throughout the year to mark the historic achievement. An annual Wall of Fame was established in 2000 to honor alumni who had "distinguished themselves within the field of criminal justice while maintaining the highest standards of integrity and character."

Since the school's inception, the number of alumni has risen to more than ten thousand students who have taken their education and occupational goals around the globe and put them to good use.

At least one exception was alumnus Donald Miller, who cast a shadow over the school's worthy reputation, now serving time as a serial rapist and murderer.

———————

As a 2006 Wall of Fame inductee, I am also a graduate of the Michigan State University School of Criminal Justice, having received my bachelor's degree the very year Miller murdered his ex-fiancée, Martha Sue Young. I went on to receive a master's degree from the school before embarking on a successful career as a literary criminologist and bestselling author. My work includes this piece about fellow alumnus Donald Miller and the havoc he brought upon the college and community as a result of his homicidal rage.

ABOUT THE AUTHOR

R. BARRI FLOWERS is an award-winning criminologist and bestselling author of more than sixty books and numerous articles and short stories. He has also edited two American Crime Writers League mystery short-story anthologies. His true-crime books include *Serial Killer Couples*; *The Sex Slave Murders*; *Mass Murder in the Sky*; and *Murder in the United States*. His criminology titles include *College Crime*; *Male Crime and Deviance*; *Female Crime*; *Criminals and Cellmates*; *Sex Crimes*; and *Prostitution in the Digital Age*. The author has appeared on the Biography Channel's *Crime Stories* episode "The Love Slave Murders" and on Investigation Discovery's *Wicked Attraction* episode "Twisted Twosome," and has been interviewed by ABC News. Flowers is the recipient of the Wall of Fame Award from Michigan State University's renowned School of Criminal Justice. In the works are true-crime tales on Bonnie and Clyde, the St. Valentine's Day Massacre, a criminology book on homicide, as well as a thriller novel set in Honolulu, Hawaii, and a young-adult mystery. Learn more about upcoming books from the author at www.rbarriflowers.com.

REFERENCES

"Admitted Killer Leads Police to Third Body." 1979. *Ludington Daily News* 89 (July 18): 205. http://news.google.com/newspapers?id=M9VOAAAAIBAJ&sjid =IkoDAAAAIBAJ&pg=5612,6918758&dq=michigan+state+university +student+murdered&hl=en.

Carpenter, Jacob. 2007. "East Lansing's Only Serial Killer Struck 30 Years Ago, Today He Is Serving His Term in Lenawee County." *State News*, November 8. http://www.statenews.com/index.php/article/2007/11/east_lansings_only _serial_killer_struck_30_years_ago.

Flowers, R. Barri. 2003. *Male Crime and Deviance: Exploring Its Cause, Dynamics, and Nature*. Springfield, IL: Charles C. Thomas.

———. 2009. *College Crime: A Statistical Study of Offenses on American Campuses*. Jefferson, NC: McFarland.

Flowers, R. Barri, and H. Loraine Flowers. 2004. *Murders in the United States: Crimes, Killers and Victims of the Twentieth Century*. Jefferson, NC: McFarland.

"The Killer Next Door." 2009. *48 Hours Mystery*. CBS News, February 11. http://www.cbsnews.com/stories/1999/01/06/48hours/main27268.shtml.

Rykert, Wilber L. 1985. "The History of the School of Criminal Justice at Michigan State University 1935–1963." Master's thesis, Michigan State University. http://www.cj.msu.edu/~history/rykert.html.

"The School of Criminal Justice—50th Anniversary Jubilee." 1985. Michigan State University, School of Criminal Justice. http://www.cj.msu.edu/~history/ 50hist.html.

State of Michigan Court of Appeals. 2000. Plaintiff Appellee v. Donald Gene Miller, May 30. http://statecasefiles.justia.com/documents/michigan/court-of-appeals -unpublished/20000530_C215237(0048)_215237 .OPN.PDF?13166 44524.

Trojanowicz, Robert C. 1985. "Michigan State's School of Criminal Justice Cele- brates 50th Anniversary." *Police Chief* 8:70–71.

Young, Sue. 2005. Lethal Friendship: A Mother's Battle to Put—and Keep—a Serial Killer behind Bars. Bloomington, IN: iUniverse.

Chapter 2

TWISTED FIRESTARTER

by Carol Anne Davis

Britain is well known for its serial killers, including the Moors Murderers, the Yorkshire Ripper, and Fred and Rose West. But few people are aware of the many deaths brought about by Peter Dinsdale, who began a murder spree when he was only twelve.

It was June 1973 when the twelve-year-old claimed his first victim. He was jealous of a six-year-old disabled boy, Richard Ellerington, whom he saw daily on the school bus, a boy who came from a loving and stable environment. Peter, who was himself disabled with a withered right hand and a partially paralyzed arm and leg, was hurting emotionally and wanted to cause the younger child even more pain.

He entered the boy's house through an open window and set the place on fire, using paraffin and matches. The parents, though injured, managed to save their able-bodied children, but despite numerous attempts to enter Richard's flame-filled bedroom, their son died. Investigators thought that the blaze might have been caused by a faulty gas oven, though no definite conclusion was reached at the time.

Twelve-year-old Peter had enjoyed watching the flames and hearing his victims' screams, so, four months later, he killed for the second time, apparently choosing his victim at random. He entered the house of an elderly reclusive man, Bernard Smythe, and set a fire close to his upholstered armchair. The seventy-two-year-old died of smoke inhalation, as he was too frail to reach the door and call for help. Peter would later say that fire was his master; that he loved watching the flames take hold.

Three weeks elapsed before the juvenile arsonist crept into the house of a thirty-four-year-old man, David Brewer, who had previously hit him for breaking into his pigeon loft. (It's likely that Peter had planned to hurt or kill the birds in an act of juvenile sadism.) He poured paraffin over his sleeping victim and set him on fire before leaving the premises. The burning man—who was already disabled following an accident at work—staggered next door, collapsed, and lapsed into a coma, dying of his burns within days. This, too, was seen as an accidental death, as the man had had clothes drying close to a paraffin fire, and it was believed that they had caught alight and that he had tried to put them out and set himself on fire. No one knew that the small, thin boy who limped and held his arm oddly across his chest had begun to kill and planned to kill again.

So what kind of upbringing produces such a troubled child? Peter was the illegitimate child of a heavy-drinking prostitute, Doreen Dinsdale. She had separated from his father during the pregnancy, and he had no part in the boy's upbringing. Within weeks of Peter's birth in Manchester, England, on July 31, 1960, she had returned to sex work and often brought strangers to their modest home. Ashamed of having a disabled child, she often left little Peter locked in his bedroom while she entertained these men. A year later, she gave birth to a girl, his half sister, who was equally neglected and failed to thrive.

Sometimes Doreen held drinking parties, and the hungry toddler would stagger around drinking dregs of beer from discarded cans. Social workers investigated to find that both children were undernourished, poorly clad, and frightened. They were taken into care for their own protection, but at that time in Britain many care homes were staffed by pedophiles, and Peter would later admit that he was frequently sexually abused. He was also sexually assaulted by older inmates; his life was a living hell.

During the next few years, Peter's life would be a case of "out of the frying pan, into the fire" as he was moved between abusive orphanages and his inadequate parent. In the 1960s, it was believed that a child should be with his mother, whatever her failings, so at age six he was returned to her—she was now living in Hull, a large industrial town in England. But she had become an alcoholic and neglected him so relentlessly that social workers soon returned him to the orphanage. They would carry out such experiments again and again over the years, sending him home to be badly treated, then taking him back when he became increasingly disturbed. Lost and alone, he often walked the streets at night, hoping that someone would buy him alcohol so that he could briefly block out the reality of his sad life.

The lack of nurturing had taken its toll on Peter's brain; his IQ peaked at seventy-five, which is educationally subnormal. (Later tests by a prison doctor would suggest that Peter's IQ was as low as sixty-eight.) He struggled to read and write and was woefully inarticulate. As a result, the other children bullied him, said that he was an idiot, and nicknamed him Daft Peter. His rage built and built. He also suffered from epilepsy, though this was controlled by medication. All that he believed he was good for was setting fires.

So far, no one had linked Peter Dinsdale's arson attacks. All the deaths were believed to be accidental, as many people in the area had paraffin fires, and spillages were common. Chip-pan fires and smoking-related deaths—when smokers fell asleep, dropped their cigarette, and set their clothes or sheets on fire—were also common occurrences at the time.

For the next fourteen months, the angry boy kept a low profile. Detectives would later speculate that he lit smaller, nonlethal fires in this time frame or that he attempted to light some that didn't fully ignite—he would admit that he lost track of the number of blazes he was responsible for. He loved to witness a conflagration; it was the only thing that made him feel special and that assuaged his rage. Watching flames destroy a building became the teenager's favorite occupation, as he had no friends, no hobbies, no interest in schoolwork, and no future plans. He would later say that he was equally happy to torch a deserted building as an occupied one, but psychologists didn't believe him, as he seemed to take pleasure in hearing cries of distress and particularly enjoyed destroying families.

In December 1974, he entered the bedroom of partially sighted and disabled eighty-two-year-old Elizabeth Rokahr and lit a fire, exulting as the blaze took hold. She burned to death, but the authorities didn't suspect that it was a deliberate attack, as she was known to smoke in bed. Neighbors told police that she was a very careful smoker, but they weren't convinced. As was often the case with a Dinsdale fire, he had started such a fierce blaze that the building was burned to the ground, leaving few clues.

For a year and a half, the boy kept his murderous desires in check, perhaps because he was spending time with a kindly foster mother. Then, in June 1976, he entered the home of a schoolmate and used paraffin and matches to set a downstairs cupboard on fire before creeping out of the apartment. The grandmother of the boy, seventy-seven-year-old Dorothy Edwards, who was babysitting her three grandchildren, got the oldest two out of the house and took them to a neighbor for safety. It was only when the neighbor asked if there was anyone else in the house that she remembered the baby sleeping upstairs. Despite herculean attempts, no one was able to save the one-year-old, Andrew Edwards, who perished in the flames. The police thought that some of the older children must have been playing with matches (though the parents protested that they didn't keep matches in the house), so it was seen as a tragic accident rather than an arson-related death. The unfortunate grandmother was so traumatized by the loss of the baby that she was later committed to a mental hospital.

Dinsdale's next victim, in January 1977, was even younger. He had been in the habit of visiting a local family to see their pigeons, but the man of the household, Peter Thacker, had challenged him over his tendency to walk into their house uninvited. The young arsonist hated being told what to do, so he became hell-bent on revenge. He sneaked into the house and set fire to the nursery of six-month-old Katrina Thacker. She died of smoke inhalation in the resultant inferno and was found lifeless in her cot.

Afterward, the teenage arsonist made a chillingly macabre visit to the funeral parlor and saw the tiny corpse. He would later say that he was sorry that he'd killed such a young child, that he liked babies. Indeed, at one point, authorities, trying to install a sense of community spirit in the too-quiet youngster, found him some volunteer work with little children. He appeared to get on well with them, as they were less threatening than his peers. He was also a religious boy who often carried a Bible and was presumably aware of the tenet that one must not harm a hair on a child's head. But detectives would later come to believe that he was incapable of true remorse, that he merely said he was sorry about the child's death, as that was what people wanted to hear.

His next eleven alleged victims—Harold Akester, ninety-five; Victor Consitt, eighty-three; Benjamin Phillips, eighty-three; Arthur Ellwood, eighty-two; William Hoult, eighty-two; William Carter, eighty; Percy Sanderson, seventy-seven; John Rilby, seventy-five; William Beales, seventy-three; Leonard Dennet, seventy-three; and Arthur Hardy, sixty-five—were killed in a single blaze. The attack took place at a home for the elderly, Wensley Lodge, also in Hull, a mere three days after the death of the six-month-old. This time, the teenager would claim that he had to break a window before he could enter the premises. He would allege that he set several fires, only leaving the building when the flames had thoroughly taken hold and that he mingled for a while outside with onlookers. He'd also later talk to detectives about hearing the old men's agonized screams.

Several of the would-be rescuers were badly burned as they tried to save the former war veterans, some of whom could be heard begging for help and pleading for divine intervention. But a thirteen-day inquiry ruled that the fire had started accidentally, as a plumber had been using a blowtorch on the premises earlier that day. So police still weren't looking for an arsonist. The plumber protested vociferously that he had followed safety procedures and wasn't responsible, but he was left unfairly with a stain on his character.

And still the carnage continued. In April 1977, Dinsdale followed yet another happy family home, returning after dark to ruin their lives forever. This time, a thirteen-year-old mentally challenged girl, Deborah Hooper, and the son of a family friend, seven-year-old Mark Jordan, died in the inferno. The latter had reached safety but went back to rescue the older girl with fatal results. The younger boy had shown a sense of responsibility and self-sacrifice that the arsonist simply wasn't capable of. Jordan was later awarded a posthumous award for bravery.

Nine months elapsed before Peter Dinsdale fatally struck again in January 1978. This time, he chose a house at random: that of twenty-four-year-old Christine Dickson, her husband, and their four sons. Peter poured accelerant, contained in a bottle of dishwashing liquid, through the mailbox slot, then pushed in a flaming piece of paper after it. In the conflagration that resulted, Christine handed her baby to a neighbor through a window before going back into the inferno in an attempt to save her other three children. But she was overcome by the heat and died alongside five-year-old Mark, four-year-old Steven, and sixteen-month-old Michael. Her husband, who was ill at the time the blaze broke out, survived.

Dinsdale would later say that he only cared about the fire and didn't think about the occupants, but in reality he was willing to ruin lives with the casualness of a person stepping on an ant. And he often hung around outside a house until the inhabitants returned, only then setting the place alight. He would eventually tell prison authorities that he often waited until 3:00 a.m. before pouring accelerant and putting lit matches through a mailbox slot, as, by then, he was sure that everyone in the household was deeply asleep.

Psychologists would later speculate that the disturbed teenager might have been suffering from seasonal affective disorder, as most of his murders took place in December, January, and February, when there is little natural light and a great deal of cold weather. For a boy like Peter, who could barely read or write and who had no job or future plans, the winters must have been excessively bleak. But he could have found casual or volunteer work and done something creative with his life rather than choose to destroy.

In June 1979, he targeted heavily pregnant Ros Fenton, torching the hallway of the house she lived in with her seven-year-old-daughter, Samantha. The woman had been preparing for bed when she saw the local boy she knew as Daft Peter loitering outside. Thinking that he was harmless, even when she thought she saw a hand flapping through the mailbox slot, she soon went to sleep. She awoke to find the house engulfed in flames, but she and Samantha were rescued. Ros spent several months in the hospital recovering from her burns and also lost the baby she was carrying. For many months, she was too ill to give a statement to the authorities, and they assumed that a visitor to the house earlier that evening had dropped a cigarette, starting the blaze.

That same summer, the young killer legally changed his name to "Bruce Lee"—also the name of the late martial arts expert and actor, whom he admired greatly. (Shortly before this, his mother had married a man with the surname of Lee, and Peter wanted to pay homage to his stepfather, a man with whom he got on reasonably well. He told some people that his name was now Bruce George Peter Lee, a lengthy name for such a small nineteen-year-old.) But Peter had none of Bruce Lee's wealth and was sometimes forced to sleep on the streets. He would later claim that he had relationships with several girls, and indeed, he had two female figures tattooed on his arm. He was desperate to assert his heterosexuality but was apparently more comfortable having same-sex relationships, as he'd been used sexually by men during the time he was growing up. As an inarticulate, often homeless, and physically unprepossessing boy, he struggled to woo girls and found it easier to satisfy the more physical demands of gay men, who preferred casual sex.

He took to loitering in public toilets and having sex with men there, sometimes for pleasure, sometimes for cash. One of his conquests was a fifteen-year-old boy called Charlie Hastie, and this boy demanded money, threatening that he would go to the police if Peter didn't give him a pound for every sex session (which apparently involved Peter bringing Charlie to orgasm by touching his penis) and that Peter would then be arrested, as Charlie was underage. Peter reluctantly paid. He was attracted to one of Charlie's sisters—indeed, he claimed to be in love with her—but the Hastie family told him that he had no chance and laughed at his relentless infatuation. It was an action that would cost some of them their lives, for Peter brooded about this injustice and decided to seek the ultimate revenge.

In December 1979, he put paraffin-soaked rags through the mailbox slot of the house that Charlie shared with his six siblings and parents, then he poured additional paraffin into the hallway before lighting the pool of fuel with two matches. Soon the small terraced house was consumed by flames. The mother, Edith, woke up and raced into Charlie's bedroom, begging him to help her save the children. He saved her life by pushing her out the window. She fell fifteen feet onto the concrete pavement, damaging her ankle, but she was soon on her feet and screaming at Charlie to jump from the house. Instead, he heroically went back into the room in an attempt to save his three brothers, one of whom, nine-year-old Thomas, was virtually immobilized by muscular dystrophy.

By now, the flames were so fierce that parts of the house had started to collapse. Charlie and two of his brothers, Peter and Paul, suffered burns over 80 percent of their bodies and died within days in the burn unit of the local hospital, but Charlie had managed to save Thomas. The other household members were fortunately not on the premises; the father was in prison, and the three girls were staying with friends.

The police knew that this was an arson attack because strong-smelling paraffin was found just inside the door, alongside two spent matches, but they had no idea who the culprit was. They began to bring in various local youths for questioning, but there were many possible suspects, as some members of the Hastie family had indulged in criminal activity and were feared and hated throughout the neighborhood. The children had been school bullies and made many enemies. For weeks, detectives followed their main lead: a note that had been sent a year before to the Hastie family, threatening to burn down their apartment. Eventually, the writer was traced. She was a quiet, law-abiding senior citizen, who was a regular at her local church, but the family had made her life hell, and she thought that sending an intimidating letter filled with swear words was the only language they would understand.

In the same time period, Peter was arrested for having sex with men in public toilets and was questioned briefly by the police. He admitted to having sexual contact with Charlie Hastie and said that Charlie had taken money from him. Later that year, he was interviewed again about his relationship with the younger boy. Acting on a hunch, the man in charge of the investigation, Detective Superintendent Ron Sagar, said to Peter that he believed he'd started the fire. Peter admitted to the arson attack and was soon speaking in detail about how carefully he had covered his tracks.

Sagar sent out for fish and chips to feed the undernourished boy and made him copious amounts of tea. His non-macho brand of questioning paid off (he was so unlike a typical detective that he was often put forward for undercover work), and Peter thanked him for treating him fairly and admitted that he'd expected the police to beat him up. Sagar paced the interviews and often broke off his questioning to allow the fragile youth to rest in his cell.

Two days later, Peter decided to make a full confession of all his crimes and gave the detective details of his fire spree. But the body count sounded so outlandish that Sagar and his colleagues wondered if the boy was a fantasist. After all, weak-minded or easily intimidated people often admit to crimes they haven't committed, and some even convince themselves of their own guilt. The detectives left him in a prison cell while they checked on his story, finding that adults and children had died as he had suggested in what were believed at the time to be accidental fires.

They then took the twenty-year-old out in a police car. He'd led such a small life that he really enjoyed being driven around the city, a place he mainly explored by walking or cycling. He pointed out all the buildings he had blitzed and explained which windows he'd broken to gain entry. He described the type of curtains he'd set fire to, the furniture in the room, and the inhabitants. It was obvious that he had been at these premises before they were firebombed and hadn't just read about them on the news. Police were shocked to find that the youth, who Sagar described as "insignificant," was claiming responsibility for twenty-six horrifying deaths.

Peter Dinsdale remained in custody while the authorities finalized their case against him. A legal report explained that he had set the fires for three reasons, namely, revenge, pathological compulsion, and because it excited him sexually. Psychologists believed that he would always become sexually aroused by the thought of setting fires and so would remain a danger to the public for the rest of his life. They found that he showed the usual pyromaniac traits of sexual sadism and paranoia, that he even wanted to set fire to his cell. He was also diagnosed as having a psychopathic personality and was described as "a highly dangerous repetitive arsonist." He had derived orgasmic pleasure from his actions; though, unlike some diehard arsonists, he could also find sexual satisfaction while having homosexual or heterosexual sex.

The prison doctor found the young man to be immature and indifferent to his deadly actions, though an EEG showed that his brain wave pattern was only mildly abnormal with no serious organic dysfunction. Instead, he was suffering from a personality disorder—hardly surprising, as his personality had formed during years in which no one cared for him and he cared for no one else. He said that he felt bad about killing children, but the doctor got the distinct impression that he was just telling people what they wanted to hear. As a child, he had been hated, hurt, and humiliated, and he appeared incapable of fully bonding with anyone. That said, he was able to make superficial friendships in prison and looked up to the more notorious prisoners, hero-worshipping them.

On January 20, 1981, at Leeds Crown Court, Dinsdale was charged under the name of Bruce Lee and pleaded not guilty to twenty-six counts of murder and guilty to twenty-six counts of manslaughter and ten counts of arson; his defense being that of diminished responsibility. Because he had admitted to the murders, the trial lasted only a few hours, and he was sentenced to be detained indefinitely in Park Lane Special Hospital (a secure prison hospital) near Liverpool.

He had favored this sanatorium-style setting, as he believed that it would be less repressive than a prison. However, he changed his mind and asked for his freedom when newspaper reports suggested that a disabled boy couldn't have climbed into houses to set the fires. This obviously wasn't true, as Peter was dexterous enough to ride a bicycle and had also briefly held down a job at the local meat market herding pigs into pens. Numerous people had seen him cycling while holding onto something in a paper bag, possibly a can containing paraffin.

He also had a connection with several of the victims. Some were from his school and traveled with him on the bus for disabled students, while others were adult neighbors whom he'd had arguments with, so it was obvious that these latter murders were grudge killings. Controversially, it was decided that he hadn't lit the fire at the home for the elderly, so his eleven convictions for this act were quashed on appeal. But the young man continued to protest that he'd set the building ablaze and that he had stayed behind on the sidewalk to hear the inhabitants shouting for help.

Some newspapers suggested that the police had coerced the vulnerable young man into making a confession to all twenty-six murders. But, far from bullying Peter, the detective in charge of the case had treated him with the utmost civility, feeling pity for the disabled young man who was so obviously a loner. In fact, Peter later wrote to Ron Sagar, thanking him again for his kindness and wishing him well.

Various prisoners also wrote to the newspapers, pointing out that Sagar had treated them fairly when they were in custody and that he had never used bullying tactics. The newspaper that had been most vociferous in its condemnation of Sagar eventually had to back down. Sagar received an out-of-court settlement, which he donated to charity. It had been a stressful and expensive time for the well-liked detective, but he had kept the full story from his wife, as he didn't want to worry her. If he'd lost the case and had had to pay substantial legal fees, they would have been bankrupt and lost their family home. Fortunately, his services to the public were later recognized, and he was named a member of the Order of the British Empire by Queen Elizabeth II. The detective (who this author interviewed at his home in Yorkshire, England, in 2002 for another book) was also renowned for his charitable work both in the United Kingdom and in impoverished parts of Africa. He also worked in that country as a criminal investigation adviser, helping to stop ritualistic killings.

Ron Sagar found that Peter Dinsdale was a typical arsonist, a loner with a great deal of resentment toward others. He had been so badly treated throughout his childhood that he had no future plans. Ron interviewed the young killer on at least twenty-eight different occasions and got to know him well—even to like him. He was able to pity the sinner while hating the sin.

Because Dinsdale pleaded guilty, negating the need for a long trial, the case received very little publicity. The trial date also occurred eighteen days after the police had at last caught the serial killer known as the Yorkshire Ripper, whose real name was Peter Sutcliffe. The British public wanted to know all about the man who had terrorized northern England for the past five years. He had claimed to be on a divine mission from God to kill prostitutes, but his victims had included six women who had no links to the sex industry, including a sixteen-year-old building society clerk and a twenty-year-old university student. At least one of his victims was still a virgin—and, as feminists pointed out—those who *were* sex workers didn't deserve to die for plying their trade.

Sutcliffe had murdered thirteen women, whereas Dinsdale had been found guilty of killing double that number, but Sutcliffe's crimes were more obviously sexual, and this made them of greater interest to the press and public. The public were also more intrigued by Sutcliffe, as he was a handsome man who was married to a pretty schoolteacher, the daughter of Czech refugees. At one time, he'd been a gravedigger, and this added to his colorful history. In contrast, Dinsdale's laboring jobs sounded dull.

The Yorkshire Ripper had an unusual modus operandi: crushing his female victims' skulls with a hammer before mutilating their breasts and genitals with a knife or sharpened screwdriver. He sometimes returned to the corpse at a later date and attacked it again. He would cut a hole in his pocket and underwear so that he could masturbate at the scene of the crime but avoid leaving behind his DNA. Conversely, Peter Dinsdale didn't physically touch any of his victims, many of whom were elderly or very young, and his sexual excitement was less overt.

Because of the lack of publicity surrounding Peter Dinsdale's crimes, various myths later grew around the case. Writers with an interest in miscarriages of justice suggested that the detectives leading the case were homophobic and had targeted Peter Dinsdale because he was a gay man. But Peter defined himself as heterosexual and seems to have had sex with men mainly for financial reasons.

There was another myth that police were actively on the trail of an unknown arsonist called the "Holocaust Man" and that they had found a piece of paper at the Hastie's fire-gutted house with a Salvation Army address on it. Several writers added that the police had gone there and searched Peter Dinsdale's room, finding a can of gasoline under the bed. This is nonsense, as the police became aware that these had been acts of serial arson only when Peter confessed to them.

Peter himself added to the legends, stating that he had been paid between £300 and £500 (around $180 to $300) for each fire that he started, but he was unable to give further details, so the prison doctor suspected these confessions were based on fantasy. The idea of being tasked with an underworld-style job and doing it well made an insignificant boy feel important. As a lone fire starter, he was simply a disturbed individual, but if he could convince the world that he had been a paid assassin, he would earn the respect of those who revere the antihero in our society.

Another likely falsehood that made the rounds was that Peter didn't kill the Hasties and that the fire was started by someone who was angry about a drug deal and targeted the wrong house by mistake.

The years passed, and Peter was transferred to Rampton Special Hospital in Nottinghamshire, England. In 1999, he was joined there by another arsonist, Richard Fielding. Fielding was an unemployed disc jockey who'd had a grudge against an old school friend. He went to the friend's London house and poured gasoline through the mailbox slot, killing four adults and three children.

In 2005, it was rumored that Peter Dinsdale had married a fellow patient, Anne-Marie Davison, though the authorities at Rampton were swift to point out that inmates who marry are not allowed to consummate their union. Male and female inmates are, however, able to socialize on a daily basis in communal rooms.

In March 2010, the much-respected detective Ron Sagar died of cancer at age seventy-five, leaving behind a wife, two children, and six grandchildren. Before his death, he stated that one day he hoped Peter would be well enough to be released.

But how likely is that? Having been raised in children's homes and having spent his entire adult life in a psychiatric hospital, he is now entirely institutionalized. Could he really cope in the outside world? And could any psychiatrist guarantee that his love of fire has completely and permanently receded and that he will never kill again?

ABOUT THE AUTHOR

CAROL ANNE DAVIS is a British writer who was born in Scotland and now lives in England. She has written the true-crime books *Women Who Kill*; *Children Who Kill*; *Couples Who Kill*; *Sadistic Killers*; *Youthful Prey*; and *Doctors Who Kill*, all of which include interviews with detectives, psychologists, and survivors. She is also the author of five realistic crime novels that focus on the psychology of the criminal mind. Before turning to writing, she was everything from an artist's model to a development worker for abused women. She's decidedly counterculture, so she refuses to use Twitter', but her website can be found at www.carolannedavis.co.uk.

REFERENCE

All information in this chapter comes from Davis, Carol Anne. 2003. *Children Who Kill*. London: Allison & Busby. Chap. 4.

Chapter 3

BEAUTY SLAIN IN BATH
The Titterton Tragedy of 1936
by Harold Schechter

O ne of the most exclusive of Manhattan addresses, Beekman Place—a two-block enclave running from East Forty-Ninth Street to Fifty-First Street—didn't always enjoy its present cachet. In the late nineteenth century, as the immigrant poor pushed steadily northward from the teeming ghettos of the Lower East Side, this well-to-do enclave became engulfed by slums. Tenements sprang up beside the handsome Victorian brownstones, while coal yards, tanneries, and slaughterhouses turned the nearby riverbank into a reeking industrial wasteland.

Its revival began in the 1920s when blue bloods like Anne Morgan (of the banking family) and Mrs. William K. Whitney set out to reclaim the area. By the 1930s, the now fashionable neighborhood was home to a particularly rich concentration of artists, writers, and theatrical celebrities, among them Irving Berlin, Alexander Woollcott, Ethel Barrymore, and Pulitzer Prize–winning novelist John P. Marquand. In later years, the neighborhood would boast such residents as John Steinbeck, Marcel Duchamp, and Noel Coward.

Among the creative spirits drawn to Beekman Place during the Depression years were Lewis H. Titterton and his wife, Nancy. A slight, sandy-haired Englishman who sported a neatly trimmed mustache and round horn-rimmed eyeglasses, Titterton had been educated at Cambridge where he specialized in ancient Mid-Eastern languages. Winning a fellowship to Harvard, he spent two years happily immersed in the study of Syriac. In 1925, still in his twenties, he was offered the prestigious post of assistant editor of the *Atlantic Monthly*. From there he moved into the book business as assistant sales manager and later associate editor of the Macmillan Company. During his spare time, he translated French novels and turned out several hundred book reviews, mostly for the *New York Times*.

In 1932—thanks to his familiarity with copyright law—he was lured to NBC as head of the literary rights department. Four years later, at the age of thirty-six, he was promoted to chief of the script division, a somewhat incongruous position for so bookish a man. Intent on elevating the cultural quality of radio programming, he commissioned scripts from serious dramatists and hosted a weekly interview program featuring eminent men of letters. Even among his competitors at rival stations he was regarded as a force for good, a champion of literacy in a world of *Amos 'n' Andy*, *Gang Busters*, and *Chandu the Magician*.

His wife, Nancy, a petite, auburn-haired woman four years his junior, was a kindred spirit. After graduating with honors from Antioch College, she had returned to her hometown of Dayton, where she briefly operated a small bookshop. In 1924, intent on pursuing a literary career, she moved to New York City, rented an apartment in Greenwich Village, and went to work in the book department of Lord & Taylor while writing newspaper reviews in her spare time. After a few years as a bookseller, she was hired by the publishing house of Doubleday Doran, where (in a grimly ironic coincidence that the tabloids never tired of noting) she helped develop the company's popular Crime Club series. She and Titterton met in 1927. After a two-year courtship, they were wed in the picturesque Little Church Around the Corner on East Twenty-Ninth Street. They lived briefly on West Forty-Seventh Street—the heart of Manhattan's notorious Hell's Kitchen—before moving to the far more congenial milieu of Beekman Place, renting an apartment in a handsome five-story walk-up overlooking the East River. "I'm so glad to get out of Hell's Kitchen," Nancy wrote to one friend shortly after the move. "Even though we had bars on the window, I never felt safe there. Nothing could happen to anyone on Beekman Place."

Applying herself full-time to her writing, Nancy achieved a breakthrough in August 1935 when her first published piece of fiction, "I Shall Decline My Head," appeared in *Story* magazine, the prestigious journal that would introduce the work of J. D. Salinger, John Cheever, Joseph Heller, and Tennessee Williams, among others. On the strength of that story—the poignant tale of an old man adrift in dreams of the past—she was given a contract for a first novel and immediately set to work on it.

Compared to the literary luminaries she counted as her Beekman Place neighbors, Nancy Evans Titterton was still an unknown. For a few weeks in April 1936, however, she became the biggest name in town.

Good Friday fell on April 10 that year. After breakfast that morning, Lewis Titterton left his fourth-floor apartment in the five-story walk-up building at 22 Beekman Place and strolled the few blocks to his office at Radio City. In his mailbox he found "an amusing letter from a friend" and telephoned his wife to read it to her. They shared a laugh over the letter before hanging up. The time was approximately 9:00 a.m. They would never speak again.

Nancy had another telephone conversation that morning, this one with Mrs. Georgia Mansbridge of 12 St. Luke's Place in Greenwich Village. They chatted for a few minutes at around 10:15 a.m. about a dinner party scheduled for the following night. "I feel sure no one was in her apartment when we spoke," a distraught Mrs. Mansbridge would tell reporters the following day. "Poor little Nancy—she couldn't fight. She had no strength, and she wouldn't know what to do. All she could do was scream."

The only person to hear Nancy scream—other than the man who raped and killed her—was Oneda Smithmead, a "colored maid" in an apartment one floor below. At around 11:30 a.m., Smithmead heard a woman call out "Dudley, Dudley, Dudley!"—the name of the building handyman, Dudley Mings. There was urgency to the cry, but since the tenants routinely shouted for Mings whenever a toilet overflowed, a ceiling light blew, or a sash-window wouldn't open, Smith attached little significance to it. Only in retrospect (as the *New York Post* reported) was "the cry interpreted as a desperate plea for the help of the only man who might be about the premises" at that hour of the workday.

Not long afterward, Wiley Straughn, a fourteen-year-old delivery boy for a local dry cleaners, the London Valet Service, arrived at 22 Beekman Place with a dress for Mrs. Titterton. He pressed the downstairs bell repeatedly but got no response. Assuming that no one was home, he returned to the shop with the dress.

Later that day, another delivery arrived for the Tittertons. At approximately 4:15 p.m., a small truck pulled up in front of 22 Beekman Place and two men emerged from the cab. The driver was Theodore Kruger, the stocky, middle-aged owner of a local upholstery shop. With him was his assistant, John Fiorenza.

A grade-school dropout with a "dull normal" IQ, a stunted personality, and a face that seemed fixed in a perpetual smirk, Fiorenza, twenty-four, shared a Brooklyn apartment with his mother, Theresa, and her second husband, Ignazi Cupani, a WPA carpenter. Withdrawn to the point of extreme social isolation, he barely communicated at home—his stepfather claimed that Johnny had spoken to him no more than seven times in the past eleven years—and didn't have a girlfriend until the age of twenty-one, when he began seeing a quiet, strictly raised young woman from the Bronx named Pauline D'Antonio. After two years of "keeping company" under the chaperoning eye of Pauline's old-country grandmother, the couple had gotten engaged. Hoping to wed in the fall, Pauline had recently taken a job in an underwear factory to earn money for her dowry.

John himself had been working at Kruger's shop for the past three years, sweeping out the place, cleaning the display windows, and helping with the upholstery, a skill he had picked up during one of his stints in the Elmira Reformatory in Upstate New York. From the age of twelve—when he was arrested for stealing a bicycle—Fiorenza had been in and out of trouble with the law. In the scheme of things, his offenses were trivial. His most serious conviction to date, on a charge of grand larceny, had resulted from the theft of two snare drums and a trombone from the basement of a neighborhood music shop. A psychiatrist who examined him at the time diagnosed Fiorenza as a "neurotic type of personality deviate" with poor impulse control, "with him, the wish is father to the thought and leads quickly to action without consideration or foresight." On two occasions, he had given in to an "uncontrollable urge to take 'joy rides,'" making off with stolen cars in broad daylight, once with the owner clinging precariously to the running board and shouting for him to stop. "Perhaps," a prominent New York City psychoanalyst named Walter Bromberg ventured, "this urge to drive cars could be interpreted as a symbolic expression of the pressure of unrecognized, powerful sexual drives." Bromberg, of course, had the benefit of hindsight. Until Good Friday 1936, no one—John Fiorenza included—realized just how dangerously explosive his sexual drives were.

Kruger, who regarded his assistant as a "good-natured" if "not very quick-witted" young man whose troubles had been "over little things," knew all about John's police record. Indeed, that very morning, Fiorenza had shown up late for work in order to keep an appointment with his probation officer, Peter Gambaro. Or so Theodore Kruger had been led to believe.

From the rear of the truck, Kruger and his assistant removed a loveseat, newly upholstered in green fabric. They had picked up the little sofa the previous day from the Tittertons' apartment and were now returning it per prearrangement. Their load wasn't heavy, and the two men had no trouble carrying it up to the fourth floor, where they found the Tittertons' door ajar. After rapping on the door and getting no response, they carried the loveseat inside and set it down in its original location in the living room. Kruger called out for Mrs. Titterton. Receiving no answer, he left the bill on the seat cushion, then motioned for his helper to follow him from the apartment. They had just started down the stairway when Kruger—thinking he would telephone Mrs. Titterton once he returned to his shop and make sure she was satisfied with the job—decided to go back and get her phone number.

"I found the phone in bedroom and took the number," Kruger told reporters later that day. "Suddenly I noticed the bathroom light was on and the door was open a few inches. I walked over and knocked. Finally I pushed the door wide open."

A woman's foot hung over the edge of the bathtub. Kruger called out Mrs. Titterton's name but the figure in the bathtub did not stir. He went closer and peered into the tub. "My knees began shaking and I felt sick," he related. "I shouted to Johnny, 'My God, something's happened to the missus! Call the police!'"

Fiorenza did as he was told. Kruger was so rattled that only much later would he recall something strange. Though Fiorenza had not yet even glanced into the bathroom, he told the sergeant who answered: "There's a woman tied up in the bathtub."

In less than five minutes, a half-dozen homicide detectives were crowded inside the Tittertons' bathroom. Inside the tub, Nancy lay on her stomach, naked except for a torn white slip bunched around her waist and the sheer magenta-colored hose hanging down her legs. Twisted around her neck was a makeshift noose, fashioned from a pink pajama top and a matching silk dressing jacket, tightly knotted together. Water dripping from the shower-head had pooled around her dark, swollen face.

From the state of the apartment, the detectives were able to reconstruct the general circumstances of the crime. There was no sign of forced entry; evidently, Nancy had freely admitted her killer. The kitchen, living room, and library were undisturbed. The assault had taken place in the bedroom, where one of the twin beds was in disarray and the victim's garter belt, brassiere, blue tweed skirt, and pink blouse were strewn around the floor, violently ripped from her body by her attacker. Ligature marks on her wrists showed that he had bound her hands together before raping her. Afterward, she had been garroted and dragged into the bathroom. An autopsy revealed that she was still alive when she was dumped in the tub and had died of slow asphyxiation.

At approximately 5:45 p.m., Assistant Medical Examiner Thomas A. Gonzales arrived on the scene. Moments later, Lewis Titterton returned from work. He had not been notified of the tragedy and was startled by the milling crowd outside his building and the fleet of police cars at the curb. He collapsed in horror at the news that greeted him upstairs.

After finishing his preliminary examination, Dr. Gonzales ordered the body removed. Lying beneath it on the bottom of the tub was a strand of cord about thirteen inches long, cleanly cut at both ends. Though it matched the marks on Nancy's wrists, it was too short to have kept her hands tightly bound. Detectives immediately deduced that it came from a longer piece of rope. Evidently the killer, intent on removing all physical evidence, had sliced off the rope and carried it away with him. In his haste, this segment, concealed beneath Nancy's body, had escaped his notice.

To the naked eye, there was nothing at all distinctive about the piece of cord. In the end, however, it would prove to be the key element in a landmark feat of forensic detection: "the string," as the *Daily News* declared, "that tied the slayer to the chair."

From the moment the story broke, the Beekman Place "Bathtub Murder" became the talk of the town, thanks to the gleefully exploitative coverage by the tabloids. Hearst's *Mirror* did its usual shameless job of turning the tragedy into lurid entertainment. On Saturday, April 11, under the headline "How Woman Was Found Strangled to Death in Murder Mystery," the paper presented the gruesome sex killing as a five-panel comic strip, complete with graphic drawings of the corpse and a fedora-wearing detective bearing a marked resemblance to Dick Tracy. The following day, its entire back page— normally reserved for the latest sports headlines—was devoted to a voyeuristic photo of Mrs. Titterton's body being removed from the apartment on its way to the morgue.

In the relentlessly titillating coverage of the case, the victim—by all accounts a demure, "owlishly solemn" woman who favored modest tweeds and sports clothes and wore her hair in a mannish cut—was portrayed as a slinky redhead who liked to parade around her apartment in a negligee, even when "delivery boys and workmen" were present. As if the particulars of the murder weren't sensational enough, the tabloids spiced up their stories with hints of sexual perversion. According to the *Mirror*, Dr. Gonzales's initial examination of the violated corpse revealed "evidence of abnormality that convinced him that only a degenerate could have committed the crime." Citing experts like Arthur Carey, former head of NYPD's Homicide Bureau, the *Daily News* informed readers that "crimes of this shocking type" are "relatively frequent," as should be expected "with so many perverted, twisted, and mentally unbalanced persons on the loose."

The *Mirror*, true to its three-ring-circus sensibility, cited experts of its own, like "Mrs. Myra Kingsley, prominent astrologist of 225 East 54th Street," who determined from the victim's horoscope "that the crime was due to the conjunction of the planet Mars—the War God—with the Sun in the Eighth house, which signifies DEATH." Mrs. Kingsley also deduced from Nancy's "chart that the murderer was an older man, and that he either came from or has gone to a distance since the crime was committed." Not to be outdone, the *New York Post* hired its own astrologist, Mrs. Belle Bart, who insisted that "the murderer is German or English, has a light complexion, takes drugs or drinks, met Mrs. Titterton in the fall of 1935, escaped from Beekman Place in a southwesterly direction, and would probably be arrested in Washington Square or thereabouts."

Within a week of the murder, the unknown aspiring author had become such a tabloid sensation that the headlines simply called her by first name: "Nancy Knew Killer," "Man of Mystery Bought Nancy Flowers," "Nancy's Husband Named Murder Suspect." Visiting from England at the time was a writer of authentic renown: Marie Belloc Lowndes, best known for her novel *The Lodger*, a thriller about Jack the Ripper made into an early Alfred Hitchcock film. On the evening of Friday, April 18, she dined with Edmund Pearson, dean of American true-crime historians. Her diary entry about the occasion records only a single topic of conversation: "All New York is horrified over the murder of a woman writer, Mrs. Titterton, strangled on Good Friday. She was about thirty and happily married." Speculating on the identity of the killer, Mrs. Lowndes could reach only one conclusion: "It was a lunatic's murder."

There was no shortage of suspects, beginning with Lewis Titterton. He was not only the victim's husband—always the likeliest perpetrator when a married woman meets a violent death—but a bookwormish Brit "whose accent and manner were alone enough to put the average detective's back up," as one commentator noted. Titterton, however, had no trouble proving he was at work all day. And even the cops most inclined to sneer at his egghead demeanor were moved by the depth of his grief.

For a few days, investigators focused on a "sandy-haired young man with needlepoint eyes and a manner that verged on the feminine" who, according to the Countess Alice Hoyos—a beautiful divorcée occupying the apartment directly below the Tittertons'—had been skulking around the neighborhood for the previous week. W. A. DeWitt, a writer for *Reader's Digest* who lived in the neighboring building, claimed that on the morning of the murder he had glanced through his window and saw a "Negro in dungarees walking across the roof of No. 22 Beekman Place from which access to the fire escape leading to the Titterton apartment was readily accessible." Other supposed witnesses pointed their fingers at "a shifty-eyed youth loitering in front of the building," "a reputedly demented man who had been annoying maids and matrons in the neighborhood," and a pair of mysterious "prowlers, one in his early twenties with several missing teeth, the other a forty-year-old man with a florid face."

From Police Chief George Fallon of Quincy, Massachusetts, came a tip about a fugitive wanted for a similar bathtub strangling in that city. Another official, Dr. Carlton Simon, "former Special Deputy Commissioner of the NYPD and present criminologist of the International Association of the Chiefs of Police," opined that Mrs. Titterton died "as the innocent victim of a sexual adventurer who, obeying an uncontrollable emotional urge, set out to talk his way into apartments in the Beekman Place district. He planned to force his attentions upon any women he met who challenged his bestial desire. Mrs. Titterton chanced to be that woman."

That Nancy had admitted her killer into the apartment and even, as the evidence suggested, allowed him into her bedroom fueled a host of prurient rumors that the tabloids were only too happy to promote. Every day brought unsubstantiated stories of another secret paramour. There was the "rejected suitor of her bachelor girlhood who had been in touch with her since her marriage." The "brilliant literary figure widely known to millions" who urged Nancy to "divorce her husband and marry him." The mysterious gentleman who, according to a neighborhood florist, "frequently bought gardenias there for Mrs. Titterton." At one point, the *Mirror* even had her consorting with "a youngish male adventurer of the type known as a 'gigolo.'"

Her family and friends reacted with outraged denials. From Dayton, her grieving mother, Mrs. Frank Evans, issued a statement affirming the warmth of Nancy's marriage. "She never mentioned the name of any other man but Lewis to me in her letters. They were completely devoted to each other." A close friend of the Tittertons, Caroline Singer—well-known writer of travel books and wife of famed illustrator Cyrus Leroy Baldridge—concurred. "I never saw more devoted persons than Nancy and her husband," she told reporters. "There was no possibility of an outside love interest in her life. She was too fastidious for anything so sordid as a semi-Bohemian relationship with some other man. She had an integrity of character which would have prevented any second-rate love affair." Besides, added Singer, even if Nancy *had* been unfaithful, she would certainly have chosen a tender and sensitive lover, not "the brute type of man" who might resort to physical violence.

The police, too, swiftly dismissed the love-affair angle. On the day of Nancy's funeral—a simple Episcopalian service attended by more than two hundred people, most from the publishing world—Assistant Chief Inspector John A. Lyons cautioned reporters not to leap to salacious conclusions. "We are satisfied now that Mrs. Titterton voluntarily admitted the man. This does not mean, however, that he was a lover or even a close friend. It may have been a salesman or repair man of some sort, someone who made a casual call."

By then, the hunt for Nancy Titterton's killer had become the biggest homicide investigation in the city's history, with sixty-five detectives on the case. On Thursday, April 16, forty of those detectives gathered for a two-hour conference at police headquarters to compare notes. Afterward, their commander, Deputy Chief Inspector Francis J. Kear, appeared before reporters to offer a bleak assessment. After running down scores of tips and following every possible lead, his men were no closer to making an arrest than they were at the beginning. "Police at a Loss in the Titterton Case," read a headline in the next morning's *Times*, while the *Mirror* declared that the murder was shaping up to be "the perfect crime." Even as New Yorkers were reading these gloomy reports, developments were taking place behind the scenes that would break the case wide open.

When Dr. Charles Norris became New York's first chief medical examiner in 1918, he immediately recruited Bellevue biochemist Alexander O. Gettler as his toxicologist. Setting up a laboratory on the fourth floor of the City Mortuary at Bellevue, Gettler quickly earned a reputation as a "modern Merlin," a master of "criminological chemistry." Newspaper photos accompanying the stories about his forensic feats invariably showed the white-coated Gettler posed with some impressive piece of lab apparatus—a kind of 1930s CSI wiz, capable of cracking seemingly unsolvable crimes with one of his "well-nigh magical scientific techniques." By the time of his retirement in 1959, he was internationally renowned as the "father of forensic chemistry," the "world's greatest test-tube sleuth." By his own estimate, he and his assistants worked on approximately two thousand cases a year. Of those, one of his greatest triumphs would be the solution of the Titterton mystery.

Studying it under his microscope, Gettler discovered that the piece of twine found in the tub beneath the dead woman's body contained a strand of istle, a stiff fiber obtained from several species of Mexican plants and used in the manufacture of cheap scrubbing brushes, burlap, and cordage. Inspector Lyons immediately had a circular sent to more than two dozen rope makers in the region: "Advise immediately whether you manufacture quarter inch hemp fiber twisted twine with single strand istle. Twine this description important in homicide investigation."

Twenty-three telegrams with negative replies came back before an executive with the Hanover Cordage Company of York, Pennsylvania, telephoned to say that his firm made a similar product. Carrying the telltale piece of twine, a detective set out for York at once, where Hanover officials confirmed that it came from their factory. They also explained that the cord was commonly used as upholstery binding.

A check of company's sales records showed that several rolls of the rope had recently been purchased by a New York City wholesaler. When police paid a visit to the wholesaler, they learned that on Thursday, April 9—the day before Nancy Titterton's murder—one of these rolls had been delivered to the East Side shop of Theodore Kruger.

Kruger himself had long been dismissed as a suspect, having been in his shop all Good Friday morning, as several witnesses testified. His twenty-four-year-old assistant, however, was a person of interest to the police. Not only had they learned of his lengthy arrest record, they had also turned up the psychiatric report that described him as a "personality deviate" and predicted that, without ongoing treatment, the young compulsive car thief would "have difficulty in learning to refrain from illegal acts from time to time."

Fiorenza was placed under twenty-four-hour surveillance. In the meantime, Dr. Gettler continued his hunt for forensic evidence that would tie the killer directly to the crime. He found it on Monday, April 20. Going over Nancy Titterton's rumpled bedspread inch by inch with a high-powered magnifying glass, Gettler discovered a single odd-looking hair, less than half an inch long. It was white and "strangely stiff," and it was certainly not human. Placing it under his microscope, he determined that it was horsehair of the type used as furniture stuffing. Obtaining a sample from the Tittertons' newly reupholstered loveseat, Gettler confirmed that the two hairs matched. There was only one plausible way that the horsehair could have ended up on Nancy's bed: the killer must have had it on his clothing when he attacked her. And he had gotten it on his clothing while working in Kruger's shop.

Questioned about his employee, Kruger insisted that, despite his various run-ins with the law, Fiorenza was "a perfect gentleman." "There was never anything about him that was bad," said Kruger. "Why, I've seen him take meat out of his sandwich for lunch and give it to our dog." He was a good worker, too, very reliable, always on time. True, he'd shown up a few hours late on the day of the murder, but he had had a solid excuse—his weekly appointment with his probation officer, Peter Gambaro.

When detectives visited the probation office in the Criminal Court Building, however, they discovered that Gambaro, a practicing Catholic, had taken Good Friday off. And no one else in the office had any memory of seeing Fiorenza that morning.

With his alibi blown, Fiorenza was immediately taken into custody and whisked to an undisclosed location in the Bronx where he underwent sixteen hours of relentless grilling. He didn't break down until 10:30 the next morning when he turned to Police Commissioner Lewis Valentine and, in a voice hoarse with exhaustion said, "Give me cigarette and I'll tell you all I know."

According to his confession—transcribed by Detective George Swander and signed by Fiorenza—he had gone to the Tittertons' apartment on Thursday afternoon, April 9, to pick up the loveseat with Kruger. As soon as he set eyes on Nancy, the "idea came to me of doing what I did to her afterward." He could see that she was too slight to put up much resistance and was so soft-spoken that she would be unable to make much of an outcry. All the rest of that day and night, he brooded on his plan.

The next morning, after telephoning Kruger to say that he would be late because of an appointment with his parole officer, he proceeded to 22 Beekman Place. In his pocket was a fifty-two-inch length of cord he had taken from the shop the previous day.

"I rang the downstairs bell. The latch sounded. I went upstairs. Mrs. Titterton answered the door. She was all dressed and had a garment—a dress or a pair of pajamas, something like that—in her hand. I told her I came about the loveseat. Just to get her in there I asked her, didn't she want to have the loveseat in the bedroom? She didn't know. But that made her go into the bedroom to see in her mind how the loveseat would look there. I went in there with her."

No sooner were they inside the bedroom than Fiorenza lunged at Mrs. Titterton. She just had time to let out a scream before he "grabbed whatever it was she had in her hand and stuffed it into her mouth, so she couldn't yell anymore." Throwing her facedown on the bed, he pulled the cord from his pocket and tightly bound her wrists. He then turned her over on her back and, in a blind frenzy, tore off her clothes and raped her. "From time to time, when she started to scream as the gag worked loose, I throttled her with my hands. She raised an awful fuss."

Afterward, as she lay whimpering on the bed, he snatched up the pajama top and a thin dressing jacket, knotted them together, and strangled her. She was still breathing when he carried her into the bathroom. He thought about filling the tub to make it look as if she had drowned, but he couldn't find the plug. Grabbing a knife from the kitchen, he sliced the rope in several pieces from her wrists. He thought he "put it all in my pocket and took it away."

He got out of the building without being seen and hurried around the corner. A block away, he tossed the cord into an ash can, never guessing that he had left a piece behind. He then ducked into a drugstore on First Avenue and called Kruger to say that he had been delayed longer than expected but was on his way.

He reached the shop at around 11:50 a.m. "I helped fix the loveseat. I didn't say anything about killing the woman." At 4:00 p.m., he "went back with my boss to the Tittertons," taking care to let Kruger enter the apartment first and discover the body.

When his interrogators asked Fiorenza why he had targeted Nancy Titterton, even he seemed baffled. "She wasn't my type," he said. "If I saw her on the street, I would not give her a second look."

The woman who presumably was his type, his fiancée Pauline D'Antonio, initially refused to believe any of it. "He did not do it," she told the reporters who swarmed to her apartment at 2385 Lorillard Place in the Bronx (just a short block away, as the tabloids delighted in noting, from the home of Anna Hauptman, widow of the convicted killer of the Lindbergh baby). "They are telling lies about him. He did not confess. He could not have confessed to such a thing. He will be back and we will be married in September."

By the following morning, however, she had undergone a change of heart. "It's all over," she said. "I can have nothing to do with him. Thank God I found out before we were married. I'd have died if he'd been the father of my child, my husband."

Informed of her comments in his cell at police headquarters, Fiorenza looked glum. "I guess she'll never come to see me now. Well, what can I do? I made a serious mistake."

Not content to titillate its readers with the lurid details of Fiorenza's actual confession, Hearst's *Daily Mirror* resorted to a stunt so brazen that it made the city's other tabloids seem like models of journalistic sobriety. Beginning on Saturday, April 25, it ran a sensational six-part series headlined "Fiorenza's Own Amazing Story" trumpeted as the exclusive firsthand account of "the events leading up to the fateful Good Friday when the body of Mrs. Nancy Titterton was found in the bathtub at 22 Beekman Place." A prefatory note claimed that Fiorenza had dictated the story from his cell in the Tombs to a staff reporter from the *Mirror* named David Charney.

According to this startling tale, Fiorenza had first encountered his future victim six months earlier when "she called up Kruger's where I worked and I went up to see her about fixing some furniture and upholstery work. She was a fine-looking woman. She had a lot of class." Much to his surprise, she "started to ask me questions about myself. Gee, I couldn't get over her being so nice to me, just a plain working fellow." Noticing the dirt under his fingernails, he felt embarrassed in her presence, but "she told me not to worry about my hands" and invited him to sit down in the living room. "She seemed anxious to talk more about me. Among other things, she asked about my fiancée. She also asked if I was interested in the arts. I didn't get that. It was very highfalutin talk." Initially flattered by her attention, he began to feel "dopey" when he realized that "she was a writer" and "was studying me like them doctors study guinea pigs to see what they got behind their minds. I was a type to her. When I left, she asked me to come back again. I was thinking of her. She was thinking of a guinea pig."

The remaining five installments of this sleazy potboiler describe Fiorenza's burgeoning obsession with the beguiling Mrs. Titterton, who comes across as a careless, high-society tease, inviting him back repeatedly to pump him for material she can use in her fiction while ignoring the erotic effect she is having on him. Before long, Fiorenza is in the grip of a "wild, uncontrollable passion" for her. "Every other woman I saw looked to me like Mrs. Titterton. I'd pick up a magazine and all the faces of the good-looking women in it were like her. Daydreaming about her, I pictured myself dressed up in a swell tuxedo, married to her. We just finished up a cocktail and the butler comes up, bows, and says the car's waiting." By its final chapter, "Fiorenza's Own Amazing Story" had turned into a cut-rate version of Theodore Dreiser's *An American Tragedy*: the story of a poor working boy engaged to a doting girl of his own class who becomes infatuated with an upper-crust beauty and dreams of possessing her. In this account, however, it is the beautiful socialite who ends up dead.

Even by tabloid standards, "Fiorenza's Own Amazing Story" was outrageous, provoking a furious response from one of Hearst's main competitors, Julius David Stern, publisher of the *New York Post*. After contacting the district attorney and confirming "no reporter from any newspaper had ever talked to Fiorenza in jail," Stern published a scathing front-page editorial denouncing the purported autobiography as "the baldest fake in years, a semipornographic thriller, so written as to blacken a dead woman's character and build up sympathy for a confessed murderer." Besides its defamation of the victim—"a woman who, during her lifetime, was respected by all who knew her"—what made "the Hearst hoax" particularly disgraceful was its potential to influence Fiorenza's future trial.

"How many prospective jurors have read the *Mirror*'s vile insinuations that Mrs. Titterton led Fiorenza on," thundered Stern, "that she encouraged him to spend time with her while she probed him for literary material?

Hearst's fake is so abhorrent that it shames the whole newspaper business. It is so dangerous that it can lead to a miscarriage of justice."

On May 19, just a month after his arrest, Fiorenza went to trial. Dressed in an ill-fitting blue serge suit, with his slick-backed black hair "accenting the whiteness of his sharp features," he sat through the weeklong proceedings with an air of bland indifference. Only once—when his stricken mother took the stand to testify (falsely) that he had been at home on the morning of the murder—did he display any trace of emotion, wiping his eyes, burying his face in his hands, and shaking his head.

After a fruitless attempt to show that Mrs. Titterton had actually been killed by a shadowy "fiend" who had been on the loose in the neighborhood at the time of the murder, Fiorenza's lawyer, Henry Klauber, switched to an insanity defense. His main witness was Dr. James Lincoln McCartney, former psychiatrist at Elmira Reformatory, who (using the now-outmoded terminology for schizophrenia) characterized Fiorenza as "a dementia praecox case." In rebuttal, the prosecution called a quartet of experts, including Dr. Perry Lichtenstein—author of, among other professional publications, a magazine article titled "Who's Looney Now?"—and Dr. Thomas Cusack, who insisted that Fiorenza was not nearly "wacky" enough to be diagnosed with dementia praecox. All four prosecution experts agreed that the defendant was "keenly aware of the nature and quality of his behavior at the time of the crime."

The conflicting psychiatric testimony left the jurors deeply divided. Retiring to the jury room at 3:00 p.m. on May 27, they deliberated for more than eleven hours without reaching a verdict. When Judge Charles C. Nott Jr. received word shortly after 2:00 a.m. that they were deadlocked, he refused to let them go to their hotels, ordering them locked up in the jury room until they came to a decision. Finally, at precisely 10:07 a.m., they emerged with a verdict. Fiorenza was found guilty of first-degree murder.

The following week, on Friday, June 6, he was sentenced to die in the electric chair. Standing before the bench in his blue suit, blue shirt, and white tie, he displayed not a flicker of emotion. He was equally impassive when he went to his death on January 22, 1937, one of four prisoners executed within a twenty-minute span that night. Accompanied by the Catholic chaplain Reverend John P. McCaffrey, Fiorenza walked calmly into the execution chamber and said nothing as he sat on the chair. The switch was thrown at 11:09 p.m. Three minutes later, he was pronounced dead.

In 1938, two years after his first wife's murder, Lewis Titterton remarried. He continued to work at NBC until 1944, when he left to join an advertising agency. His departure was bemoaned as a significant loss to the medium. "I do not know of any individual who has stood for quality broadcasts more steadfastly than Lewis Titterton," wrote playwright and producer Blevins Davis in the *New York Times*. "A brilliant scholar, linguist, and editor, he used his influence to bring great masterpieces of literature to radio." Another admirer was Max Wylie, Titterton's counterpart at CBS, who praised him in print as "the most just, the most catholic and impartial appraiser of material in radio today."

Nearly twenty years later, Wylie himself would suffer a devastating tragedy when his daughter Janice was slain in her Upper East Side apartment along with her roommate, Emily Hoffert, a crime that became known in the tabloids as "The Career Girl Murders." But that is another horror story.

ABOUT THE AUTHOR

HAROLD SCHECHTER is a professor of American literature at Queens College, the City University of New York. His essays have appeared in various newspapers and magazines, including the *New York Times*, the *Los Angeles Times*, and the *International Herald Tribune*. Among his more than thirty published books are a half-dozen historical true-crime narratives, including *Killer Colt*; *The Devil's Gentleman*; *Deranged*; *The Serial Killer Files*; and *The A to Z Encyclopedia of Serial Killers*. The author has also written a series of mystery novels featuring Edgar Allan Poe, and an anthology of American true-crime writing published by the Library of America.

REFERENCES

Block, Maxine, ed. 1944. *Current Biography: Who's News and Why, 1943*, p. 770. New York: H. W. Wilson.

Blum, Deborah. 2010. *The Poisoner's Handbook: Murder and the Birth of Forensic Medicine in Jazz Age New York*. New York: Penguin Press.

Brewster, Dorothy, ed. 1936. *A Book of Contemporary Short Stories*. New York: Macmillan.

Edmiston, Susan, and Linda D. Cirino. 1991. *Literary New York: A History and Guide*. New York: Gibbs Smith.

Evans, Colin. 2008. *Blood on the Table: The Greatest Cases of New York City's Office of the Chief Medical Examiner*, pp. 69–71, 79–80, 85–92. New York: Berkley Books

Farber, James. 1936. "Murder Victim Won Honors as Student." *New York Daily News*, April 11.

Faurot, Joseph. 1936. "The Inside Story of New York's Bathtub Slaying." *Official Detective Stories II* 7 (July): 4–5, 7, 43, 44.

Lowndes, Susan, ed. 1971. *Diaries and Letters of Marie Belloc Lowndes 1911–1947*, p. 138. London: Chatto & Windus.

New York Daily Mirror. 1936. April 11–18; April 21–23; April 25–30; May 22.

New York Daily News. 1936. April 11–16; April 22; May 23; May 25; May 27.

New York Post. 1936. April 11; April 14; April 16; April 21–23; April 25; May 1; May 26.

New York Times. 1936. April 11; April 17; April 19; April 22–23; April 26; May 20–21; May 26–29; June 6; January 22, 1937; March 26, 1944, sec. X.

"Obituary Notes: Nancy Evans Titterton." 1936. *Publishers Weekly* 129, no. 16 (April 18): 1614.

Porter, Edward Sefton. 1962. *Conscience of the Court*, pp. 175, 179–80. Englewood Cliffs, NJ: Prentice-Hall.

Titterton, Lewis H. 1944. In *Current Biography: Who's News and Why, 1943*. Edited by Maxine Block, pp. 768–70. New York: H. W. Wilson.

"Woman Writer Slain in Home." 1936. *New York Daily News*, April 11.

Chapter 4

THE EVIL AT THE ANGEL INN

by Linda Rosencrance

It was sometime in the beginning of 2001. The woman was sitting at the bar of the Angel Inn, located in Guilford, New York, and owned by Oxford residents Peter Wlasiuk, a former truck driver, and his wife, Patricia. The woman chatted with Peter for a bit. But she didn't quite understand why, out of the blue, he started talking to her about killing someone. It was all too macabre.

"It would be easy to kill someone and make it look like a drowning accident," he said. "But you have to be smart, you can't just drown them and, say, throw them in the lake because they could test the water in their lungs and tell whether or not it came from the lake. Say I wanted to put someone in Guilford Lake . . . the thing to do would be to get a bucket or a container of water from the lake and drown them in that, then throw the body in the lake."

Thirty-five-year-old Patricia "Patty" Wlasiuk, a registered nurse, finished her shift in the intensive care unit of The Hospital in Sidney, New York, at 11:00 p.m. on April 2, 2002. When she got home, she and her husband, Peter, thirty-three, allegedly argued about who was supposed to have picked up the kids at the babysitter's.

Aggravated, Peter called the babysitter, Joyce Worden, and told her they would be driving over together to get the children—Peter had an eight-year-old daughter from a previous marriage, and he and Patty had two younger daughters. Patty also had a teenage son from a previous relationship who lived in another town.

It was after midnight on April 3, 2002, and Veronica Palmer, who lived about one hundred eighty feet away from Guilford Lake, was watching television. She was just about to turn it off and head to bed when she heard a door slam, shattering the otherwise quiet night.

Around 12:30 a.m., Steven Schweichler and Thomas and Jessica Becker were suddenly awakened by a hysterical Peter Wlasiuk banging on the walls and front door of their lake house begging for help.

When the trio answered the door, Peter told them to call 911. He said he and his wife, Patty, were on their way to pick up the couple's children at the babysitter's; he had swerved to miss a deer, and their truck plunged into Guilford Lake. He escaped, but, try as he might, he just couldn't pull Patty out of the truck. As Thomas dialed 911, Jessica thought it was odd that although Peter was drenched, his hair didn't appear wet.

After Thomas called 911, he, Steven, and Peter drove down to the lake to try to find Patty. When they got to the shore, the men saw the headlights of the truck shining beneath the surface of the lake. Realizing the truck was too far out, not to mention that the water was too cold, Thomas went back to the cabin to get his wet suit and his rowboat.

Steven stayed onshore and tried to get Peter to tell him where Patty was. But Peter was so incoherent; Steven couldn't even figure out if he had been able to get her out of the truck.

Feeling helpless, Steven decided to swim down to the truck, which appeared to be at least eighty feet from shore. But as he started to wade into the water, Peter told him to stop because it was too dangerous.

When Thomas finally returned with the boat, he and Steven tried to get to the truck, but it was impossible because the water was so cold. Thomas was freezing and having a hard time speaking and breathing.

As the two men were searching for Patty, Chenango County deputy Dwight Meade was driving nearby on Country Route 35. He heard the call from dispatch about a pickup truck that had veered off Route 35 and had plunged into the lake, so he sped to the scene. After hearing the call come in for a diver at around 12:40 a.m., state police diver and investigator Jamie Bell immediately grabbed his gear and took off for the lake with some other troopers, changing on the way. They arrived at about 12:52 a.m.

At the scene, Bell finished putting on his gear and went into the forty-degree water at about 12:56 a.m. The Wlasiuks' 1998 dual-wheel, one-ton truck had plunged into the water and rested on the bottom of the lake about seventy-five feet from shore, the eerie red glow of the taillights still visible.

Bell swam to the truck and then dove down about twelve feet in the frigid water. The first thing he found was a sweatshirt. Then he saw a leg and a foot and realized he had found a person.

Grabbing Patty's body, Bell swam to the surface yelling, "I've got her." Thomas Becker and Chad Brown, an EMT from Oxford, moved Becker's rowboat close to Bell and helped him lift Patty's body into the boat.

Deputy Meade was the first law-enforcement officer on the scene. When he arrived, he found Peter standing next to Country Route 35 soaking wet and shivering profusely. Meade escorted Wlasiuk into the backseat of his patrol car, cranked the heat up, and raced down to the shore to offer his help. When the Guilford ambulance arrived, Meade got Peter out of the cruiser and brought him to the EMTs. Marlene Martin, the first EMT to examine Peter at the scene, was struck by the fact that Peter's hair wasn't wet. Additionally, she thought his behavior was a bit over the top.

Other emergency personnel started working to try to revive Patty after she had been pulled from the lake. Meade then began a search of the area where the accident occurred. He found tire tracks on the far shoulder across from where the truck went into the lake. The tracks appeared to have been made by the Wlasiuks' truck. Meade cordoned off the area with traffic cones to protect potential evidence.

When Chenango County sheriff's deputy Clarence Ellingsen got to the scene at 12:50 a.m., he was ordered to stay with Peter, which he did, until about 4:45 a.m. Ellingsen first talked to Peter when he was in the back of the ambulance wrapped in a blanket. Like Jessica Becker and Marlene Martin, Ellingsen thought it was odd that Peter's hair was neat, not to mention bone-dry. Ellingsen also noticed that Peter's lips were rosy red and his speech was perfect, not what one would expect from someone who had been struggling in icy water.

As Peter talked, Ellingsen wrote some notes in his notebook. Initially, Peter told him that he had grabbed Patty and pulled her out of the truck, but she slipped from his grasp as he made his way to the shore. He said when he got to shore, he called out her name several times, but, getting no answer, he went to a nearby house for help.

Tow truck driver Daniel Spencer was summoned to the scene to pull the Wlasiuks' truck out of the lake. When he brought it to shore, it took a few minutes for the water to empty out of the truck before the deputies could check it out.

Ellingsen rode in the ambulance with Peter to babysitter Joyce Worden's home so Peter could get some dry clothes. Peter and Ellingsen got to The Hospital in Sidney—where Patty had worked—at around 1:45 that morning. Patty had been pronounced dead on arrival at 1:20 a.m. It was left to supervising nurse Carol Olmstead to tell Peter that Patty had passed away. When he heard the news, Peter, who had been calmly sitting on one of the stretchers, held his hands up and started shaking, but he didn't cry.

Peter told Olmstead that Patty was a nurse and always wanted to help people, so he wanted to donate her organs. He also told Olmstead that he had to have her cremated right away.

The emergency room doctor who had pronounced Patty dead examined Peter for hypothermia an hour later. But Peter showed no signs of hypothermia. In fact, his body temperature was 99.5 degrees, above the normal core body temperature of 98.6 degrees.

A technician from The Hospital drew Patty's blood—Peter had insisted she be tested to prove she wasn't drunk. It was then that Ellingsen noticed some bruises on Patty's forehead and chin. When the nurses turned her over to take her body temperature, Ellingsen also saw some bruises on her back. The technician gave Ellingsen Patty's blood sample. Because he didn't have anywhere to put the vial of blood to keep it safe, he put it in his pocket. When he got back to the station, he turned it into the evidence room.

Forensic pathologist James Terzian of Lourdes Hospital in Binghamton, New York, conducted the autopsy on Patty's body at 9:30 a.m. on April 3. His preliminary finding was probable drowning, pending toxicology reports. But that determination soon changed.

During the autopsy, Terzian found burdocks—weeds commonly known as sticky burrs—in Patty's hair and on her clothes. He visited the lake but didn't find any burdocks there. However, when he went to the Wlasiuks' house as part of his investigation, he found burdocks everywhere. Terzian then conducted a more complete autopsy on Patty and determined that she had died of asphyxiation consistent with smothering rather than with drowning. He reached this conclusion because a drowning victim's lungs are quite heavy and filled with water—Patty's were not.

The doctor also found other evidence that Patty had been smothered. For one thing, there were tears on her inner lip, which most likely meant that someone had put a hand over her mouth, putting pressure on her lips and teeth. He also found a bruise on Patty's back and abrasions on her forehead and chin. And because there was swelling and hemorrhaging associated with her injuries, they had to have been inflicted before she died. Terzian believed that Patty died either insider her house or just outside, and that she had been facedown when she was being smothered.

At the hospital, Peter told Ellingsen that he and Patty had left their house at a quarter past twelve in the morning to pick up their kids at the babysitter's. Peter said he had been waiting for Patty to get home from work for quite some time. When she finally arrived, the couple argued about who was supposed to pick up the children; they then decided to drive over to Joyce Worden's place together.

So Peter called Joyce to tell her they were on their way to get the children. Joyce suggested that it made more sense for the kids to stay the night at her house. But Peter said Patty refused to let the kids stay there—apparently Peter, Patty, and Joyce had been engaging in a three-way sexual relationship since September 2001, but Patty was not very happy that Peter and Joyce were spending time together alone. According to Peter, Patty stormed out of the house without saying a word and got into the truck. Peter followed.

On the way, Patty, who was driving approximately sixty miles per hour, rolled down her window to flick out a cigarette. When she turned back around, she saw a deer in the road in front of the truck. Peter said she swerved and hit a small post. The truck fishtailed, then plunged into the lake. As the cab was filling up with water, Peter said he couldn't pull his wife out of the truck. When Ellingsen told Peter that his second story didn't match his first one, Peter said he was very upset and confused.

Sergeant Richard Cobb, who was in charge of accident reconstruction for the Chenango County sheriff's office, arrived at the scene of the accident around 2:00 a.m.

After being briefed by Chenango County sergeant Scott Carpenter, Cobb started taking photographs and examining the tire tracks that had been marked off. He noted the location where the tires of the truck had made their impressions in the dirt. Then he sketched out the hypothetical trajectory of the vehicle. Cobb's investigation indicated that the truck made a gradual curve from the road toward a thirty-three-foot-wide opening on the shore—the only opening not protected by guardrails. In fact, it was the only open access to the entire lake on County Route 35.

During his investigation, Cobb didn't find anything to indicate that the truck had been going fast when the accident occurred. Nor did he find any skid marks or yawing (marks made during a skid when a vehicle rotates along its vertical axis), indicating that the driver had been in full control of the truck. Cobb also didn't find any evidence of acceleration or deceleration or any indication that any attempt was made to stop the truck from going into the lake. Cobb also based his determination on the STAR report—written by the Michigan State police regarding accidents that resulted in vehicles being submerged in water.

After his investigation, Cobb determined that Patty hadn't been driving the truck when it plunged into the lake. Cobb theorized that Peter Wlasiuk had killed his wife, placed her in the bed of the truck, drove the car to Guilford Lake, and left it about eighty feet from the edge of water, parked on or near the road. Cobb firmly believed that Wlasiuk then put the truck into drive and watched as it became submerged in the lake. His conclusion was partly based on the fact that investigators found Patty's pager and strands of her hair in the bed of the truck.

Cobb also based his findings on the burdocks in Patty's hair and on her clothes when her body was recovered from the lake. And although there were burdocks on the driver's side door, there were none on the seat, which should have been the case if she had been driving. The burdocks probably came from Peter, who had them in his shoes, which were recovered later at the scene. But they were not found in Patty's shoes. During their investigation, police found eighteen strands of Patty's hair in a burdock bush by the pool in the Wlasiuks' backyard. Police theorized that Peter murdered Patty in their yard, put her in the bed of their truck, drove to the lake, and let the truck roll into the water.

After Patty's death, Peter seemed to be more focused on money than on how he was going to live without his wife. On April 3, just before 8:00 a.m.—less than seven hours after his wife's death—Peter Wlasiuk called lawyer Hugh Leonard of Binghamton to file a claim on his damaged truck. The truck was insured by New York Central Mutual Insurance Company, and Leonard had been retained by the insurer.

Several months later, during the insurance company's investigation, Peter told Leonard that Patty turned the vehicle around in the middle of an argument because he suddenly realized she had been drinking. He said Patty stopped the vehicle and began a "K-turn" in the middle of County Route 35; then she inadvertently hit the gas, causing the truck to go through the guardrail and into the lake. Peter said he lied about Patty swerving to miss a deer because he didn't want the police to arrest Patty for a DUI.

Around noon on April 3, Peter called Donald Beckwith, the insurance agent who had sold him a $100,000 life insurance policy on Patty just three months earlier. The couple needed to take out the policy so they could get a business loan to purchase the Pillars bar, which they renamed the Angel Inn. But Peter became angry with the agent when he mentioned that the company was allowed to contest the payment for up to two years in case there was a false statement on the application. Peter didn't even seem to be sorry about losing his wife; he seemed only to be interested in the money from the life insurance policy.

On April 5 at around 1:20 p.m., Peter went to the Chenango County sheriff's office to meet Detective Sergeant James Lloyd to pick up Patty's jewelry. Much to his shock, he got more than he bargained for when, about ten minutes after he arrived, he was being accused of murdering his wife and was read his rights. Regardless of his surprise, Peter initially decided to talk without an attorney present.

Lloyd told Peter he wanted to clear up some rumors that Patty might have been drinking the night she died. Peter said that wasn't true. Then Lloyd asked Peter if he was having a sexual relationship with his children's babysitter, Joyce Worden, who was also the entertainment director at the Angel Inn. During the police investigation into Patty's death, people who knew the Wlasiuks said that Peter was having sex with Joyce. They also told police that Peter had physically and emotionally abused Patty.

Initially, Peter denied it, but when Lloyd told him Joyce had already admitted it, he claimed that he, Joyce, and Patty had been involved in a three-way sexual relationship. He also claimed that he and Patty had such a special bond that she even allowed him to see Joyce alone.

Lloyd also challenged Peter's story about the accident, confronting him with the results of Cobb's investigation. Peter told Lloyd that when the truck went into the water, he opened the door to escape. But that couldn't have been the case, because when police checked the truck after it had been pulled from the lake, both doors were locked—and Patty wasn't inside the cab of the truck; she was in the water.

When Lloyd started to ask Peter if he had ever abused Patty, Peter said he needed to talk to his attorney, effectively putting an end to the interview. So Lloyd let Peter leave. Just three days later, at 8:21 p.m. on April 8, 2002, Peter Wlasiuk was arrested for the murder of his wife, Patricia. He was indicted on a charge of second-degree murder on April 12. Prosecutors believed he murdered Patty for money—$330,000 from the life insurance policy and death benefits from The Hospital where Patty worked—and to be with Joyce Worden. After Peter's arrest, his parents received custody of the couple's children.

Peter went on trial for Patty's murder on November 6, 2002, in the Chenango County Court. Lloyd, Cobb, and other members of the Chenango County sheriff's office testified about the investigation. Cobb testified as to his opinion of the accident scene, referencing the STAR report. Chenango deputy Gerald Parry told jurors about Patty's diaries, which he'd found at the couple's Oxford home. In the diaries, Patty detailed her relationship with Peter. In one of her entries, Patty said she had been having nightmares and flashbacks because she believed that Peter could kill her if he was angry.

Some of Patty's friends testified that Patty often had injuries she said Peter had caused—like a boot mark on her chest where he had kicked her. At one point, Patty told a friend that she planned to leave Peter and was waiting for the right time. Others testified about the way Peter abused Patty. One of Patty's coworkers at The Hospital, also a registered nurse, told the jurors about a fight the couple had had in the fall of 2001. She said Peter once held a loaded shotgun to his wife's head. Patty told the nurse that she could never leave him because he'd kill her first.

Peter's attorney, Frederick Neroni, put Peter on the stand to testify in his defense. On the stand, Peter admitted he initially lied to Deputy Ted Ellingsen about what had happened the night his wife died. Sometimes weeping on the stand, he told the jury his version of the events leading up to his wife's death.

Peter said he lied because he wanted "to downplay her drinking" since Patty had five convictions on her record for driving while intoxicated. Peter was afraid that if she was arrested for driving drunk again she might lose her driver's license as well as her nursing license. Peter said he was scared for Patty because he thought she was still alive.

During his testimony, Peter said that Patty put the truck in forward and drove into the lake after the pair had argued because she was drunk.

"It felt like a big log flume," Peter told the jurors. "One minute you are at the top of the hill and the next minute you are in the lake." He said he climbed over his wife—kneeing her in the head—then escaped through the driver's side window.

Peter explained that when he learned that Patty was dead, he thought that God had taken her away because of the sexual relationship the Wlasiuks had had with Joyce Worden.

Chenango County district attorney Joseph McBride went after Peter like a pit bull, confronting him about the numerous contradictions in his story. According to Peter, the only lie he told was that Patty swerved to miss hitting the deer.

Under questioning by the prosecutor, Peter also said that he had never hit Patty—not that night or any other night. Peter also told the jurors that when the truck started going into the lake, he braced for impact. And despite the fact that the truck had traveled nearly seventy-five feet into the lake, Peter said he never tried to jump out.

During the trial, the prosecution called fifty-one witnesses to the stand, while the defense called seven. On Thursday, November 21, 2002, after deliberating for a little over four hours, a jury of nine women and three men found

Peter Wlasiuk guilty of second-degree murder. On Friday, January 17, 2003, Peter was sentenced to twenty-five years to life in state prison.

But that wasn't the end of the story.

Peter filed an appeal, and on August 31, 2006, the New York State Supreme Court Appellate Division's Third Judicial Department ruled that a "litany of errors effectively deprived the defendant of a fair trial" and threw out his conviction.

The appellate court ruled that Judge W. Howard Sullivan, the judge who presided over Peter's trial, should not have let prosecutors introduce evidence that Peter had been violent with Patty on a number of occasions. The appellate court also said the judge should not have allowed Patty's letters and diary entries to be admitted into evidence.

And finally, the appellate court ruled that the prosecutor overstepped his bounds by repeatedly expressing a personal opinion concerning the merits of particular evidence, disparaging Peter and characterizing his testimony and that of his witnesses as "lies," as well as maligning the defense counsel and his arguments.

The court also questioned Richard Cobb's expert opinion, as it relied too heavily on the STAR report, the credibility of which the county court had never really established. Since much of Cobb's expert opinion was based on that report, the appellate division had no choice but to call his whole expert testimony into question.

The appellate court's ruling stated that although many of the procedural errors taken by themselves seemed to be "harmless," taken together they could infringe on the defendant's rights. The court said the most important consideration was "the cardinal right of a defendant to a fair trial."

Peter Wlasiuk was again indicted for Patty's murder in 2007. He was retried in the Chenango County Court in 2008. Testimony in Peter's retrial began on September 9, 2008. Prosecutors called fifty-eight witnesses, and the defense, nine. This time his new attorney, Randel Scharf, did not put Peter on the stand. At his second trial, prosecutors alleged that Peter wanted to get rid of Patty so he could get the insurance money and buy a bar in Binghamton.

On September 26, 2008, after deliberating seven hours over two days, the jury of eight women and four men found Peter guilty of murdering his wife.

The deciding factor in the guilty verdict was some notes on a piece of evidence submitted by the defense that referenced Patty's diary. The notes were written on a report made by the state police forensic science lab and entered into evidence by Scharf.

On one page of the report, an officer had written about something he had read in Patty's diary—that Patty was afraid Peter would seriously injure or kill her. The officer also noted that Patty was upset by Peter's continuing sexual affair with Joyce Worden. Patty's diaries, however, were not allowed into evidence because of the appellate court's ruling.

The jurors asked the judge if they could consider the officer's notes as evidence. He said they could, and less than half an hour later, the jurors sent a note to the judge that they had reached a verdict—they found Peter guilty of second-degree murder, the same verdict the jury in his first trial had reached.

After the verdict, Scharf said the judge had made a huge error when he said the jury could consider the notes as evidence without being told they had been written by an officer, which meant they were not necessarily true.

On November 17, 2008, Peter Wlasiuk was again sentenced to twenty-five years to life for the murder of his wife, Patricia. At his sentencing, Judge Martin Smith told Peter he hoped he would never be paroled because he was "a person society needs be protected from."

Peter Wlasiuk is serving his sentence at the Attica Correctional Facility. He has vowed to continue his fight to prove his innocence.

ABOUT THE AUTHOR

LINDA ROSENCRANCE is a freelance writer and editor in the Boston area. She has worked for more than twenty years as an investigative reporter, writing for the *Boston Globe* and the *Boston Herald*, as well as for many community newspapers in the metropolitan Boston area. She is the author of four true-crime books, *Murder at Morses Pond*; *An Act of Murder*; *Ripper*; and *Bone Crusher*, for Kensington Publishing. She is currently working on her fifth true-crime book for Kensington, *The Killer Debutante*.

REFERENCES

All quotations are from Peter Wlasiuk's first trial, which took place on November 6–
    21, 2002, in the Chenango County Court, Norwich, New York. State v. Peter
    Wlasiuk, 2002-35-V.

On December 29, 2011, the Appellate Division of the New York Supreme Court
overturned Peter's second murder conviction. See http://decisions.courts.state
.ny.us/ad3/Decisions/2011/102275.pdf.

The court ruled that Peter's second trial lawyer was ineffective. The court also
said his attorney should have challenged a biased juror as well as hearsay evidence that
Patty feared Peter would kill her.

At the time of this writing, the Appellate Division had sent the case back to
Chenango County Court for further proceedings.

Chapter 5

NIGHTMARE ON SPANISH CREEK

by Robert Scott

I t's not often that a true-crime case turns into a modern ghost story, but that is exactly what happened in the small Northern California town of Keddie. It all stemmed from a quadruple murder, so bizarre and so bloody in its details that the town never recovered from the shock. When the word "ghost town" began to be applied to Keddie, it had more than just one meaning.

In 1981, Keddie was a popular vacation locale not far from the famed Feather River Canyon in the Sierra Nevada Mountains. Situated along sparkling Spanish Creek, Keddie boasted numerous cabins and a resort atmosphere. People came to fish, hike, horseback ride, or just relax. But after the madness of April 1981, there was little in the way of relaxation for anyone there.

It all began innocently enough, with a teenage boy, two teenage girls, and a young boy who lived in Cabin 28 in Keddie with their mother, Glenna Sue Sharp, thirty-six. The family had been renting the cabin since October 1980. Glenna often went by the name Sue or Susan. Her children were John (Johnny), fifteen; Sheila, fourteen; Tina, thirteen; and Ricky, who was still in elementary school. The older boy and girls were just normal teenagers who liked to hang out with their friends and had never been in trouble with the law. In many ways, they enjoyed an idyllic lifestyle in the small mountain community.

Johnny had an older friend, Dana Wingate, seventeen, and they would occasionally hitchhike to the largest town in the area, Quincy, about seven miles away. Johnny was in middle school there, and Dana was in high school. For them, and all the others in the Sharp family, April 11, 1981, started out like any other spring day.

Around 1:30 p.m., Sheila Sharp rode with her mother to pick up Johnny and Dana at Garsen Park and then drove them back to Keddie. Sometime after 3:30 p.m., Johnny and Dana hitchhiked back to Quincy, where they may have visited a friend at Brown's Trailer Park.

In the late afternoon, a woman named Donna Williams picked up Johnny and Dana and gave them a ride from the Big O Tires store in Quincy down the road. The boys got out and went to visit another friend in the area.

A lazy afternoon passed in Cabin 28. In the evening hours, a man named Thomas Schmidt gazed at the cabin. He noted a woman, probably Sue, doing dishes in Cabin 28 around 8:00 p.m. A short time later, Sheila, who was visiting a friend in a nearby cabin, came back to Cabin 28 to get some bedclothes. She planned to stay with the Seabolt family, who lived in the cabin next door.

Sheila grabbed her things and then went to watch television with the Seabolts at their cabin, which was only a few feet away from Cabin 28. For some reason, Paula and Pearl Seabolt looked out a front window that evening and noticed a green van parked outside of Cabin 28 at around 9:00 p.m. They did not know who owned the green van.

Tina Sharp was also watching television at the Seabolt residence, and she asked at one point what time it was. When Tina found out it was 9:30 p.m., she said good night and went home to Cabin 28. Already there were her mother, young brother Ricky, and his friend Justin Smartt. Justin was going to spend the night at Cabin 28.

Ricky Sharp would recall later that his mom was lying on the couch watching television, wearing a towel-type bathrobe. Tina was wearing a blue shirt, blue jeans, and tennis shoes before going to bed. Ricky was sleepy and went to bed sometime before 10:00 p.m., as did his friend Justin.

Around that time, a man named Timothy left the Backdoor Bar in Keddie and saw a dark-colored "boxy" van parked across the bridge by a pond. He did not recognize the van. Also at around that time, several people who knew Johnny and Dana saw them on the road hitchhiking back to Keddie. A few of these people later thought Johnny and Dana stopped at a party, but just whose party it was could not be determined.

Not only was the green van observed in Keddie that night; a small brown car, perhaps a Datsun, was also parked near Cabin 28. Like the van, witnesses didn't recognize this vehicle. The one thing that stood out was the fact that the car seemed to have a tire that was going flat.

Sheila went to sleep at the Seabolts' residence sometime between 11:00 p.m. and midnight. Right around that same time, a man named Donald Davis drove by Cabin 28 and noticed that the front porch light was not on. This was unusual, as Sue always kept her front porch light on during the night hours.

Closer to midnight, two people who left the Backdoor Bar noticed a stranger's car coming across the narrow Keddie Bridge into the cabin area. A resident of the area, Karl Spang, witnessed a small light-colored car pass slowly by Cabin 28 around that same time.

Things became somewhat murky at this point. Marilyn Smartt, Justin's mother, later said that she overheard two men talking at the Backdoor Bar. One of them said, "Yo, Bo, let's go." The other man replied, "Just a minute. I'm so mad. Boy, the way I feel, I'd like to kill somebody!"

At around 1:30 a.m., Michael Plyer was awakened by his girlfriend, Barbara Meyer, in their cabin. She told him, "Listen." He did, and they both thought they heard muffled screaming. It was hard to tell where it was coming from. After a while Michael and Barbara went back to sleep.

Around 7:00 a.m. on April 12, Sheila Sharp awoke at the Seabolts' cabin, then returned home to Cabin 28. She opened the door and rocked back in horror. There on the couch was her mother, bludgeoned and butchered. Lying on the floor were the bodies of Johnny and his friend Dana. They, too, had been murdered. The whole place looked like a slaughter pen. There was blood on the walls and blood on the floor. Sheila had been sleeping less than twenty feet away, and had not heard a thing.

In shock, she ran next door and told neighbors what she had just witnessed. Soon a call went out to the sheriff's office about the murders. When Plumas County sheriff's office deputies arrived, Tina Sharp was nowhere to be found. But incredibly Ricky Sharp and his friend Justin Smartt were fast asleep in a back bedroom, only a few feet from the carnage in the front room. They had not heard a thing.

Officers found two bloody hammers and a bent knife in Cabin 28. It was apparent by the savagery that had occurred there that the killer or killers had done a lot more than it took just to kill the victims. They had butchered them in what appeared to have been a frenzy.

An all-points bulletin was put out for Tina Sharp, and local hospitals were contacted in case a killer or killers had been injured in the struggle and were seeking medical attention.

Already the questions were beginning. How could Ricky and Justin have slept through the murders? It was obvious that a great deal of noise must have occurred with the pounding of hammers and the cutting of knives. The boys said they hadn't heard anything—but Justin's story would change significantly.

Why hadn't anyone in the Seabolt cabin, especially Sheila, heard anything? After all, she was sleeping only a few feet away. Had the victims known their attacker or attackers and let them in? Police eventually divulged information that one victim had been gagged, but that the other two had not. Why hadn't those two cried out?

And why hadn't Tina been killed there? Why was she missing? Was she part of all of this or just another victim?

Yet another interesting question came up when Deputy Coroner Douglas McAllister talked to a reporter. McAllister said that he didn't believe illegal drugs were involved, nor did he think burglary was a factor. If the murders weren't drug related, then why the savagery of the killings?

*

Soon there were two Department of Justice investigators on scene, as well as two FBI agents, Dick Donner and Larry Ott. The FBI agents had been called because it appeared that Tina might have been kidnapped and possibly taken across state lines. Nevada was not that far away.

Rumors were rampant in the area. Stories ran the gamut, from crazed satanists committing the crime to Johnny and Dana selling illegal drugs to the wrong people. Sheriff Douglas Thomas quickly tried to put a damper on the satanist theory. He told a journalist, "There were no markings on the wall, no candles brought or anything that would suggest an occult-type murder." And, for some reason, Sheriff Thomas seemed to be sure that the murders were not drug related, even though some of Johnny and Dana's friends had by this point admitted to smoking marijuana.

How had the killer or killers gotten in and out without being detected? Investigators spoke with a man who had walked right by Cabin 28 at 2:00 a.m. Other people had driven by at all hours of the night. Not one of them saw anything amiss.

Sheriff Thomas did have a couple of theories. One was that Sue, Johnny, and Dana all knew their attackers. Maybe they thought that, once they were tied up, they would just be robbed, and so they kept quiet until it was too late. The other theory was that Johnny and Dana had walked in just as Sue was being attacked and were overpowered before they had a chance to respond.

The Plumas County sheriff's office had scent-dog teams out looking for traces of Tina Sharp, but no evidence was found. This led investigators to deduce that Tina had been driven away from the scene of the crime rather than dragged from the cabin and down the street, where her scent would still be apparent. Sheriff Thomas announced, "We've talked to a lot of people, and we've got a lot more to talk to." In fact, he commented that every time his officers talked to one person, this led to two more people to contact. The list of people kept getting longer and longer.

By the second week after the murders, the *Feather River Bulletin* ran the headline "Tina Sharp Feared Dead." Despite the use of jeeps, scent dogs, and an intensive grid search of the area, not one trace of Tina was found. The FBI was starting to back off from the case. At that time, kidnappings generally involved ransom demands, and no such demands had been forthcoming about Tina. Whether she had been kidnapped for some other reason remained unknown.

Sheriff Thomas did say that authorities continued to add names to the list of teenagers who had known Johnny and Dana, and they wanted to talk to them. One story making the rounds was that the two boys had been planning on going to a party either in or near Keddie. What was known for certain was that the last valid sighting of the pair had been around 10:00 p.m. on April 11.

In a vast understatement, Sheriff Thomas declared, "The investigation is not moving as fast as we would like it to."

One of the children who did survive the massacre was Ricky Sharp's friend, Justin Smartt. He later told authorities of a dream he'd had concerning that night. "I am on a passenger boat. Somebody got thrown out and there was a fight. He had long black hair and his hair was combed back. He had black glasses with a gold frame and dark lenses. He had a moustache, jean jacket, blue jeans and wore cowboy boots. He had a hammer in his left hand and it had a wooden handle.

"Johnny and Dana fought the man. Dana was almost drunk. Johnny was thrown overboard and then Dana. The man ran away. A body was lying on the bow. Sue, she had black hair and a sheet over her. I looked under the sheet and she was slit in the chest. Everybody gathered around her and wanted to go to shore."

Justin's dream was significant. Sue Sharp had indeed been stabbed in the chest. Justin continued describing his dream. "I was down by Sue, trying to take care of her. All the blood was coming down and I was trying to patch her up with a blue and white flowered rag. I threw the rag in the water."

Later, Justin told a polygraph operator that he believed he had actually witnessed the murders. This testimony differed from Justin's dream description. Justin said that he had heard a noise and awoke. He went to the bedroom doorway and peeked into the living room. Sue was lying on the sofa, and two adult males were standing in the middle of the room. One did have black hair combed back and dark glasses, while the other one had brown hair and wore blue jeans and army-type boots.

According to Justin, Johnny and Dana came in through the front door. Johnny began arguing with the two men, and a fight started. Dana tried to get away and fled toward the kitchen, but the brown-haired man struck him with a hammer, and Dana fell to the floor. Sue rushed to Johnny's aid, and Justin returned to his room and hid behind a door.

It's not clear what he could have seen at that point, but he did say that the two men tied up Johnny and Dana. So Justin must have been able to see the living room from wherever he was hiding.

Justin went on to say that Tina came out of her room, dragging a blanket, and asked, "What's going on?" The two men rushed forward, grabbed Tina by the arm, and dragged her out the back door. Justin claimed that Tina had cried for help. If she did, no one in the area heard her.

Justin told the polygraph operator that the black-haired man was the one who "cut Sue in the middle of her chest." Justin said the man used a pocket knife. Authorities had found a pocket knife in the living room with a bent blade. The blade might have bent if it struck bone.

Marilyn Smartt later told authorities that Martin Smartt "hated Johnny Sharp with a passion." Marilyn even claimed that Martin had burned some item in the fireplace in the early morning hours of April 12. And it's worth noting that Martin Smartt and his friend John "Bo" Boudee (spelled "Boubede" in some reports) had been at the Backdoor Bar the evening of April 11. It was Bo who had supposedly said, "Boy, the way I feel, I'd like to kill somebody!" A few hours later, Johnny, Dana, and Sue were dead, and Tina Sharp was missing.

Also of interest to the investigators was the fact that Justin later said that two days after the murder, he'd told Martin, "I have to protect, Sue." As he'd said this, Justin apparently demonstrated someone trying to stab Sue with a knife, as he tried to ward off the stabbing. According to Justin, Martin grabbed him and said, "Never talk about that again!" Try as they might, however, the authorities could not pin the murders on Martin Smartt and John Boudee.

It would make sense that Martin did not go into the room where Ricky was hiding if he knew that Justin was also in there. It was obviously a different matter when Tina woke up and wandered into the front room. Her presence in the room immediately made her a target. Even with that information, however, investigators couldn't quite bring together the loose ends to tie Martin Smartt and John Boudee to the murders.

Of course, the biggest "loose end" was what had happened to Tina. Her jacket was eventually found beneath a building that children of the area called their "clubhouse." The jacket had blood on it.

Three years passed with no resolution to the case. Then, in 1984, the improbable happened. Tina Sharp's skull was discovered. Strangely, it was found fifty miles from Keddie, near the small town of Feather Falls. Authorities wondered why the skull had been found there. Had Tina been murdered there and her body left in the forest? Or had she been killed in Keddie and then dumped near Feather Falls? And why Feather Falls? It was not on a direct route from

Keddie. In fact, a person would have to take many back roads just to get there from Keddie.

These and many other questions have never been answered. But one thing was certain. The small resort town of Keddie never recovered from the horrific murders in Cabin 28. Keddie was now seen by many as a dark and dangerous place. The killer or killers had never been arrested, and if such a terrible crime could happen once, then why not again?

People moved away, tourists did not return for vacations, and slowly, over time, many cabins and residences were abandoned. These empty cabins became hangouts for teenagers and homeless people. Cabin 28 in particular became derelict. Many locals said it was now haunted. Some claimed that at night, blood-curdling screams could be heard coming from the abandoned house. It took on the names "The Murder House" and "The Ghost Cabin."

The once-popular resort community of Keddie began to falter and die. Attempts to revitalize it never amounted to much. A few homes and cabins remained inhabited and well maintained—the residents refusing to be driven out by ghost stories. But many cabins were abandoned and fell into disuse, adding to Keddie's ghostly appearance.

In 2004, the infamous Cabin 28 was finally condemned and torn down. Now only a depression and a few bits of boards and foundation are left as testimony that it ever existed. Yet, even now, there is something threatening and desolate about that spot. The very ground seems to be haunted by what happened there in the early morning hours of April 12, 1981. When the killer or killers enacted a horrendous slaughter of horror and blood, they might as well have stuck a knife into the heart of Keddie.

ABOUT THE AUTHOR

ROBERT SCOTT is the author of sixteen true-crime books, including *The Last Time We Saw Her*; *Married to Murder*; *Driven to Murder*; *Dangerous Attraction*; *Unholy Sacrifice*; and *Most Wanted Killer*. Scott's book *Shattered Innocence*, details the Jaycee Lee Dugard case. Scott has appeared on television programs on TruTV, the E! network, and Investigation Discovery.

REFERENCES

"Cabin 28," Detailed Timeline, posted by "Jesse W." Keddie Murders Forum, December 22, 2008. http://www.keddiemurdersfilm.com/forum/.

Feather River Bulletin. 1981. (Plumas County, CA). April 15–20.

Sumner, Bernie. 2008. "The Unsolved Keddie Murders." Find Target Articles, May 26. http://articles.findtarget.com/articles/culture_and_society/crime/the_keddie_murders/e.

Chapter 6

THE GRIM KEEPER

by Katherine Ramsland

The superintendent of *polizia* in the province of Reggio Emilia had a problem. Over the past eight months, two elderly women had gone missing from the same neighborhood in Correggio, but there were no leads. They were just gone, as if they'd never existed, save for the silent testament of personal mementos in their abandoned homes. Tension had been in the air all over Italy, the pungent echo of Mussolini's frustration with Hitler's aggression. The Pact of Blood ensured that if either of them declared war, the other would support it. Mussolini had waffled several times on his stance of neutrality, renaming the agreement the Pact of Steel to soften it for his people. But Hitler had tested him by invading Czechoslovakia and Poland, and from towns and villages all over Italy young men had been joining the army in great anticipation. *Il Duce* had punished France on several scores by supporting Franco's victories in Spain, but England and France then jointly declared war on Germany. All eyes had turned to Mussolini.

It was at the close of 1939, as Italy neared a tipping point, when the first woman, Faustina Setti, vanished from Correggio. People did go missing that year—lots of them—after Mussolini established the Chamber of Fasci and Corporations. Some believed that Italy would fare badly in the impending war, and everyone worried about what would happen to their jobs and homes. It was understandable that those who had found stability elsewhere had moved on.

But the superintendent knew that elderly women whose lives were clearly settled here should not be missing. They wouldn't just leave their families and friends without a word. And, actually, both of these women had made a noticeable effort to assure their acquaintances that they were fine, writing an abundance of letters just before all communication had ceased. The similarities were eerie.

Faustina Setti had lived alone her entire life, without husband or children, but at age fifty, she had plenty of ties to the area. The police had questioned a number of people who knew her, but everyone seemed genuinely puzzled. Many had received a letter from her around the same time, and the messages were pretty much all the same. She'd told them she was in Pola (also spelled Pula), but no one knew where she was staying or whom she was visiting. She'd said she was happy, but when she failed to return, they'd grown worried. She didn't have enemies—not even jealous friends. She'd simply gone to Pola and disappeared.

Detectives had tried to piece together a timeline, but whole segments of the life of this woman who'd lived and traveled alone remained shrouded. She'd left behind no diary or calendar that revealed her plans. It appeared that she'd taken a suitcase and some clothing, so the investigators could only conclude that whatever had happened to Faustina Setti had probably occurred in Pola.

Austria had ruled the province of Pola until after World War I, when it became part of Italy. With a second major war looming, Pola's location on the southern tip of the Istrian peninsula made it a particularly vulnerable region. It was a significant seaport and industrial center, as well as a popular tourist destination, thanks to its ancient amphitheater and famous Roman temples. It drew many types of people, including criminals looking for an easy con. With so many outsiders entering the city, streetwise thieves could overpower a naive woman like Faustina Setti, with no one the wiser.

A check in this area had turned up no reports of Jane Does or women in hospitals recovering from an attack. Beyond that, the police in Correggio had few resources to track down the missing woman. The nation needed such resources for more pressing matters, especially in June 1940, when Mussolini finally led the nation to war. The superintendent had shelved the investigation of Faustina Setti pending a solid reason to believe she'd met with foul play. For all anyone knew, she'd decided to start her life over elsewhere; perhaps she was having a secret affair. But then, eight months later, another woman around Faustina's age vanished from the same neighborhood, giving the police a reason to worry.

Like Faustina, Francesca Soavi had written to her relatives early in September that she was leaving town to take up work in Piacenza. She had a job there, she'd assured them, set up by a friend, and they'd hear from her soon.

These letters had been mailed from Correggio on the same day. However, as time passed, no one heard anything more. Neighbors and relatives consulted with one another, but the quick rash of letters was the last communication anyone had received. The police moved in, albeit with considerably diminished resources, but it seemed as if this woman had been taken up into the sky. Aside from the message in her letters, there was no evidence that she'd even left town. Worse, they found no trace of her presence in Piacenza, bringing them back to Correggio.

Among those questioned was Leonarda Cianciulli, a local shopkeeper who'd known both women. She lived in a whitewashed house along the canal from which she sold herbs, baked goods, and soaps. An amateur poet, the plump, middle-aged woman with salt-and-pepper hair had a reputation for dealing with the occult, so area residents often asked her to reveal their future. The superintendent had believed it was worth a trip to see if the missing women had consulted her.

A motherly sort, Signora Cianciulli welcomed the investigators, inviting them in and offering coffee. Over the course of an hour, they learned that she'd once married a government clerk, from whom she'd separated, and she had four children. A year earlier, her eldest son had joined the army, and she was quite proud of him. As she urged them to try one of her chocolate tea cakes, she told the same story they'd heard from everyone else. She even showed them the letters she'd received from her missing friends. Both had assured her they were fine, and Leonarda told the detectives that when she'd heard about Faustina and Francesca, she'd made a point to read their fortunes. Her special vision had confirmed that they were well and happy. She believed it was just a matter of time before they'd reveal their plans to worried friends.

The investigators left her house thinking that Signora Cianciulli was a bit strange, but they were satisfied that she knew no more than anyone else. They'd reached an impasse.

Leonarda waved at their backs and smiled. It had been almost too easy. But then, she'd always had a persuasive charm. That's why she'd succeeded so well, even without the support of a husband.

Leonarda Cianciulli *knew* things; she understood how the dark forces worked. The police were ignorant. They operated on an entirely different plane. They could never comprehend what she'd done—what she'd *had* to do—but she felt perfectly justified. The proof was evident. She was merely making the forces work *for* her. And after all she'd been through over the past forty-seven years, she believed that she deserved something better.

Leonarda had gotten a miserable start in life. Born a bastard in Montella di Avellino, the result of a rape, she'd known from her first awareness that she reminded her unhappy mother of this brutal attack. She'd felt unwanted, and on at least two occasions, she'd tried to escape the pain of abuse and neglect by erasing herself from existence. Still, she'd made it through adolescence before she'd finally spotted a way out: she had eloped with Raffaele Pansardi, a registry office clerk who made a meager living. Young and naive, he had loved her like no one ever had. He'd been her savior.

However, this union had only deepened the rift between Leonarda and her mother. A female child—even a detested one—offered struggling families a means via marriage to elevate their status, so plans had long been under way to marry Leonarda to a man with considerable social standing. By eloping with a clerk, she'd ruined everything. Her mother was livid; rather than welcome her new son-in-law, she'd cursed the newlyweds.

Leonarda had moved with Raffaele to the town of Lariano in Alta Irpinia. To her horror, the curse followed her. Hoping for a large family that she could smother with love, she'd given birth to one child after another, but three miscarried and ten died young. Left with only four, she'd visited every practitioner of magic she could find, seeking signs of hope. She believed that this dark cloud that hung over her could be defeated.

One day, Leonarda paid a palm reader and waited anxiously for good news. The oracle studied the lines of her right palm with a serious expression. Leonarda barely breathed.

"Hmm," the woman said under her breath. "Let me see the other one."

Leonarda offered her left palm. She tried not to tremble as she felt the warmth from the reader's hand and watched the lines deepen around her mouth.

The reader squinted hard at her with a fierce glint in her eye before saying, "This is not good. One hand tells me you will end up in prison. The other indicates a criminal asylum. I don't know why, but it is inevitable. It will be one or the other."

Leonarda withdrew her hand in shock. She did not believe it, and yet her life had been filled with terrible things. What if she went mad from disappointment and committed a crime? She told herself to be more watchful. But she continued to consult prognosticators, and another revealed something worse, "You will live to see all of your children die."

Leonarda could barely understand. Unlike her mother, she loved her children. She was fully devoted to those who'd survived, and she routinely said prayers for the souls of the thirteen who'd already departed. She went home from these occult sessions deeply wounded. Why were the forces so firmly aligned against her? What had she done? She knew she had to find a way to appease them.

On top of all her grief, in 1930 an earthquake destroyed her home, forcing the family to move to Correggio, in the Po Valley of northern Italy. Here, Leonarda had opened her shop to sell charms. She loved helping people. She baked cakes, made herbal remedies, and offered a range of homemade soaps and perfumes. She also became an amateur poet and studied the occult to learn how she might avoid the dire things predicted for her. As a result, she gained so much knowledge that she started to offer advice to friends and customers. She quickly learned that telling people what they wanted to hear was always better than delivering bad news. They happily paid a fee and went away satisfied. They also returned, so this business put a little money in Leonarda's pocket, as well as giving her the feeling of power. She sensed if she learned the future's signposts, she could redirect the dire predictions for her own life. Fiercely protective, she was determined that no dark force was going to claim her remaining children.

But then her oldest son, Giuseppe, shocked her. Now a young man, he'd observed the country's unrest and the number of his friends enlisting. As Italy opened a front in Africa and prepared to support Germany's war effort in Europe, he made a decision.

"I'm going to join the army," he told his mother.

Leonarda was stunned. As if walking blindly toward his destiny, her favorite child was placing himself in the greatest possible danger. He knew nothing of the terrible prophecy, but she had not forgotten. It seemed clear to everyone during the fall of 1939 that Italy would soon be sending forces into other countries and that many of those troops would die. Leonarda knew from what she'd read in her books of mystery that one paid for a life with another life. To save Giuseppe, someone else must die. She looked around. Then she spotted the solution.

Faustina Setti, a neighbor, had been unmarried her entire life, and she wanted a change. She had saved up thirty thousand lire, and she'd offered it all to Leonarda to find her a mate. Leonarda was only too happy to assist. She knew she could easily "send" Faustina to a distant town and disguise her intent as a "service." She told Faustina that she knew about a man in Pola who would be perfect for her, but she insisted that this arrangement would work out only if Faustina did everything she was told. She could not deviate from the instructions even a little, or it would all collapse. Faustina gave her word. She desperately wanted to meet her heart-mate.

"Keep what I tell you a secret," Leonarda insisted. "If you reveal it to anyone, you will never meet him."

The first task, Leonarda said, was for Faustina to write notes to all her close relatives and friends. She was to keep these notes with her and mail them when she reached Pola. She could then tell anyone who might be worried that she was fine—just visiting a friend. If she followed all these steps, Leonarda assured her, and paid the fee, Faustina would meet the man she'd been waiting for her whole life.

Excited, Faustina set about writing letters and postcards to everyone she knew. Perhaps she included people to whom she hadn't spoken in a while, just to strengthen the magic. She didn't understand how this exercise would work, but the stakes were high, so she asked no questions. When she was ready, she packed her best dresses, bundled up her correspondences, and took everything over to the poetess. Faustina dreamed of the romance she'd never had.

"Have a glass of wine before you go," said Leonarda. "To celebrate."

Faustina held up her packet of letters, all ready to be mailed, and paid Leonarda's fee. "I'm ready to leave."

"Then sit for a moment."

They went into the kitchen and talked for a few minutes about Faustina's preparations before she urged, "Tell me again about this man. I'm so anxious to meet him." She took a sip of the deep-red wine.

Leonarda smiled. "You'll soon see for yourself."

"He has a nice house?" Another sip.

"You'll be quite surprised."

"And he . . ." Faustina stopped for a moment. Her eyes fluttered and her face flushed.

"You're overexcited," Leonarda said. "Take a breath."

"Sho . . . heesh . . . am I . . . ?"

Leonarda watched her struggle to speak. She smiled. The drug was working.

"I'm going . . . itsh time . . ."

"Here, my dear, lie down a moment. You look pale."

Leonarda waited patiently as Faustina fell into a stupor. When Faustina lay still and her breath went shallow, Leonarda was relieved. She knew the time was right. Everything was moving according to plan.

She'd been preparing all day. She'd never done anything like this before, but her son's life was in jeopardy. Thinking of Giuseppe, she picked up a hatchet with a sharp blade, raised it high, and swung it hard, slamming her friend on the skull. She did this several times, casting blood across the floor and onto a wall. Faustina jerked twice before she lay still, but clearly she was dead. Leonarda looked at her victim in triumph. Now her son would be safe. She'd made the necessary sacrifice, and she'd enriched her family as well. Since Faustina had to die and would no longer need her money, there seemed no reason not to take it.

But Leonarda also had a body lying in front of her, and a lot of blood. She bent over and steadied herself, then gripped Faustina's traveling dress and dragged the corpse into a large closet with an overhead light. Shutting the door to ensure privacy, she picked up a thin saw, a boning knife, and a sharp cleaver, and then prepared an area where she could work without interruption. Positioning Faustina's corpse faceup, Leonarda placed the saw blade on the woman's cold skin, against her shoulder, and pushed down. The skin yielded but did not break. Leonarda applied her full strength to the task, using a mallet to dig the blade in. She pushed and pulled on the saw, assisted with the knife, until she had broken through the skin. She worked her way through muscle and bone to remove the right arm, gathering the blood as it flowed from the open wounds to set it aside. It was a messy, time-consuming business, but she continued. After disarticulating the body, Leonarda removed the head, reminded only briefly by the sagging face that this woman had once been her friend. Before she was finished, Leonarda had cut the corpse into nine separate pieces, each just the right size for her largest kettle.

She'd already prepared her soap-making ingredients—resin, aum, and caustic soda—although she used considerably more for this grim deed than for her typical recipe. These she boiled before dropping the hands and arms into the bubbling pot, and then the feet and legs. As she was about to toss in the head, Leonarda held it by the hair and looked into the dead face, its hemorrhaged eyes slightly open. She whispered a quick "*grazie*" and then dumped it in with the rest. Finally, she added the chest and abdomen.

The room temperature was nearly unbearable, but for hours Leonarda stirred, holding a cloth over her nose against the noxious fumes. Throughout the night, she thought of her son as she watched the flesh melt off the bones, and the bones eventually dissolve into a thick, blackish sludge. This mixture she allowed to cool until she could pour it into a series of buckets. Once this task was done, she took the buckets, one at a time, and dumped the contents into a septic tank. Then she returned for the most intriguing task. She knew where the true power lay.

Leonarda lifted the basin of blood she'd drained from Faustina's body. By now it had thickened and congealed, so she spread the sticky stuff onto flat pans. These she placed into a warm oven. Every so often she would test it, and when the substance was dry and hard, she cooled it until she was able to grind it into a brownish powder that would cut into flour. Mixing this concoction with eggs, sugar, and milk, she added a touch of chocolate, pulling a wooden spoon through the mixture until it was just the right texture. She was pleased to see that the blood and chocolate had blended so well. Leonarda rolled and patted the dough with her hands, placing small mounds onto flat pans. When she pushed them into the hot oven, it wasn't long before their cooked fragrance filled her home. Once these fine little tea cakes were ready, she placed them in a container.

Now, for the last step: the deflection. Leonarda went out with Faustina's packet of letters and put them into the mail. Let those who sought her look for her in Pola. She was now sure that she'd defied the curse. She'd saved her son. Even if he went to war, he was protected. His fellow soldiers were going to be amazed by his uncanny luck. She'd done the best she could for him.

For weeks, Leonarda served the special tea cakes to people who came to visit, and she enjoyed knowing that they were consuming the very person about whom they were gossiping. Faustina was *there*, inside them. It was almost too funny. In fact, to ensure her son's good fortune, Leonarda gave him several cakes. He went off with his friends to prepare for battle, and whenever he sent her a letter, she was relieved to see that the magic was working.

But then Mussolini entered the war, and Leonarda started to worry. Had the sacrifice of Faustina been enough? Not well versed in this particular area of dark magic, she grew more anxious with each passing day. She looked for another sacrifice.

In early September, her friend Francesca Soavi came by. They had tea as Francesca described how depressed she'd been lately. She didn't know where she would get money to maintain her home or to buy food. She wondered if the war had affected Leonarda's business.

Leonarda was about to console her when she got a better idea. She assured her friend she could look into the future for her. She told Francesca to return the following day.

"I'd be so grateful! Please tell me if there's any hope."

The next day, Leonarda told Francesca what she'd learned: there was a job at a school for girls in Piacenza, but getting it required a specific ritual. If Francesca followed Leonarda's directions, step by step, the job would be hers.

"You must write letters to all of your family and friends," Leonarda instructed, "to assure them you're fine, but you must tell no one where you're going until after you arrive. From there, you can mail the letters."

Francesca was excited. The job sounded exactly right for her, and at her advancing age she had few options. She packed her clothes and prepared to leave. Then she walked over to Leonarda's canal-side house to say good-bye and to thank her. In her pocket she had her packet of letters and three thousand lire.

Leonarda offered Francesca some wine, and they sat down together. In a repeat of the previous scenario, she watched Francesca fall under the drug's spell, grabbed her hatchet and cleaver, and once more boiled up a pot of human soap. Two sacrifices would surely please whatever forces controlled her son's fate. This was all too easy. In fact, this time she used some of the hot sludge to make candles and soap for her shop. It took just a bit of perfume to mask the odor, and finding a good use for the transformed flesh meant she had to carry less of the smelly stuff to the septic system. She was getting good at this! To honor her son, Leonarda lit several of the candles.

As Francesca's family and friends grew increasingly more worried, discussing the matter with Leonarda over coffee and cake, they fell into despair. Francesca had uncharacteristically vanished. They were certain she'd come to harm. Leonarda handed out bars of soap, *gratis*, and reassured them that there was no cause for alarm. But her son was still away, and she grew worried again, so she began to look for yet another "sacrifice."

She set her eye on neighbor and client Virginia Cacioppo, a former soprano of some renown. Virginia, now fifty-three, had come to Leonarda, desperate for employment and willing to pay a great deal, so the poetess took advantage. She told Virginia that she'd found work for her as the secretary of a wealthy man in Florence.

"But you must do as I say and tell no one," she warned, "or you'll lose the position."

Virginia agreed to everything, preparing herself just as Faustina and Francesca had done, and on September 30, she brought a payment of fifty thousand lire and a handful of valuable gems. Leonarda accepted it all with feigned gratitude and offered Virginia a glass of wine to see her on her way. Soon Virginia's remains were going into the pot and her blood into the oven. Not long after, Leonarda had another batch of tea cakes.

Virginia's sister-in-law walked into the police station. She was nervous, but she knew what she'd seen. Virginia Cacioppo had entered the soap-maker's house, she told them, and then had disappeared. Virginia's letter, which arrived a few days later, told of her great good fortune in finding a position, but when time went by and no one heard more from her, this woman was certain something was wrong—especially with two other women still missing.

The investigators considered what they had: three women from the same neighborhood had all disappeared within a short period of time, all had written similar letters, and all knew Leonarda Cianciulli. Yet she was a popular, middle-aged woman. What reason would she have to harm them? Still, she was a solid person of interest.

The superintendent brought Leonarda in for questioning. At first she seemed confused, but the police reassured her that they just had a few items to discuss. To their surprise, she readily confessed. In fact, she seemed happy to provide the details of what she'd done with each and every one of the missing women, as if she was proud of it. Those who listened to her talk about how she'd murdered, dismembered, and boiled three women in the superstitious belief that it would protect her son were stunned. Some of them remembered with distaste the chocolate cakes she had served them. Had they inadvertently consumed human blood?

How could any woman, they wondered, do this to one person, let alone three? She was a wife and mother, a woman who wrote poetry. It baffled everyone who heard about the case, but, strangely enough, an American psychiatrist had the answer.

During the time that Leonarda Cianciulli had transformed into a remorseless serial killer, prison psychiatrist Hervey Cleckley was writing a groundbreaking book, *The Mask of Sanity*. He was aware that during the early part of the century, the condition called "constitutional psychopathic inferiority" had been a vague diagnosis that encompassed too many different types of conditions to be diagnostically useful. It had evolved from other equally vague diagnoses from the past century, based on the observations of asylum directors and a handful of criminologists. In the prisons, Cleckley had met some rather distinct and charming manipulators who seemed to be in a category all their own. They could dupe people easily and had no remorse for their trespass against others, not even for murder. Cleckley called them psychopaths.

He described them in *The Mask of Sanity* as being agreeable and affable on first impression. For all intents and purposes, they are alert, able to engage in conversation, quite charming, and even funny. They appear to have genuine interests, and one would notice nothing particularly odd about their manner. In fact, they often seem quite well adjusted. Despite their tendency to lie to and con others, they don't come across as oily, artificial, or slick. Yet they have the capacity to plot against you even as they reassure you about their true friendship.

Cleckley had studied many convicted psychopathic offenders, but he had also analyzed such conniving people in professional and political life. They were present inside prison and out. The cleverest of them were not murderers; rather, they had applied their manipulative skills to social trespass for self-enrichment. Devising sixteen distinct clinical criteria for assessing these psychopaths, Cleckley described them as being rich in the following traits: charming, manipulative, irresponsible, self-centered, shallow, lacking in empathy or anxiety, and likely to commit more types of crimes than other offenders. When violent, they were more impulsive, more likely to recidivate, and less likely to respond to treatment.

At this time, most mental health professionals viewed psychopaths as male, and it would be decades before anyone would study female inmates to see how psychopathy manifested in women. Generally speaking, clinicians referred to female psychopaths as morally insane. But Leonarda Cianciulli, the "soap-maker of Correggio," was already showing the world that she was on the same level as remorseless males who dreamt up hideous crimes, fully appreciating that they were wrong. God had not commanded these murders, as a deranged lunatic might insist; Leonarda had done so, based on ignorant superstition. But even if she could somehow justify the "sacrifice" for her son, the dismemberments, the making of soap from human flesh, the drying of blood to make flour for cooking—these things moved her into the area of an extreme criminal deviant.

At her trial in Reggio Emilia in June 1946, Leonarda's testament, titled "An Embittered Soul's Confessions," provided her official statement. A correspondent for *Time* magazine described how the hefty serial offender "gripped the witness-stand rail with oddly delicate hands and calmly set the prosecutor right on certain details. Her deep-set dark eyes gleamed with a wild inner pride as (according to him) she concluded: 'I gave the copper ladle, which I used to skim the fat off the kettles, to my country, which was so badly in need of metal during the last days of the war. . . .'"

As she coldly described what she'd done with the women—her friends— she mesmerized the entire court. About Virginia Cacioppo, for example, the

Italian sources quote her as saying, "She ended up in the pot, like the other two ... her flesh was fat and white. When it had melted, I added a bottle of cologne, and after a long time on the boil I was able to make some most acceptable creamy soap. I gave bars to neighbors and acquaintances. The cakes, too, were better: that woman was really sweet."

Leonarda Cianciulli was diagnosed as "manic," which meant that her behavior was at least partly compulsive. However, she was found to be criminally responsible: she knew what she was doing and that it was wrong. She received a sentence of thirty years in prison and three years in a criminal asylum in Pozzuoli—exactly as the palm reader had foreseen. She was in the asylum when she died at the age of seventy-six from cerebral apoplexy on October 15, 1970. (It remains unknown from available sources whether she outlived her surviving children.)

The Ministry of Justice Department of Prison Administration in Rome offers criminological exhibits to the public on the Via del Gonfalone, and among them is a glass case that houses artifacts from the investigation of Leonarda Cianciulli. These include the trivet for the pot in which Leonarda boiled her victims into soap, and the hacksaw, kitchen knife, hatchet, and hammer that she used to kill and carve them up. Two films and several stage plays were based on this case.

While female serial killers are more prevalent than many people believe, a murderess like Leonarda Cianciulli, who dismembered her victims for occult purposes and cooked and consumed their blood, is quite rare. It's the kind of story one might find among fairy tales about witches rather than as a case in a criminological museum. A coldhearted psychopath who even fed the blood of victims to others—she's almost too evil to believe.

ABOUT THE AUTHOR

DR. KATHERINE RAMSLAND is an associate professor of psychology at DeSales University in Pennsylvania, where she also teaches criminal justice. She has published over nine hundred articles and forty books, including *The Mind of a Murderer: Privileged Access to the Demons That Drive Extreme Violence*; *Inside the Minds of Serial Killers*; *The Forensic Psychology of Criminal*

Minds; Beating the Devil's Game; A History of Forensic Science and Criminal Investigation; Inside the Minds of Healthcare Serial Killers; and *The Human Predator: A Historical Chronology of Serial Murder and Forensic Investigation.* For seven years, she contributed regularly to Court TV's (now TruTV) *Crime Library* and now writes a column on historic and investigative forensics for the *Forensic Examiner.* She has appeared on numerous cable network documentaries and programs on NPR, as well on as such programs as *The Today Show, 20/20, Montel Williams, Larry King Live,* and *E! True Hollywood Story.*

REFERENCES

Bolognini, Mauro. 1977. *Gran Bollito.* Triangolo Film, Italy.

Cleckley, Hervey. 1988. *The Mask of Sanity: An Attempt to Clarify Some Issues about the So-Called Psychopathic Personality.* 5th ed. St. Louis, MO: C. V. Mosby, 1976.

"The Correggio Soap-Maker." 2003. *Museo Criminologico Catalog,* pp. 23–25. Rome, Italy.

"The Correggio Soap-Maker." Museo Criminologico Exhibit. Ministry of Justice. Rome, Italy.

"Foreign News: A Copper Ladle." 1946. *Time,* June 24. http://www.time.com/time/magazine/article/0,9171,852845,00.html (accessed September 2010).

Hibbert, Christopher. 2008. *Mussolini: The Rise and Fall of Il Duce.* New York: Palgrave Macmillan.

Ivelja-Dalmatin, Ana. 2009. *Pula.* Tourist Monograph.

Ramsland, Katherine. 2007. *Beating the Devils Game: A History of Forensic Science and Criminal Investigation.* New York: Berkley.

Chapter 7

THE ALASKA MAIL-BOMB CONSPIRACY

by Burl Barer

Peggy Barnett dreamed of George Kerr. Cute George. Puppy-dog George. Peggy is pregnant with her husband's child, but she dreams of twenty-year-old George Kerr. The dream excites Peggy, and she breathlessly recounts every erotic detail to her brother, Doug. He likes to listen.

The way she tells it, the images begin slowly, teasingly, mounting in intensity, and climaxing in glorious irrevocable finality.

The dream is always the same: She drives down a quiet country road. Standing up ahead, straddling the center line is boyish, denim-clad George Kerr. He doesn't move. She guns the engine, picking up speed as the adrenaline roars fire through her veins.

WHAM!

When the impact sends Kerr's shattered body careening in a flailing arc over the hood of the car, Peggy's heart almost bursts. She stops the car, gets out, and looks back at Kerr's twitching limbs. Little George is still alive. Peggy smiles. This is her favorite part. She walks to where he lies broken on gravel, blood bubbling between his lips, eyes staring in shock and disbelief. Peggy Barnett, devoted wife, loving mother, Jehovah's Witness, leans over and snaps Kerr's neck with her bare hands. Warm blood runs out of his mouth, over her wrists, pours down her palms, and drips sticky, wet splotches on the dirt.

"I hope you washed the blood off before you woke up," says Doug with a grin. "You know what the Bible says about blood." And they both have a good laugh about dead little puppy-dog, baby-faced George Kerr.

On September 14, 1991, a very pregnant Peggy Barnett drove her nine-year-old daughter two miles from her house to the Anchorage mail facility. Peggy was on the verge of going into labor, the road was rough and bumpy, and there was a homemade bomb in the car. Arriving safely at the post office, she mailed the nondescript package to George Kerr in Chugiak, fifteen miles northeast of Anchorage. David Kerr, George's father, picked up the package from the Chugiak post office three days later and took it back to the family home. David and his wife, Michelle, were standing in the kitchen when he decided to open it. The explosion was so intense; neighbors feared there had been an earthquake.

The blast destroyed the kitchen, living room, dining room, and hallway; shredded the rafters; and lifted a section off the top of the house. David Kerr, forty-four, died instantly. A piece of cartilage from one of his knuckles was found on the roof.

Michelle Kerr, found coated in a thick layer of insulation and blood, was lifted from the rubble and rushed to the emergency room. Though blinded, bloody, and burned; with both eardrums ruptured; numerous facial bones broken; no sense of smell or taste; thousands of shrapnel wounds; and a nearly destroyed airway, she begged paramedics and doctors to save her life.

"The ambulance personnel kept Michelle Kerr alive and engaged in conversation on the way to Humana Hospital," recalls US Postal Inspector Jim Bordenet, who worked this case from the beginning.

> The Anchorage Police met the ambulance when it arrived. I have a copy of the actual Anchorage Police Department's audio tape of Michele Kerr, recorded at Humana Hospital, as she was being removed from the ambulance. Given her severe injuries, and the possibility she would not survive, they asked her to talk in hopes that she could give them a clue, or more, as to who would do this horrible thing. On the audio tape, you can hear the siren, and Michelle's struggling for breath. Her speech was garbled, her voice hardly audible due to the blast damage to her mouth and face. Yet, Michelle summoned the strength to say, 'The package was addressed to George. It was from the State of Alaska.' And then she said the most amazing and insightful thing, 'Doug did it. Doug Gustafson did it.' She then lapsed into unconsciousness.

Michelle finally "woke up" about six weeks later to a sufficient extent that US postal inspectors could talk to her. She remembered David bringing the package inside the house; that he remarked it was from the state of Alaska and was addressed to George. As her husband tore at the outer wrapping, the next feeling she experienced was "like I was melting into the floor." Her eardrums were blown out, so she heard nothing. She just felt a tremendous pressure—then nothing.

How did she surmise that Doug Gustafson was involved? Given the family history with their son George and the Gustafsons, her comment was right on.

It was no secret that Douglas Gustafson and his cohort, Raymond Cheely, despised young George Kerr, had knowledge of explosives, and liked to blow things up. Gustafson and Cheely, however, had perfect alibis. They were already in prison for murder.

SMILEY AND LIZARD

Raymond "Smiley" Cheely and Douglas "Lizard" Gustafson are neither bright men nor endearing characters. They are convicted teenage murderers. Cheely's nickname derives from his continual grin; Gustafson earned his reptilian moniker by a chilling lack of human warmth. Naturally, they became the best of friends.

Attending Alaska's Chugiak High School, they dissipated their midteen years in repeated displays of antisocial behavior committed with a core group of recalcitrant would-be hard-asses: Travis Smith, Eric Evans, Shayn Nicolaysen, Mike Connor, Chris Robinson, and George Kerr. Cheely, the pack's undisputed leader, acquired his authoritative position in ninth grade.

His ticket to social prominence was a provisional driver's license and ownership of a large Chevy carryall. "Everyone liked Cheely because he had a big Suburban and would organize parties," recalls Travis Smith. "He could get a lot of people in it."

Cheely's gang was fearless and well aware that as long as they were under eighteen, there would be little price to pay for their decidedly criminal hijinks.

"We were once stopped while driving down a road clubbing mailboxes," remembers Eric Evans. "Ten cops pinned us down and pulled guns. We all got off because the cops forgot to read us our rights." He also said they would shoplift smokes and tools because they "didn't have anything else to do."

Smoking cigars behind the Kerr's home, the boys accidentally burned down a shack. They thought that was cool and soon began experimenting with explosives, building bombs with one-by-eight-inch pipes and using gunpowder for the bang. Mostly, they hung out at Cheely's house, where, in the acres of secluded woods, they could target practice and blow up old cars.

Chris Robinson, whose father worked as a corrections officer, was one of the first to realize his playmates were playing with fire. Although he continued to consider the guys his friends, he left Cheely's gang when they started breaking the law.

Soon to follow in his footsteps was Shayn Nicolaysen, who was convinced that Cheely was going down.

When they were high school sophomores, four members of the gang went to Alaska Sales and Service, busted open lockboxes with a sledgehammer, and drove off with three new Chevy trucks. For a week, the boys went four-wheeling on dirt roads, drove the trucks to school, and parked them at night in the Eklutna gravel pit. Cheely had told them how they could find wrecked S10s and swap out the serial numbers and enough parts to call the trucks their own. Cheely was an expert on such matters, as his parents owned Eagle River Auto Parts.

Smith, Connor, and Evans were headed for an Anchorage Denny's® restaurant in one of the stolen trucks when the cops spotted them. Soon, they were behind bars at the McLaughlin Youth Center, ordered to pay restitution, and placed on probation. While Cheely was never fingered in those thefts, he had driven the boys to Alaska Sales and Service and provided the sledgehammer. No one ever mentioned his name to the cops.

Ironically, two years later, Smith got a call from Alaska Sales and Service informing him that he'd won the car dealer's annual giveaway of five hundred silver coins worth $4,000. When Smith got his first car, he started spending less time with Cheely and more time with George Kerr and Eric Evans, known as "The Burn Brothers" because of their habit of snuffing out cigarettes between their pressed forearms.

Cheely and Gustafson graduated with the class of 1990. Cheely's parents had high hopes for him. They bought a full-page advertisement in the back of his high school yearbook and plastered it with photos of his youth, proclaiming how proud they were of their son.

Exactly what they were proud of is not clear, as it couldn't have been the pregraduation burning of his 1988 Chevy pickup, apparently as an insurance scam, or the reported theft of a Chevy pickup from Alaska Sales and Service.

According to court testimony, Cheely had salvaged enough parts to make the new truck look like his old one. He got caught when high-school authorities called police to check a pump-action shotgun hanging in the truck. Even in Alaska, weapons are not allowed on school property. Although law officials were never able to prove the truck was stolen, Cheely was convicted for another Chevy truck theft the same year he graduated from Chugiak High.

The summer after graduation, Cheely confronted a friend accused of stealing money from his parents' store. When she denied it, he tied her spread-eagle between two trees in the woods near his parents' Eklutna home. He left her there screaming for fifteen minutes before returning to rape her. When he finished, he apologized and promised to be her protector from then on.

By late summer 1990, Cheely's gang had diminished to the troubled trio of Cheely, Gustafson, and baby-faced dropout George Kerr, one of three children from his father's previous marriage.

George's dad, David Kerr, knew the boy was a handful, but he and his new wife, Michelle, did everything they could to provide a stable home. Unfortunately, George felt more at home riding in the backseat of Cheely's car.

One night, the three young toughs broke into a contractor's cache of dynamite and used it to blow up abandoned cars, planning to sell the balance to pay for beer, movies, and cars. In October, the boys broke into Mike's Quality Meats in Eagle River and stole about $20,000 in cash. The money was split three ways. Gustafson, who always wanted to be a sniper, took part of his cut and ordered a $1,700 HK-91 semiautomatic rifle from Jumbo's Ammo Cache in Chugiak.

THE TRAGIC DEATH OF JEFFREY CAIN

When Gustafson's sniper rifle arrived on October 19, 1990, the trio's unproductive Alaskan adolescence climaxed with the senseless slaying of twenty-year-old Jeffrey Cain.

It was Cain's misfortune to be a passenger in Robert Chamberlain's red Toyota* when it passed the AMC Eagle driven by nineteen-year-old Raymond Cheely. Also in the Eagle were Doug Gustafson and George Kerr. The three teens were heading to the Big Timber Motel in Anchorage to rent a room for the night and to "party" with affordable intoxicants and rentable women.

When Cheely and Gustafson decided that the Toyota had cut them off, the pursuit to "get them" was on. The Eagle accelerated to catch up; Cheely maneuvered his car into a position no more than fifty feet behind so that Gustafson, armed with the HK-91 assault rifle, could get a good shot.

With no other cars in sight, Gustafson leaned out the passenger side of the Eagle and squeezed off one shot. The bullet smashed through the Toyota's rear window, struck Cain in the head, and killed him instantly.

Gustafson, Cheely, and Kerr watched the Toyota drive away and thought Gustafson had missed. The three boys continued on to party at the Big Timber Motel. The next morning, Kerr awoke early because he had to get to work. He grabbed a cab home, where he saw the morning newspaper. He realized that Gustafson hadn't missed and called the boys at the motel and told them what happened. They told him to keep his damn mouth shut. Kerr realized that if he didn't take immediate action to protect himself, his life and future were in immediate danger. Hanging out with teenage tough guys was one thing, but murder was something else. It was then that George Kerr went to his boss and told him what happened.

"By sheer coincidence, his boss's attorney was there at the same time," says Jim Bordenet. "He rightfully told the kid to go to the police, and do so immediately." George went to the police station, told the cops everything, and agreed to wear a hidden recorder to tape incriminating conversations with Cheely and Gustafson.

While David Kerr thought his son was at work, George was really with the police getting wired up. Finally, George called his father, explaining what happened the night before and how he planned to help the police.

When George called his dad, he had no idea that Cheely was there at the house. Cheely was obviously there to make sure that George hadn't rolled over on him and Doug, though he'd told David Kerr that he needed David's help to repair his truck.

David Kerr apparently did his best to cover up the nature of George's call, trying to not tip off Cheely that George had gone to the cops. As a precaution, the cops sent George to talk to Doug Gustafson. Meanwhile, the police contacted everyone on the fringe of Cheely's shrinking gang and got two of them to also wear wires.

The comments of Doug Gustafson captured on tape by George Kerr, plus incriminating statements made by Cheely recorded by another undercover wire, were crucial to the arrest and successful prosecution of Cheely and Gustafson for the murder of Jeffrey Cain.

This was Anchorage's first drive-by shooting, and the media coverage was extensive. Cheely's lawyer filed a motion for a change of venue, submitting more than twenty-four newspaper articles covering all aspects of the case, including characterizations of both Gustafson and Cheely, the latter of whom was described as a lead troublemaker and a gun nut, as well as other negative characterizations.

Several of the newspaper stories reported that Cheely maneuvered the car so that Gustafson could get a clear shot, that police suspected Cheely had hidden the murder weapon, and that both men had threatened others not to testify against them. The newspaper coverage also detailed past crimes such as burglary and theft in which the two were suspects.

Cheely's argument was simple and direct. Getting a fair trial with presumption of innocence was going to be impossible because the case had already been tried in the press. Despite this intense media coverage, the court ruled that a change of venue was not required. (This became a matter of intense scrutiny and scholarly study in later years.)

George Kerr became the state's star witness. Although hostile and childishly belligerent on the stand, he gave eyewitness testimony, ensuring convictions.

Doug Gustafson, skinny and wan, displayed little emotion when the guilty verdict against him was read. Raymond Cheely, blond and stocky, smirked cockily when his own verdict was announced. Judge Milton Souter sentenced Cheely to sixty years in prison. Judge Karl Johnstone sentenced Gustafson to sixty-five years.

"No prison sentences were sweeter to hear," commented *Anchorage Times* columnist Terry Carr. "No two people more deserved to go to jail for the biggest part of their lives."

THE HIT LIST

Everyone thought George Kerr had done the right thing. His father, an exemplary and admired engineer at Elmendorf Air Force Base, who had served with distinction aboard the nuclear submarine USS *James Madison* during the Vietnam War, was proud of George for "doing the right thing" by going to the police, being honest about everything, and helping bring Cheely and Gustafson to justice.

Cheely and Gustafson felt differently. They wanted George dead. Not the least bit shy, and far from being the model prisoner, Cheely devised elaborate plans for his post-release lifestyle of revenge. "I'm gonna dig a pit under my house," he said to a fellow inmate, "so I can starve and torture the motherfuckers to death."

Not everyone had to wait sixty years for retribution. Cheely compiled a hit list of future victims and kept it stashed in his cell. Fellow inmate Garland Green said that he saw the list Cheely had written on a torn piece of yellow legal paper. According to Green, Cheely hid the list under papers on his nightstand. Once Green got a look at it, Cheely stashed it between his mattress and the wall.

The hit list included the district attorney, police officers, all the jurors who found him guilty, and the judge who presided over the case. At the top of the list was baby-faced George Kerr.

Doug Gustafson was also unimpressed with George Kerr's unflinching honesty following the death of Jeffrey Cain. After all, reasoned Gustafson, Cain's death "wasn't premeditated and it wasn't intentional. What happened that night was a one-in-a-million shot that nobody ever intended." His reasoning, of course, was faulty and contradicted by facts and forensics. Gustafson knew exactly what he was doing when he leaned out the window with his brand-new sniper rifle, and Cheely didn't maneuver behind the car in which Cain was riding by happenstance.

In the months following Cain's death, Gustafson refused to admit that he had even pulled the trigger, which could be why his sister and brother thought he was innocent. Apparently convinced that their brother was railroaded, they were ready to help when he convinced them to kill the chief witness against him.

In Doug Gustafson's own words, "Exterminate the witness and maybe you win the case."

ENTER THE INSPECTORS

Within two hours of the explosion at the Kerr home, an investigative task force was formed led by the US Postal Inspection Service, with assistance from the Anchorage Police Department and the US Department of the Treasury, Bureau of Alcohol, Tobacco and Firearms (ATF). Inspector Russel Mabry was named task-force leader. Within twenty-four hours, the task force numbered twenty-seven inspectors. By September 24, 1991, the number had expanded to nearly fifty.

The US Postal Inspection Service's Crime Laboratory personnel from both the National Forensic Lab in Washington, DC, and the Western Regional Crime Lab at San Bruno, California, responded to the crime scene within the first twenty-four hours. Inspectors Doug Pulling and Mathew Allen were called to lend their combined forty-eight years of experience to Inspector Mabry, and a tactical operations center was set up at Anchorage police headquarters.

Forensic experts and ATF special agents spent two weeks at the crime scene removing furniture, ceiling joints, and roofing material that filled hundreds of industrial-sized evidence bags. These bags were taken to an indoor storage site where they underwent further screening.

David Kerr's body was removed from the blast site within twenty-four hours. An autopsy revealed that an item embedded in his body turned out to be a small component available only at Radio Shack. Three more weeks were devoted to sifting through the debris looking for bomb components and/or bits of mailing wrapper.

Despite published statements by federal authorities that they had no suspects, investigators spent part of the day contacting people with connections to the previous year's fatal highway shooting of Jeffrey Cain, warning them to be careful of packages in the mail. In an effort to protect Michelle Kerr, authorities did not reveal to the press or public that she had emphatically named Gustafson as the one responsible for the bomb.

At first consideration, the prospect that Doug Gustafson, who had been transferred to a high-security facility at Seward, Alaska, on September 3, 1991, could have been directly involved seemed highly problematic. After all, prison authorities routinely monitored his activities and recorded his phone calls.

However, recording is one thing and listening is another. Upon investigation, it was discovered that no one at the prison had ever bothered to play back the tapes.

Inspector Mathew Allen persistently listened to hour after hour of Doug Gustafson's tiring telephone banter. One particular conversation was recorded on September 5, 1991—twelve days before the explosion. Gustafson was giving his sister, Peggy, instructions about fixing her car. In reality, he was telling her how to build the bomb to kill George Kerr.

Allen called in Inspectors Mabry and Pulling, and the more they listened, the more they learned. The conspiracy to murder Kerr involved Peggy, Doug, their brother Craig, Raymond Cheely, and mutual friend Joseph Ryan. Doug told Peggy that when it was all done, he'd sit back in his cell, "smoke a nice juicy cigar, down a glass of spirits, and laugh so hard."

The phone recordings also revealed Peggy's erotic dream in which she kills George Kerr with her bare hands after hitting him with her car. "That excerpt was included in the original charging document filed against Peggy, which formed the basis for her initial arrest," recalls Jim Bordenet. "They were also used as part of Inspector Mabry's exhaustive fifty-nine page Affidavit filed with the US District Court in Anchorage in support of the Government's Application for Authorization to conduct Title III electronic surveillance against a number of targets—including placing listening devices at certain residences and locations; and conducting wire taps on certain telephone numbers, including the line leading into Peggy's residence. These were, indeed, her own words which came back to haunt her."

Once investigators got approval for the wiretaps, they were able to utilize some of the prison tape recordings. Using the high standards established to protect privacy, authorities could record only conversations that were obviously related to the crime.

Rotating teams began covering "target" telephones and open microphones twenty-four hours a day, and a listening post was established at the Anchorage General Mail Facility. According to Jim Bordenet, "The number of people wire tapped in Alaska for this investigation was unprecedented."

Meanwhile, postal inspectors, Anchorage police, and ATF agents stepped up the pressure and began serving search warrants. In their search for evidence, they had to rely on full Arctic survival gear and snowmobiles, thanks to weather conditions that included −30 °F windchills, blowing snow, icy roads, and head-high snowdrifts.

On April 1, 1992, charges were filed in federal court against Doug and Craig Gustafson, Peggy Gustafson Barnett, and Raymond Cheely for mailing the explosive that killed David Kerr and grievously wounded Michelle Kerr.

Thirteen days later, a federal grand jury returned a ten-count indictment against Craig, Peggy, and Raymond. Joseph Ryan would also face indictment on seven counts for conspiracy to construct and mail the fatal bomb. Ryan, who worked selling toys at Fred Meyer, arranged for the explosives and blasting caps to be in a paper bag in his car at work, which he'd left unlocked. Peggy went to Fred Meyer, where Ryan gave her the heads up; she then went to his car, got the bag, and went home to make the bomb.

According to Bordenet, "Peggy took the stuff home, and Craig helped her make it all work. In fact, Craig heard the explosion. Peggy was in the hospital with her new baby at the time David Kerr was being killed."

According to Doug Gustafson, the mail bomb idea was all his, and he seemed to display a certain criminal pride in excluding Cheely from any potential credit. "This was a Gustafson project," insisted Doug Gustafson. "Smiley did not know the bomb was built. He did not give the orders for it. Did not finance it. When it was mailed, he didn't know it was mailed."

Doug claimed the plot had begun before he was found guilty in the Cain shooting, and that his brother Craig originally agreed to help him out, even going so far as to build a bomb and attach it to Kerr's car. "He had second thoughts," said Doug Gustafson, "and he went back and removed it."

"First we were going to poison Kerr," explained Doug Gustafson. "We took a variety of steps to use ricin from the castor bean of the castor plant. We were trying to go to the local greenhouses or nurseries to see if they had any of those plants."

When that proved too difficult, Doug decided to design a new bomb. "It was going to be a shrapnel device with several thousand BBs," he explained in his deposition. "Most all of my explosives I keep in my mind. I had no books. I used a calculator to figure out the BB spread at fifteen feet of shrapnel, how many per-square-inch average, things of that nature."

Gustafson also made sure that the mail bomb looked as if it were an official package from the state crime laboratory. "I wanted to have official government letterhead," Gustafson said, "so that he would think it was something related to the case from the government, so he would be put off guard. I also wanted him to open it privately without anyone else around, thinking it was of a private nature."

The bomb that killed David Kerr and disfigured his wife was not built to Doug Gustafson's exacting specifications, "but it was the same basic design, the same circuits, the same switches, the same everything except the wrong size packaging and absent the shrapnel."

These slight variations, insisted Doug Gustafson, made an important difference: "If my detailed plans had been followed," he said, "we would not have been caught."

Catching them was easy. Gustafson and Cheely were not hard to find. They were in prison. Keeping track of Craig Gustafson was another matter.

HOLLYWOOD AND CRIME

On March 12, Craig Gustafson called postal inspectors to his home and confessed his role in the mail-bomb incident. It may seem peculiar that he was not immediately arrested, but that is not unusual in a conspiracy situation.

Authorities were in no hurry to arrest Craig. According to Bordenet, "He was the lynchpin to the entire case. We wanted him out there on the street interacting with and talking to people. If there were others involved, we wanted to know."

On March 29, immediately prior to the filing of federal charges, Craig left home for a quick trip to the store. He didn't come back. Craig Gustafson was now a fugitive from justice.

"At first we thought he may have killed himself," said Bordenet. "He was overcome with guilt about what happened to David and Michelle Kerr. He wrote a series of letters when he vanished, including one to a Postal Inspector to whom he had become close. They all sounded like Goodbye Cruel World letters. I thought maybe we would find his body in the woods after the snow melted. I was wrong. He went Hollywood on us."

Craig Gustafson flew from Anchorage to Seattle, then hitchhiked fifteen hundred miles to Los Angeles. He lived on the streets for nearly three weeks until he ran out of money and was robbed of most of the paltry possessions he had acquired on the road.

"Craig kept calling his girlfriend from various pay phones," recalls Bordenet, which immediately alerted postal inspectors from the Los Angeles division. "Thirty Postal Inspectors were mobilized to arrest Craig Gustafson," Bordenet said, and "he told his girlfriend, Barbara, that he was ready to turn himself in, but he kept calling from different phone booths. We had Inspectors fanning out, checking and re-checking those phone booths, but Gustafson kept moving around, never staying on the line long enough to trace the call."

With less than one dollar in his pocket, he decided to place another collect call to Barbara. This time, she kept him talking long enough for postal inspectors to trace the call to a phone booth in the lobby of the Roosevelt Hotel in Hollywood.

The broke, hungry, and tired fugitive was not alone at the Roosevelt. In an odd twist, at the same time Gustafson was on the phone to Alaska, the hotel was being used as a movie set for the Wesley Snipes/Dennis Hopper film *Boiling Point*.

Former US Secret Service agent turned screenwriter (*To Live and Die in L.A.*) Gerald Petievich was on the set at the hotel when ten arresting agents interrupted the filming to grab Gustafson. The agents were stopped on their way into the lobby and were filmed entering the building. Petievich, seeing several familiar faces among the invading agents, thought it was all a practical joke and teased agent Tom Dugan with the quip "It's nice to see you guys still work late on Friday nights."

There was a $10,000 reward for information leading to the capture of Craig Gustafson. On the phone to his future wife, Barbara, Craig insisted that she claim the reward for herself. She did.

"The check was for $9,000. I bought a car for the family," recalls Barbara. When welfare officials learned about her windfall, they cut off her monthly check. With the money spent, she was back on welfare.

The task force's activities didn't end with the arrest of Craig Gustafson. They were still trying to acquire enough evidence to charge Joseph Ryan for supplying the explosives, and they also had to prepare for the upcoming trials.

WANTON AND FREAKISH

The Department of Justice decided to seek the death penalty against Doug Gustafson and Raymond Cheely if they were convicted of murder by mail. This decision sparked intense discussion and attracted the attention of legal scholars and defense attorneys across America. There was a strong argument that the federal death penalty was in violation of the United States Constitution, and that the government couldn't apply it to Gustafson and Cheely.

On July 15, 1992, Craig Gustafson pleaded guilty to causing the mailing of the mail bomb, and he agreed to testify against Cheely and Ryan. Both he and Peggy were promised that they wouldn't have to testify against their siblings. Craig got twenty-two and a half years in prison. He is currently incarcerated under an assumed identity in a secret location as part of the witness protection program. He makes about $100 worth of collect calls to Barbara monthly. She, too, was offered enrollment in the witness protection program but decided it was too restrictive.

Throughout all this drama, no one seemed to notice that the state of Alaska had never filed one single criminal charge against any of the mail bomb conspirators. This wasn't an oversight or an accident. It was because of an agreement reached at the onset of the investigation.

"The Acting U.S. Attorney had reached agreement with the Anchorage Prosecuting Attorney that the feds would take the lead in both investigative and, hopefully, the follow-up prosecution aspects of the case," recalls Bordenet. "The 'locals' raised no objection. Given the tremendous costs involved in this matter, about three million dollars in direct expenses, this made sense. We [Postal Inspection Service, ATF, FBI] had the resources, and we had made the on-the-ground practical arrangements with the Anchorage P.D. to that effect."

On May 7, 1993, Doug Gustafson sat before US District Court judge James Singleton. Michelle Kerr and several family members were present for most of Doug's rambling, twenty-minute statement. He never intimated any regrets other than having failed to kill George Kerr, and he concluded with the reassuring statement "I do not plan any further bombings."

Doug Gustafson received a sentence of life in prison without parole, plus thirty years. The trial of his sister Peggy was scheduled to take place in the Los Angeles federal courthouse.

Peggy entered a plea of guilty after much negotiating between numerous lawyers. She also acknowledged her part in the conspiracy during a dramatic videotaped interview with postal inspectors. She admitted everything and denied nothing. It was, after all, a dream come true. Peggy found it interesting that mailing the bomb cost her only $2.22.

Doug also took a guilty plea to avoid the death penalty. These were all federal charges, and the state of Alaska suddenly jumped in to complain that the feds were making deals that included an arrangement with the state to not file any charges against Peggy and Doug.

According to Bordenet, "Finally, after some near long-distance fisticuffs . . . the matter was resolved. All the while, the Federal Judge was sitting there wondering if he should go forward with jury selection. The Judge really put everyone's feet to the fire."

Dennis Barnett, Peggy's husband and the father of her two children, had no prior knowledge of his wife's deadly intentions or activities. Outside the courtroom, he announced plans to file for divorce. No one was particularly surprised.

Peggy's defense attorney, Phillip Weidner, asserted that his client suffered from a "hormonal imbalance" and did not realize that the explosive was powerful enough to kill. He requested that Judge Manuel Real excuse Peggy from prison and allow her to simply be on probation.

Sending four pounds of high explosives through the mail was not indicative of a childish prank, and it was deemed obvious from the recorded conversations that Peggy knew damn well that the intention was to cause death and destruction.

"When I saw Peggy in Los Angeles," recalls Bordenet, "I couldn't believe it was the same woman. She had lost everything. Both her brothers were going to prison, as was she. She lost her husband, her children, her career—and for the rest of her life she would have to live with the knowledge that she killed David Kerr and disfigured Michelle Kerr. That burden almost destroyed Craig. I could see it was eating away at her as well."

Peggy was sentenced to twenty-four years and four months imprisonment, followed by three years of supervised release. "The sentences announced today," said US Attorney Robert C. Bundy, "are continuing testimony to the Alaska Mail Bomb Task Force's diligence and determination to bring everyone who participated in the heinous crimes against David and Michelle Kerr to justice."

Raymond Cheely and Joseph Ryan did not plead guilty. Far from it. Despite Peggy's confession, Doug's conviction, and Craig's guilty plea, Cheely and Ryan entered pleas of not guilty. While the prosecution sought the death penalty for Cheely, the Ninth US Circuit Court of Appeals in San Francisco ruled that the 1988 laws allowing prosecutors to seek the death penalty were written in such a broad and indiscriminate manner as to set the stage for capital punishment in a way that may be "wantonly and . . . freakishly imposed."

It was also ruled that Cheely's Miranda rights were violated by postal inspectors when they interrogated him on September 20, 1991, three days after the mail-bomb explosion. Hence, any incriminating statements made by Cheely would not be admissible at his trial.

PRESUMED PREJUDICE

Because of the case's extensive publicity in Alaska, Cheely asked for another change of venue, as did Ryan. This time, the court ruled in their favor. The trial was held in February 1995 in Tacoma, Washington.

Raymond "Smiley" Cheely trimmed his beard and cut his hair before the trial. He didn't want to look like a criminal. There was also another significant alteration in his demeanor. With great effort to resist a natural impulse, Raymond Cheely stopped smiling.

The defense was not lax in their duties toward their clients. Cheely's attorney, Rich Curtner, reminded the jury that the mail bombing was "a family affair," and that the family was the Gustafsons. "They are the people who made this bomb, they are the people who mailed it. They are the ultimate dysfunctional family to say the least. The tragedy is that all three Gustafsons got deals in exchange for guilty pleas leaving only Cheely and Ryan to stand trial."

Joseph Ryan's attorney, Fred Dewey, portrayed his client as a hardworking, not particularly smart guy who wasn't involved in any plot of any kind. His only error was being a good, loyal friend. He simply was asked, as a favor, to move some perfectly legal items off the property as a favor to Cheely and his parents, and he had insisted that he had no idea how they were going to be used. Yes, he delivered items that eventually were used to make a bomb, but he didn't make it, deliver it, or even see it.

The entire case against Ryan and Cheely was, from a defense perspective, composed of testimony from jailhouse snitches, thieves, con men, ivory poachers, and murderers.

The prosecution trotted out prison informants so crooked they couldn't lie straight in bed, who changed their stories with disconcerting rapidity and were decidedly recalcitrant when confronted about their blatant dishonesty.

When one of them testified under oath that Raymond Cheely was involved in an activity that a simple fact check revealed was a complete impossibility due to him being in solitary confinement at the time, the witness coldly replied, "I can't concern myself with the moral dilemma of lying to you."

The dubious veracity of the prosecution's witnesses was offset by their number, and the essential point repeatedly established was that there was communication and conspiracy between Gustafson and Cheely, despite their being in different locations in the prison system.

Testimony confirmed that notes had been passed between the two, and that they both called the same people at the same time so they could have their conversations connected and speak to each other. Gustafson even knew about Cheely's hit list and had a note sent to him to get rid of it because there was going to be a shakedown.

Samuel Dimmick, an inmate who shared a cell with Doug Gustafson, not only told of note passing but also gave the jury an unusual insight into how informants are treated or mistreated. While he was at first cooperative, Dimmick later regretted his involvement and became less enthusiastic. As a result, he was subjected to what is called Diesel Therapy. "When I cooperated, they flew me to Los Angeles for the trial, but when I wasn't cooperative, they made me spend endless days on a Greyhound* bus being shuttled from one federal penitentiary to another all along the West Coast as punishment."

The prosecution brought forth seventy-six witnesses, most of whom were either inmates or former classmates or cellmates of Cheely who didn't take his rants of revenge seriously until the Kerr's house erupted in a deadly explosion.

"Peggy testified against Cheely and Ryan," recalls Jim Bordenet, "and so did Craig Gustafson, but neither the prosecution nor defense wanted to chance putting Doug on the stand. He had been showing increased signs of mental problems, and there was no way of knowing what would come out of his mouth."

Lest anyone forget the victims, the prosecution projected David and Michelle's wedding picture followed by graphic photos of David's mangled body and Michelle's melted face. One of the jurors almost vomited.

Cheely was convicted on all eight counts of the indictment, including one charging him with making a bomb with intent to kill. Joseph Ryan was found innocent of all charges against him and sentenced to fifty-seven months in prison. (Yes, you read that correctly.)

INVENTING A CONVICTION

Joseph Ryan was found guilty of illegal possession of a firearm, despite never having been charged with that crime. "It must have come as a surprise when, after several days of deliberation, the jury asked the district court whether 'an explosive on its own' would constitute a firearm, 'or do you have to have a bomb to be a firearm,'" stated circuit judge Reinhardt in May of 1997. "Both the government and the defense appear quickly to have grasped that the jury was inquiring as to whether it could convict Ryan on a theory not before it and on which it had not been instructed . . . in other words, whether the 'firearm' could be just parts and not the completed bomb itself. The government immediately proceeded to urge that the court give an instruction that contained a new, different, and expanded definition of 'firearm.'"

The jury convicted Ryan for possession of commercial explosives and blasting caps—a fact that was not even at issue at trial. He was never charged with a crime relative to this possession and was never allowed to defend himself against the charge.

Ryan was convicted on a theory not charged in the indictment or advanced at trial. One would think that Mr. Ryan would get a kind letter of apology and minimum wage for the time he spent in prison, but the court decided that while the matter was certainly troubling, and that it was not proper at all, they were going to let it slide. They did, however, reverse their previous ruling that Joseph Ryan pay $750,000 in restitution to Michelle Kerr and the estate of David Kerr.

"The jury's guilty verdicts against Raymond Cheely and Joseph Ryan are continuing testimony to the Alaska Mail Bomb Task Force's diligence and determination to bring everyone who participated in the heinous crimes against David and Michelle Kerr to justice," remarked US Attorney Robert C. Bundy at a joint press conference with Gerald Miera, postal inspector in charge, Seattle, Washington.

"I have not been involved in any similar case during my twenty-five years in the Postal Inspection Service which demanded so much from so many," said Miera. "Throughout this ordeal, there were countless examples of personal sacrifices made by investigators which took a heavy toll on their families and health, but we remembered that scene at the Kerr residence on September 17, 1991. That was the constant reality check which kept us focused on the mission."

"We have an obligation," said Miera, "to vigorously investigate any misuse of the mail which puts innocent persons at risk. No postal crime is more serious than the intentional placement of an explosive device in this nation's postal system."

The guilty verdict was announced at 10:30 a.m. on March 13, 1995. For the first time since the grueling trial began, Michelle Kerr began to sob. She was still crying at 1:45 p.m.

In July of 1995, Michelle Kerr read her prepared victim impact statement at the sentencing of Raymond Cheely. Shaking with anger and outrage, she gave her righteous indignation full voice at full force. When she spoke of her personal pain and anguish and of the horrid destruction for which Cheely was responsible, he audibly chuckled. Cheely received two life sentences with no chance of parole. When the punishment was announced, he laughed.

"No amount of justice can compensate the Kerr family," noted Assistant US Attorney Joseph Bottini. "I hope they can find some peace in knowing that these defendants will pay heavily for their crimes."

THE MOST UNLIKELY ALLIANCE

There was additional compensation for Michelle Kerr when she sued the state of Alaska for negligence. "She lost her husband, her home, her health, and her career," said Kerr's lawyer, Bill Bankston, to the jury hearing her case. "State officials are 100% responsible because they did nothing to stop the mail bomb conspiracy which was hatched in a state prison."

The jury heard how Michelle was pelted by three thousand pieces of shrapnel and that her eyes were still filled with glass. Her medical bills already totaled more than $400,000.

Testifying by deposition in support of Michelle Kerr was Doug Gustafson, the man who took full credit for the bomb that killed her husband and destroyed her life.

"Gustafson said he felt sorry for Michelle Kerr," explained Jim Bordenet, "because she was not his intended victim, and neither was her husband. He only wanted to kill George Kerr. Besides, Doug Gustafson said that he wanted to cost the state millions of dollars."

The state added the Gustafsons, Cheely, and Ryan as codefendants to share the costs should Kerr win her case. An Anchorage jury awarded close to $11 million in compensation for medical, property, and other losses but ruled that only 12 percent of the money should come from the state of Alaska. The rest of it should come from the other defendants, who had no money. Michelle Kerr, who had been offered $2 million to settle out of court but turned it down, wept in the courtroom.

No amount of money would bring back Michelle Kerr's life, health, or happiness, but the full amount, minus lawyers' fees, would certainly have made a difference in her quality of life.

In the final analysis, the Alaska Mail Bomb Conspiracy had numerous lasting impacts far beyond the devastation to the families of all involved, and the case demonstrated beyond any doubt the dedication and professionalism of the United States Postal Inspection Service as one of America's premier law enforcement agencies.

"The successful resolution of this case," stated US Attorney Robert Bundy, "is a tribute to the integrity of our evidence; the persistence of the investigators; the determination of the prosecutors; and above all, Michelle Kerr's courage throughout the entire ordeal."

Postal inspector Gerald Miera was unstinting in his praise for not only his investigators but also for those from other agencies who labored so intensively for such a long period of time.

"These prosecutors have now lived this case for several years," said Miera.

"It is significant that I recently had the privilege of representing Chief Postal Inspector Kenneth J. Hunter in presenting Mr. Bottini and Mr. Bonner with the Inspection Service's highest honor—the Chief Inspector's Award. It recognizes these individuals' outstanding dedication to duty as demonstrated by their tenacity, diligence, and professionalism in successfully prosecuting the defendants."

Miera also had high praise for the investigators whose work was coordinated by postal inspectors Russel Mabry, Doug Pulling, and Mathew Allen, and also lavished praise on the agents and representatives of the ATF, Alaska State Troopers, Alaska Department of Corrections, forensic experts from the Postal Inspection Service, and Anchorage police officers.

It was in this recognition of exemplary interagency cooperation that Miera presented the Chief Inspector's Award to Anchorage chief of police Kevin O'Leary. Chief O'Leary was recognized for coordinating his departments' resources in support of the task force.

"We represent many agencies," said Miera, "but we had a single goal—to identify and put away those who so callously misused the United States Mail to commit this crime."

Despite the consummate professionalism and dedication of the US Postal Inspection Service, it seldom receives the recognition it deserves as a highly effective and efficient law enforcement agency. In 1998, Showtime aired the film *The Inspectors*, which was based on the Alaska case. The last time the agency had been portrayed in a motion picture was 1949's *Post Office Investigator*.

The public's lack of appreciation for the US Postal Inspection Service irritates Jim Bordenet, even after his retirement. "I saw a news feature on television," Bordenet laments, "and it said there was a raid conducted by the FBI assisted by postal workers. It sounded as if letter carriers came running in. Nothing against letter carriers, but for heaven's sake, the United States Postal Inspection Service is an honest to God law enforcement agency of the Federal Government. It's like we're Rodney Dangerfield. At least with the Alaska mail bomb case, we finally got some recognition and respect."

ABOUT THE AUTHOR

BURL BARER is an Edgar Award winner and two-time Anthony Award nominee whose books have been translated into seven languages. His true-crime classics include *Murder in the Family*; *Mom Said Kill*; *Broken Doll*; and *Fatal Beauty*. The year 2012 will see two Burl Barer true-crime releases: *Head Shot* and *Body Count*. Barer hosts *True Crime Uncensored* on Outlaw Radio and cohosts the syndicated television show *True Crimes* with Don Woldman on the American Horrors channel.

REFERENCES

Anchorage Daily News. The online archives of this newspaper do not extend to the 1990s. Hard copies or microfilm editions may be available through your local library or interlibrary services.

Bordenet, James D. 1994 and 2011. Interviews with the author.

U.S. Postal Inspection Service Bulletin. 1993. A quarterly publication of the US Postal Inspection Service. Vol. 44, no. 4 (Summer/Fall 1993): 7–14.

US Postal Inspection Service complete media documentation file prepared by James D. Bordenet and shared with the author on November 8, 1994. This file, which the author used for reference, contained every mention of the case in every publication worldwide, although the most extensive print coverage was in the *Anchorage Daily News*, beginning with the first issue following the highway murder of Jeffrey Cain.

Chapter 8

THE TROPHY WIFE

by Camille Kimball

On St. Patrick's Day 2010, Jamie Laiaddee, a thirty-two-year-old medical sales rep, ran errands around town. A University of Michigan graduate, she now lived in Chandler, Arizona, twenty-five miles east of downtown Phoenix. At five feet four inches, one hundred thirty pounds, with shiny black hair bouncing across her shoulders, Jamie owed her honey-toned skin and almond-shaped eyes to her Thai heritage. Her most memorable features were her fresh face and eager smile.

Jamie deposited checks at the Wells Fargo drive-through, got the oil changed in her Ford Escape®, and bought office supplies at Staples. At 6:30 p.m., she took a call from a roofer who had done work on her house.

The roofer was the last known person to speak to Jamie alive.

While Jamie was a friendly, intensely loyal young woman, she was also intensely private: it wasn't until two and half months later that her friends really understood that she had vanished.

Jamie Jean was born on October 12, 1977, the younger of two daughters, to Sompsonge and Vunnee Laiaddee. Immigrants from Thailand, the Laiaddees settled in California. Firstborn Pavaree, often called Pepper, thrilled her parents by going to medical school, serving her residency in neurology. Jamie felt the pressure to achieve similar success. In 1995, she left home to begin college at the highly respected University of Michigan.

During Jamie's senior year, she and six other girls rented a house together at 516 Walnut in Ann Arbor. Thereafter, they called themselves the "516 girls." After the women graduated, they stayed close, serving as bridesmaids and, when the babies started coming along, as godmothers. Jamie traveled far to attend these weddings and baptisms, for the women had scattered to places as far-flung as Germany, Russia, and Australia. She enthusiastically took on each new godchild, generous with gifts and fond attention.

But Jamie's relationship with her own family had taken a different course. In a move uncharacteristic of the normally loyal and cheerful girl, Jamie stopped talking to her parents and her sister. The senior Laiaddees had urged Jamie to follow in the footsteps of Pavaree and go to grad school. But for Jamie, the competition with Pepper was over. Jamie moved to Arizona and settled into a career in medical-equipment sales instead. She did well for herself professionally and began building her nest egg. In 2004, just a few days before her twenty-seventh birthday, she closed on a house of her own.

Jamie may have all but cut ties to California, but she took her affection for the University of Michigan with her to the desert. She became an active member of the school's local alumni association. The alumni not only met formally on a regular basis for business but also informally every Saturday at a pub to watch the Wolverines play football. Jamie also began donating cash and her frequent-flier miles to current U of M students to help them travel from Arizona to campus.

In 2006, Jamie met the handsome Bryan Stewart through the alumni association. He was five feet nine inches tall, and his blue eyes topped off the well-muscled frame of a professional fitness instructor. Although fiercely connected to her girlfriends from the class of '99, Jamie kept a tight filter on herself. She *gave* a lot, but she *shared* sparingly: generous to a fault with her time and her money, she kept her feelings, fears, and disappointments locked away. As she and Bryan began to see each other outside of alumni meetings, she kept the romance under tight wraps until it had fully bloomed.

Jamie's friend Gretchen wrote to her on Valentine's Day 2007. "Now that you have a man, you've probably forgotten about me—your forever Valentine." Gretchen was cheered by the comfort that thoughtful Jamie had sent along, "PS thanks for the package, although I haven't opened it yet. I was waiting for today!"

Jamie's friend Jennifer, another of the 516 girls, was beginning to hear about Bryan by May. She wrote in an e-mail: "So a personal trainer, eh?? Sounds like he's bound to be a looker!!!" In a statement very telling of Jamie's private nature, Jennifer begged for details and was "hoping to get more information out of you soon."

Things had gotten off to a good start with Jamie's and Bryan's mutual ties to the University of Michigan. But they needed more. Bryan was an intensely physical man with strong opinions, while Jamie was an office professional with a temperament remarkable for its moderation. To make for a closer connection as a couple, Jamie decided to adopt Bryan's hobby, camping.

Jamie had been driving a silver Honda Accord®, but after taking up camping, she bought an SUV, a 2007 gold Ford Escape, so much more suitable for hauling camping equipment. Bryan introduced her to one of his favorite spots: the Mogollon Rim, a long finger of plateau with an abrupt drop-off located hours away in northeast Arizona. Bryan and Jamie also hiked nearby in the McDowell Sonoran Preserve, a natural desert splendor abutting the city of Scottsdale.

Jamie had not traded in the Accord. Bryan began using it to get to work at the gym. By the summer of 2007, twenty-eight-year-old Jamie Laiaddee and her boyfriend with the Apollo physique were a hot item, and Jamie's college friends cheered from afar.

In late August, Jamie was away on one of her frequent business trips for Cayenne Medical, a Scottsdale-based company specializing in complex artificial ligament replacements for knees and shoulders, when she received a strange e-mail. At the bottom, the sender identified herself as "Michelle." But the message itself was from Bryan.

"I am locked up at Durango Jail. . . . The police impounded the car. . . . I am still in the dark about why I was arrested." He went on to give her detailed instructions for visiting the jail. He finished with a request: "I can't arrange bail but you can. Please get me out of here."

In a postscript to this alarming note, Michelle introduced herself as the fiancé of an inmate housed near Bryan. Michelle said Bryan had no other way to contact her.

Jamie's response was curiously calm. "Michelle, thank you for sending the message from Bryan. I will be flying back this afternoon and hope to arrange bail for him soon. If you need anything, please feel free to call me."

Jamie may have been so calm because she had already received a heads up on the matter in what must have been an upsetting late-night phone call. She had already purchased an Internet background check on her boyfriend before Michelle's message had arrived.

Jamie must have been reassured by the background report, because she asked the company for a refund and received it. In any case, there was little to be found on Bryan Stewart of Phoenix, Arizona. Maybe a traffic citation or two. Whatever had happened that night in Phoenix must be a terrible mistake that they would face together. Jamie, above all, was loyal.

In a spacious luxury home in northwest Phoenix, an alarm shrilled through the night. It was Tuesday, August 21, 2007, nearly midnight. While patrol cars raced to the scene, homeowner Daniel Baker cautiously approached his garage. With adrenalin pumping, Baker found himself confronting a powerfully built white man breaking into his Mercedes®. The burglar rushed passed him, right into the house.

Police officers gave chase, and the burglar ran through the house and easily scaled the backyard fence, dropping down onto the grounds of an expensive private school. A helicopter kept a spotlight on him. He gave a brief struggle when the ground officers caught up with him in a baseball field.

The man gave his address as the very swank 11210 North Biltmore Drive #175, an address redolent of golf courses, legacy mansions, and historical resorts. The man getting cuffed protested. Why all the fuss? He had been walking home and took a shortcut through the school field. He had merely taken a wrong turn by mistake.

The suspect was found to have a car waiting nearby. Using the plate number, police came up with the name of the rightful owner: Jamie Laiaddee.

The burglar was none other than the man who coached well-to-do Scottsdale clients on the finer points of curls and crunches: Jamie's Adonis boyfriend, Bryan Stewart. Police called her in the middle of the night. They told her they were seizing the Honda. A day later, she received the note from Michelle.

On Saturday, Jamie paid $3,600 in cash to bail her boyfriend out of jail.

The pace of the e-mail traffic between the college girlfriends had stepped up at the end of August. The 516 girls peppered Jamie with questions about Bryan.

Was she bringing him to an upcoming wedding? Would they finally get to meet this glamorous character? Jamie delicately avoided answering these questions. It was mortifying to the professional young woman to have a jailbird boyfriend. And more cash would be required to get the Honda out of the impound lot. How could she confide in her girlfriends about such a thing? She would have to handle this on her own.

Unable to show up for work, Bryan resigned from Red Mountain Gym and told his employer that he'd "had an incident with Jamie" that made him break up with her. It would be in "poor taste to reveal what she did," but the end result was that he no longer had transportation to get to work.

The same day, he moved forward with exciting new plans: he would open a gym of his own. He registered a company name with the Arizona secretary of state.

In spite of his statement that he had ended his relationship with Jamie due to her ominous-sounding behavior, Bryan asked his girlfriend to invest money in his new gym and peppered her with requests for favors. Jamie, on yet another business trip, congratulated him on the business plan and apologized for being in meetings all day, unable to do the favors. But she wanted to know about his court date. Did he have a public defender lined up? After much dodging, he reassured her that he didn't really have a court date, just a "meeting" with the lawyers. He was sure the whole mess would be cleared up after that.

As for his new gym, as generous and trusting as she was, even Jamie did not have all the money he needed. Bryan approached a few of his best clients to ask them to invest, and he also worked on designing a web page. While he was thus carrying on in his new life as an entrepreneur, Bryan quietly missed his first court date on the burglary case.

A few weeks later, Bryan again failed to appear. Perhaps it had slipped his mind as he contemplated his new duties as a defender of democratic ideals. In early October, he had joined a group of Arizona vigilantes. In his letter to the Minutemen, Bryan talked about his desire to "do my part in helping to defend the U.S. and Arizona constitutions."

While Bryan was busy defending Arizona's constitution, that state issued a bench warrant for his arrest. Jamie would lose her $3,600. A new court date was set, but Bryan did not show up for that one either. A new bench warrant was issued.

Jamie, seemingly unaware of the truth of these developments, was getting requests from friends for Bryan's photo. She wrote back that he disliked having his photo taken. "I was hoping to get a better picture of Bryan, but no luck." In the meantime, she did have some photos that were taken in a dimly lit bar. In closing, Jamie refers to a recent wedding and gives a glimpse into her relationship with her boyfriend. "P.S. Yes I caught the bouquet. Bryan was not happy. . . ." In the accompanying photo attachment, Bryan is looking down and away, seemingly trying to thwart the photographer.

A few weeks later, Officer Rainey of the Phoenix Police Department pulled over the silver Honda. Rainey found Bryan in the driver's seat and the outstanding warrant in the database. "Stewart was arrested, handcuffed to the rear and double-locked, transported to the . . . 4th Avenue jail, and booked." Rainey also wrote down that Stewart "gave the wrong name and Social Security Number initially."

Now that he was caught, Bryan complained to the court that he was the innocent victim of "undelivered mail." But the post office had determined that that the Biltmore Drive address was purely fictional. Then he told the court that for the last year and a half he had lived at 330 North Eucalyptus Place, Jamie's house in Chandler.

Jamie paid bail again, this time $5,000. Bryan Stewart was charged with second-degree burglary, forgery, resisting arrest/physical force, and second-degree criminal trespass.

In May, Bryan took a plea deal. Instead of burglary, he pleaded guilty to trespass in the first degree, a felony. In exchange, he got two years probation and no jail time.

Bryan's stories explaining his repeated need for bail must have been convincing. His next infraction occurred soon enough, and when probation officers came looking for him, they found him at the Eucalyptus Place house. Or rather, it was Jamie who came to the door when they knocked.

A probation officer wrote in Bryan's file: "A field contact was attempted wherein the defendant's girlfriend initially stated he was home, but later returned to the door explaining that the defendant did not want to speak with this officer."

In August, all the turmoil seemed to be calming down. Bryan was set up with terms of probation, and Jamie got her $5,000 back. She bought tickets for a football game at the University of Michigan and also the airfare to get the couple there. But Bryan failed to appear in court that month as well, and yet another bench warrant was issued.

In October, Jamie paid out a new bond for Bryan. The same day she handed over that cash, Jamie and Bryan boarded their flight to Ann Arbor. In the big Michigan versus Michigan State football game, the Wolverines lost: 35 to 21. But Bryan gained something he valued highly, photos of himself attending a Michigan home game.

Two days after the couple's return to Arizona, the Maricopa County Probation Department was looking for Bryan again: "Defendant arrested at his residence [Jamie's house] for having an outstanding warrant . . . booked into 4th Avenue jail."

Jamie continued to bail Bryan out over the next six months, and he continued to miss court dates.

In April of 2009, evidence of strain in Jamie's relationship with Bryan finally began to appear. She wrote to her friend Cathy, "Bryan and I are fighting over little things and it culminated in a huge fight." Jamie continued that they had worked it out, but now she "would love" to talk with Cathy about someone new she had met, who "gave me serious doubts about Bryan and me."

By midsummer, however, she was still with Bryan, who now needed a broken tooth fixed. Jamie arranged for a dentist appointment—and paid the bill. The next day, she sought out a female client of Bryan's from the gym. In a detailed and masterfully diplomatic letter, Jamie sought the suspected "other" woman's help. But the note contained one or two blunt statements: "I know that you probably don't know the situation between Bryan and me and what has happened over the years. I am just looking to get someone to tell me the truth about what happened on Saturday and Bryan's cover-up and lies."

In spite of her concerns, that day Jamie also paid out over $700 for airfare to California, a Hilton Hotel room, and fees for Bryan to attend a personal-training certification conference.

But soon, all the trouble with Bryan took a backseat. Due to the vicious economy following the collapse of AIG, Lehman Brothers, Fannie Mae, and so many other financial institutions that year, Jamie was suddenly laid off from her job at Cayenne Medical.

Jamie simultaneously made cutbacks in spending and set forth on a methodical enterprise of job hunting. She made hundreds of cold inquiries and alerted her extensive personal network that she was looking for work. She took on two temporary part-time jobs, one as a personal assistant and the other as a telemarketer.

In October, she wrote to her friend Sheila that "it has been really hard since I was laid off. I was the breadwinner and Bryan was the 'trophy wife.' Now he doesn't quite understand that we can't always live the same lifestyle without my income."

Yet, always the good and compliant girlfriend, she continued to try to absorb his opinions and tastes. Prior to meeting Bryan, Jamie had moderate political views. But during late 2009, as Jamie struggled with the bills, Bryan, who had by this time joined the Tea Party, booked her as a guest speaker on healthcare for the John Birch Society, and she came through for him. But he did not get a second job, as Jamie had hoped. Instead, Bryan spent his free time becoming a member of Oathkeepers, a group that desired to clear up the "mistaken belief" by the military that they "must follow any order the President issues."

Jamie's own cutbacks hurt. She was upset to miss the wedding in Baku, the oil city on the Caspian Sea, of her friend Cathy. Jamie refused to let the bride pay her way. In spite of the belt-tightening she was imposing on her own household, Jamie still made her regular charitable contributions that Christmas season, not even decreasing the amount from previous years. Instead of using her frequent-flier miles for herself, she continued to donate them to the students. She increased her volunteer work, taking on Save the Family. She also added Sun Valley Hospice, where she made home visits to elderly patients.

As things darkened between the trainer and the out-of-work sales professional, Jamie withdrew more and more from her closest friends. During January 2010, the shadows seemed to hang very heavy over the house on Eucalyptus Place. To recent bride Cathy she wrote, "I have bad days and good days. Good days are when I don't break down and cry. Those days are few and far between. I haven't been sleeping very well and wake up in the middle of the night in a panic." She stated, "I have been trying to distance myself from everyone. . . . And I just can't stand people feeling sorry for me anymore."

But things finally began to look up when Jamie got a job offer from Care-Fusion. The desperate feeling of unemployment could be put behind her. It was not quite the job of her dreams, though, so she continued to look. She had high hopes after an interview in Denver but was sorely disappointed when, on February 22, she learned that she had not gotten it. She accepted the position with CareFusion, a supplier of everything from hospital-grade dispensers of hand soap to comprehensive hospital data management. The company issued her a laptop, a cell phone, and an American Express® card.

Meanwhile, evidence of more trouble between the couple surfaced. Bryan had called Arizona Public Service Company, the power company, and asked for a new-service hookup to be installed at an apartment in Scottsdale.

Days later, on March 17, Jamie used the CareFusion credit card to buy office supplies. After doing her errands, she went home and paid a bill online. The roofer called. At 7:34 p.m., an e-mail in her account arrived about a high-paying dental sales job in Portland. The message was clicked and moved to her "save" folder. The next e-mail, a forward of grocery coupons from Bryan, was time-stamped 7:58 p.m. That one was never opened.

The next day, Jamie was scheduled to work at CareFusion. She never showed up.

Two weeks after Jamie had failed to show up for her new job, Bryan got an e-mail about an upcoming Michigan alumni board meeting. He responded, "I'll be there . . . don't hold your breath on Jamie." To an invitation for Easter, he wrote, "I'll be there . . . don't know about Jamie." Bryan also wrote that day to a training client named Lori that his former relationship with Jamie had been "poisonous." He seemed to openly acknowledge his former role as "trophy wife," telling Lori that he now had ten clients a day, "that's good now that I am taking care of myself."

He soon told alumni board members Marlene Buffa and Penny Pease that Jamie had gotten the job in Denver. The women said that must be why she had not responded to their recent attempts to reach her. Bryan agreed.

Easter Sunday was on April 4, 2010. Friends and family gathered at Penny's home for an Easter celebration. At this party, Marlene and Penny pressed Bryan for more information on Jamie. They said it wasn't like her to ignore messages. Bryan thought it was weird, too.

Jamie's closest friends lived far away in different time zones—some even past the international dateline. Correspondence could be slow. But her local friend, Penny Pease, noticed it had been over a month since she had heard from Jamie, the move to Colorado notwithstanding. Penny felt certain Jamie would still want to help the young students trying to attend the University of Michigan.

Penny wrote at the end of April, "Jamie, I understand you are now a Colorado resident. . . . We miss you here and hope you are still an Arizona girl." Penny went on to describe a physics student from rural Arizona who had been accepted into a PhD program. Penny said that they needed Jamie's vote for a scholarship and were hoping to add her frequent-flier miles as well. Penny, in a discreet acknowledgment of Jamie's long silence, wrote "I know you are probably crazy busy," but she hoped Jamie would find the time to help. She signed it: "We miss you."

But both the appeal to Jamie's generosity for the students and to her sense of fondness for her friend went unanswered.

A week later, on May 5, the first e-mail expressing concern for Jamie's whereabouts arrived in Jamie's inbox. A friend from her professional world in medical sales, Karlynne Martin, asked flat out, "Are you ok? Haven't heard from you."

No answer.

On May 7, board members Penny Pease and Marlene Buffa started comparing notes. Penny had given up on the physics student, but now she had a Navajo student with an internship at NASA she hoped to help. Marlene e-mailed Jamie, "Can you please extend Penny the courtesy of a response? I know you've moved and apparently don't want anything to do with Arizona anymore."

Penny also followed up with a note directly to Jamie. Trying hard to reach Jamie's soft heart, Penny wrote about the student's bleak childhood. Penny padded the letter with abundant personal chat, filling Jamie in on various family matters.

But no response ever came. When Penny made one more appeal on behalf of the Navajo student, for the first time she let in a note of impatience. Shouldn't Jamie give her the courtesy of a response?

The people at CareFusion had given up on their new hire. They had sent several messages and a certified letter asking her to bring back the valuable items they had given her, including the phone she wasn't answering. A supervisor came out to the house on Eucalyptus Place. He found no one there. He knocked next door. The man didn't know his neighbors, but he had often seen a man and woman at that house. It had been several weeks since he had seen the woman.

In May, Bryan got pulled over for a traffic violation. He was driving the gold Escape. To the cop, who noticed the car was not registered to him, Bryan explained that he was buying it from owner Jamie Laiaddee, currently paying $250 a month.

At Gold's Gym, people noticed Bryan was driving Jamie's SUV regularly to work, even though he had made it abundantly clear that he had left Jamie and called her "psycho" to many of his exercise pals. Bryan explained that she couldn't drive both cars to Colorado so had left one here in his keeping.

As summer approached, Penny decided that Jamie's behavior over the last two months was more than irritating—it was frightening. She wrote, "Please just write a quick e-mail to tell us you are ok, please. We are worried about you."

On May 28, over the course of several hours spent on e-mails and phone calls, Penny and Marlene pressured Bryan to report Jamie missing. He said Chandler Police Department had already rebuffed him because he was not a relative. Then call her father, they pushed back. Bryan had vaguely dark opinions about Mr. Laiaddee, and, in any case, there was no way to reach the man.

Penny looked up the phone number for Sompsonge Laiaddee on the Internet and gave it to Bryan. Call him, she insisted.

In late afternoon, Bryan told the women he had spoken to Mr. Laiaddee, and the man had told Bryan to back off. So Penny called Mr. Laiaddee herself and then learned the truth. Jamie's father had become frantic upon hearing the news. He had just finished reporting Jamie as a missing person.

Patrol Officer Daniel Shellum had already been dispatched to the house on

Eucalyptus Place, arriving at 6:30 p.m. After a preliminary check in the vicinity, including hearing from the neighbor about the CareFusion supervisor and the woman resident disappearing while the man still showed up, officers broke in. They saw a woman's purse on the kitchen table; piles of unopened mail, including utility bills and mortgage notices; a pair of women's prescription eyeglasses; and a cartridge of birth control pills, with only four pills missing.

They could see the silver Honda in the garage, but where was the gold Escape? Had Jamie driven to Colorado? Was she stranded off a remote mountain road? Had she driven off to an entirely new life in parts unknown, to Canada or Mexico? How could she do so, without her personal items? Had the Ford been used to abduct her?

Finding the Escape was key to finding out what had happened to Jamie.

While Detective Nathan Moffat took over as lead detective and found DMV photos of Jamie and Bryan, Detective Jesus Deanda ran the license plate number of the Escape through the License Plate Recognition (LPR) database, a sophisticated network of cameras that can read license plates. The technology is put into use when a car trips a sensor at a toll road or passes a lift-gate to a restricted access area. Deanda found that the gold Escape had been recorded by an LPR camera in the area of Raintree Road in Scottsdale. He grabbed his keys and headed out there.

At about half-past midnight on May 29, Deanda spotted an apartment complex with a lift-gate. He turned in, but since he couldn't get past the gate, the detective started executing a U-turn.

As Deanda steered away, a car pulled in after him. Deanda, figuring he could follow it in, converted his U-turn into a 360-degree circle. As he completed the maneuver and arrived behind the second car, Deanda realized he was staring at the very license plate he had been searching for. As the driver leaned out the window to enter the access code, Deanda recognized him as Bryan Stewart.

The Escape pulled forward as the entrance barrier lifted, and Deanda followed in his unmarked car.

He radioed in his sighting of the Ford and tailed it as it wound around the apartment complex. At the Chandler Police Department, others were busy running more checks on Bryan Stewart. They found an outstanding traffic warrant.

Deanda's car was equipped with emergency lights and a siren, so he conducted a traffic stop. Stewart, exiting the SUV, walked toward him.

Deanda said, "Do you know why I'm here?"

"No," Stewart answered.

"Well, I'm here regarding your girlfriend—"

"You mean my ex-girlfriend," Stewart interrupted.

Deanda asked the man driving Jamie's SUV to come down to the Chandler Police Department voluntarily to talk about her disappearance, but Stewart said he would rather not do it tonight. He asked to go in to his apartment to relieve himself.

Deanda wrote in his police report: "I believed that Stewart was now nervous and for some reason he needed to go inside his apartment. I noticed that he began to walk around as if he was thinking what to do next."

Stewart was not allowed back inside. He was arrested on the outstanding warrant. He was taken on the thirty-minute drive to the Chandler Police Department. Officers wrote in their notebooks that he no longer asked for a restroom, though he was offered the use of one several times.

Detective Moffat entered the small interview room at Chandler Police Department headquarters where Bryan Stewart was waiting.

After talking to Stewart for a while, Moffat's internal sensors started clanging. "I believed he was lying. It takes focus and concentration to lie," Moffat said. "So I divided his attention."

While Stewart was looking at papers, Moffat asked him where and when he went to high school, then immediately called him on his response when the years of his high school attendance did not match up to his stated birth date.

"I was held back," Stewart quickly explained.

"Twenty-four-year-olds are not allowed to go to high school," Moffat shot back.

Later Moffat described this moment. "Until we pulled him over, I had no reason to believe he wasn't Bryan Stewart. Now I knew his story was falling apart. I didn't know who I was talking to."

Stewart told Moffat that he had broken up with Jamie on the seventeenth of March. Nevertheless, the two had platonically shared a bed that night with the understanding that she'd be moving to Denver without him in the morning. Before dawn, he had headed out for the gym, leaving a sleeping Jamie behind. When he returned after noon, a set of luggage was gone and so was she.

The detective made him repeat several times that neither he nor Jamie had gotten out of bed during the night.

Up to now, Moffat had been a good listener. But he was about to spring.

Moffat asked him why the gold Escape had been tagged on LPR cameras around fifteen minutes before midnight on March 17. Stewart was clearly surprised. After thinking for a few minutes, Stewart decided Jamie must have slipped out while he slept and then returned without his ever becoming aware of her absence.

The detective then revealed where the gold Escape had been tagged—at the Raintree address. Bryan's confusion and discomfort increased. He couldn't understand why Jamie would be there.

Slapping the LPR photo down on the table between them, Moffat ended the charade. Even Bryan Stewart could not deny that the photo showed his face. The interview soon ended. Bryan Stewart stayed in jail. And there was no kindhearted Jamie to bail him out.

Searching the Raintree apartment, officers saw a framed University of Michigan diploma for Bryan Stewart, BS in education physiology, displayed on the wall; a birth certificate in the name of Bryan Stewart; and a state of Michigan ID card for Bryan Stewart. But as they rifled through papers, a thick envelope addressed to "Rick Valentini" caught their eye. Inside it they found divorce papers for Rick Valentini. Why would Bryan Stewart be holding divorce papers for Rick Valentini?

Cutting the lock off Bryan's storage unit with bolt cutters, the first thing police saw inside was a shovel with a lot of dirt on it. Near the shovel, officers were alarmed to see a sawed-off shotgun and a large quantity of plastic sheeting.

The shotgun wasn't the only weapon. There was a .25-caliber semiautomatic handgun in the storage unit, and in the apartment there were several other firearms and hand weapons such as hatchets and swords. Little wonder their subject had wanted to go back inside his apartment before he was handcuffed.

Inside the storage unit police also found a state of Michigan seal embosser and a birth certificate in yet another name, Ricky Wayne Schmidt. Throughout the search, they found paperwork with several different social security numbers. Things began to make sense when they found a book titled *The Modern Identity Changer.*

Crime-scene investigators searching the gold Escape found a red stain on the center console. It tested positive for blood.

Within days of Bryan Stewart's incarceration, other inmates were reporting that he was afraid he would soon be charged with the murder of his girlfriend. Stewart had allegedly stated to his cellmates that her body would "never be found" and that "cops already had the murder weapon"—the shotgun from the storage unit.

One snitch was told to let Stewart know that he had a friend who could do some errands for him on the outside. The friend's name would be "R. J." Stewart was quick to take the bait. Soon he had arranged to have R. J. go to Gold's Gym to pick up his stuff. Whenever R. J. was needed for Bryan's various tasks, a series of different detectives took on the undercover role. Detective Moffat put $200 of county money on Stewart's jail account. To Bryan, the money appeared to come from R. J.

Meanwhile, a woman named Mary Sowers had been hired to clean out the abandoned apartment on Raintree. Mary was working in the kitchen when she picked up a box of oatmeal. The box just didn't feel right. Taking the lid off, she discovered a handgun hidden inside.

Although Bryan Stewart had long told his Arizona friends that both his parents died in a fiery car crash in 2001, Moffat easily found the man's mother, Debbie Valentini, alive and well and living in California. She hadn't heard from her son in many years. She told detectives he had been born Ricky Wayne Schmidt in 1969. Debbie had later remarried, and her children had taken on their stepfather's name, Valentini. Ricky had gone to kindergarten and every grade since as a Valentini. She had never heard the name Bryan Stewart.

Ricky's childhood had been rough—rough on the family, that is. Ricky's brother told the detective he'd had a hard time with him. Ricky's sister told police she was afraid of him.

Ricky had had such behavioral problems that Debbie said a counselor had given her an unusual prescription: keep the child in the garage where he couldn't disturb others. He could come inside for meals. When Ricky was sixteen, Debbie had let him out of the garage and turned him over to foster care.

As a young adult, Ricky ended up with an aunt, Donna, who told Moffat that her nephew had parked a U-Haul® truck at her house for a week. Privately, Donna came to suspect that Ricky had stolen the truck. It fit in with another incident that was about to come to a head.

Unbeknownst to Donna, Ricky had approached her own elderly aunt, Rose, for money. The eighty-one-year-old had given him a $2,000 check, but she made him promise he would not cash it until she had time to transfer funds. Ricky promised. Later, he returned to Rose. He convinced her something was wrong with the check. Rose wrote him a second $2,000 check.

Donna was shocked when her elderly aunt called her from jail. Rose had been arrested, booked, fingerprinted, and mug-shotted. The charge? Check fraud.

Donna went rushing down to the jail. As she untangled the mess, she found Ricky had cashed the first check instantly after receiving it, despite his promise. He had pocketed a total of four grand while an eighty-one-year-old female relative went to jail.

Donna kicked Ricky out.

But Ricky fared much better with women who were not his relatives. Soon he was married and had a baby of his own. Although the good-looking young man had no trouble attracting women, his relationships often took a dark turn. Donna told detectives that she was once at his apartment while his wife, Wendy, was out. Donna heard a thud and the baby start to scream after Ricky scolded her. Donna ran into the nursery where Ricky claimed the infant had "fallen" in her crib. Donna concluded that Ricky had dropped her. Donna stayed with the baby, afraid to leave the room while her nephew was still there, until Wendy came home.

Ricky then joined the army and was sent off to Fort Lewis, Washington, south of Tacoma, where his young family lived. But Ricky did not like army life or family life. He went AWOL. When military police caught up with him in Florida, he stabbed one of them in the hand. Rick Valentini spent the next two years in an army jail. By the time he was twenty-three, Rick was not only on his way to a dishonorable discharge from the US Army; he was also being sued for divorce and child support.

Rick wasn't alone for long. During the mid-1990s he was married to a woman named Catherine, and she gave him a second daughter. This second marriage didn't go any better than the first one had.

Divorce documents found at the Raintree apartment showed the name of yet a third woman. A "Cynthia Valentini" had married Rick in 2000. A stunning brunette with a lucrative career as a bank vice president, Cynthia had sent the divorce papers to Rick from Florida. Years after leaving his Valentini identity behind, "Bryan Stewart" had written to his financial adviser to not send mail to a certain address, because "I do not want anyone at that address stealing my financial info." Cynthia Valentini was living at the address at the time. Yet Bryan was still using her credit card to pay for things for himself, such as an apprenticeship program in fitness training. It seems that Bryan's career as a "trophy wife" had begun long before he met Jamie Laiaddee.

It is doubtful that Jamie knew about Bryan's marital history. All the papers were under the name "Valentini," a name Jamie had certainly never heard of.

Piecing together Bryan/Rick's life story, Moffat confirmed there had been no University of Michigan education, either. University officials denied they granted a degree in "education physiology." Nor did they have a Bryan Stewart, Rick Valentini, or even Ricky Wayne Schmidt anywhere on their rolls. They pronounced the diploma displayed in the Raintree apartment a blatant forgery.

A small print shop was tracked down. An older woman at the shop readily admitted to having made up the University of Michigan seal embosser. She remembered the customer, Bryan Stewart, telling her it was to be a birthday gift for someone. She was upset to learn that it had been used to forge documents.

It also seemed that Bryan Stewart had changed his beliefs as often as he changed identity. The religion listed on his dog tags was Mormon. But one e-mail trail led to a woman practicing the pagan religion. Bryan had written to her that he had been raised Presbyterian. Now he wanted to pursue the religion of his "Scottish ancestors." Bryan wanted to learn all about Druidism, to connect to his "authentic" heritage.

Eventually, Bryan wanted to meet R. J. in person. A professional undercover cop, maintaining the personal style of an underworld figure, Detective "Smith" easily fit the part. He showed up at the county jail and introduced himself to Stewart as R. J.

Bryan wanted R. J. to sell more of his belongings. In giving instructions, he referred to his "cereal" several times, saying, "that's a hint" after each mention. R. J. indicated that he did understand. This exchange was repeated again and again and again.

Bryan had no way of knowing that the gun from the oatmeal box was already in police custody, thanks to the housecleaner, or that all his secrets were being gathered by his "friend" R. J., who was one undercover cop after another.

Over the next year, police made jail visits with snitches, ran errands posing as R. J., conducted surveillance, and plunged into the records left by Jamie Laiaddee and Bryan Stewart/Rick Valentini/Ricky Wayne Schmidt. They concluded that Jamie Laiaddee, beloved of friends, family, coworkers, roommates, and godchildren, had been murdered sometime between 7:34 p.m. and 11:45 p.m. on March 17. The window of time between 7:34 p.m. and 7:58 p.m.—the time between when Jamie had last saved an e-mail and when Bryan had forwarded her the coupons—was particularly suspicious, as Bryan had never sent these coupons to Jamie before, and she directly received a set from the grocery store anyway. It looked like he had been trying to establish some sort of electronic alibi.

A timeline showed that Jamie's methodical behavior ceased and Bryan's impulsive behavior took over her life just as St. Patrick's Day had expired.

First there was the LPR photo at 11:45 p.m. of Bryan in the gold Escape entering the Raintree apartment complex. At 2:00 a.m. on the eighteenth, Jamie's personal American Express card was used from the Raintree apartment to buy $160 worth of camping goods online.

The day after Jamie's disappearance, Jamie's CareFusion American Express card was used for an ATM cash advance of $503. Over the course of the week, several more attempts at a cash advance, all unsuccessful, were made on this corporate card.

On March 21, using one of Jamie's personal cards, Bryan signed up for accounts with online dating sites SpeedDate™ and eHarmony®. He joined at least seven other dating services over the next few days. Police found that he often used the screen name "Thorinin the Dolphin" for these profiles. For pictures, he used the photos Jamie had taken of him in Ann Arbor on the trip that she had paid for, while simultaneously paying his bail. He looked like a happy alumnus of the school, smiling broadly in his blue and gold shirt, posing with players, at the stadium gate, and with the Wolverine statue. In the section of the profile asking about kids, the father of two school-age daughters wrote, "None, I don't think I ever want kids." He met up often for casual sex with women he culled from his online flirting. He nearly got scammed by online dater "Oksana," who wanted him to send money to the Ukraine.

Several online purchases were paid for using Jamie's cards over the next few weeks and sent to her house on Eucalyptus but addressed to Bryan Stewart: a teepee-style tent, a University of Michigan football jersey, a seventy-inch African spear, a Bowie knife, and two swords. Video beginning on March 18 showed Bryan shopping alone at Target, Walmart, and Costco with Jamie's credit cards.

Well before Jamie had vanished, Bryan had sent a message that suggested her disappearance had been premeditated. "Seriously, I don't know what is happening with Jamie," he wrote to a friend in early February, "but I know she wants out of Arizona REALLY bad." Bryan shared her alleged desire to move out of Arizona with several people for weeks before she went missing. But police found her correspondence frequently asking for job referrals in Arizona and expressing the specific desire to friends to find a way to stay where she was.

Police also found that late on the afternoon of what may have been her last day alive, Jamie had sent a message to her lawyer friend David Beauchamp, making tentative plans to meet up. Beauchamp told police that she had once told him she was afraid of her boyfriend. Beauchamp had advised her to call police. She had responded, "I don't think they could protect me from him."

From the jail snitches police learned that the potential motive for Jamie's death had been that she had begun talking to other men. Her brief mentions to her girlfriends that she had "met someone" seemed to enforce this theory.

In jail conversations reported to police Bryan was alleged to have said that men could hit women under certain circumstances. Pointing to a picture of Jamie in the newspaper, he allegedly continued, "She learned that." According to the snitches, Bryan supposedly made statements that Jamie had been blasted with the shotgun and "cut up."

Whether Jamie ever understood the truth about Bryan's "trespassing" case is unknown. But had she been able to attend his next court case, she would have learned a lot about her boyfriend. Bryan went on trial on fraud and weapons charges in June of 2011. As a personal trainer, he'd had close-buzzed hair and a bulked-up frame. After a year in jail, his hair was curled over his collar, his face had thinned out, and his frame had become slender, less menacing.

In court, Bryan was confronted by the man whose social security number he had frequently used over a period of years. Quintez Braxton, a strapping marine, took the witness stand and told the court good-naturedly that he had not known that anyone was using his social security number all this time. At the defense table, dishonorably discharged Rick Valentini had to listen. Braxton testified that he had been serving his country in Iraq, Korea, and Afghanistan. The active-duty marine, smiling calmly, said that in such dangerous places he had other things to do than check his credit rating.

The courtroom was small. During breaks, jurors passed right behind the defense table. Bryan stood up and faced them, a hopeful and friendly look on his face, as they walked within twenty-four inches of him. They typically stared straight ahead rather than meet his imploring gaze.

After all the witnesses had spoken and all the evidence had been laid out, Defense Attorney Marie Farney argued to the jury that her client, to whom she continued to refer to as Bryan Stewart, had meant no harm.

"What does one do when you find you have no identity?" she asked. Bryan had been inspired by the events of September 11, 2001, she told the jury, reading from a letter he had written from jail to his aunt Donna. He wanted to die a hero, like those who had rushed to help on that terrible day. From that thought, he soon he realized he should live like a hero, too, she said, still reading from the letter.

What's wrong with creating the identity you want to live? she asked the panel. He was not trying to harm anyone, she said; "He was trying to live a life." The bottom line, she thundered to the jurors, is that "the state cannot prove he is *not* Bryan Stewart until they can tell you who he *is*."

The jurors deliberated for about one day. Bryan again wore his hopeful face as court reconvened. But as guilty verdicts were announced, one after another, forty times, Bryan's mask of congeniality abruptly fell away. His face took on a look of disgust; he shook his head and muttered angry words to himself. It was Marie Farney's turn to put on a mask. Though she was sitting right next to him, she sat stone-faced, pretending not to notice her client's outburst.

Jamie's body has never been found. Jamie's parents, whose love Jamie somehow failed to feel in all its warmth during the last years of her life, made tearful appeals on television and traveled to Arizona to search, to put up fliers, and to talk to anyone who would listen.

Jamie's friends—including the 516 girls—have not given up the search. They organized a Facebook® page, made appeals to crime-television-show celebrities like Nancy Grace and Jane Velez-Mitchell, and succeeded in bringing national exposure to Jamie's case. The friends hope that someone somewhere saw or heard something that might lead to the discovery of Jamie's remains. Campers on the Mogollon Rim or hikers in the McDowell Sonoran Preserve, Bryan's frequent haunts, might one day find something that unlocks the tragic mystery of Jamie's fate.

For all of Jamie's care and concern for others, the one thing she failed to see was how much people cared for her. In trying to put her best face forward, she disguised her needs from those who would have rushed to her aid. The one person she did trust with her deepest layers of self, her "trophy wife," turned out to be the one person who did not see her beautiful soul but instead saw a revenue stream, a possession, something to be extinguished when he could no longer control her.

ABOUT THE AUTHOR

CAMILLE KIMBALL is an Emmy award–winning investigative reporter, former newspaper columnist, and longtime broadcaster. Her books include *A Sudden Shot*; *What She Always Wanted*; *The Mammoth Book of Tough Guys*; and more to come. She can be seen on such television shows as *Wicked Attraction*, *Scorned*, and several others, as well as on film in the Swiss documentary *Debra Milke*. Find supplementary material, photos, updates, and new cases at her website www.camillekimball.com.

REFERENCES

Arizona court documents housed at Maricopa County Clerk of the Superior Court, 601 W. Jackson Street, Phoenix, Arizona.

Author's notes during attendance of trial for Maricopa County Criminal Case #CR2010 007708001.

City of Chandler Police Report #10-06-0454 (including e-mails, transcripts, and other primary documents).

Goldstein, Michael, deputy county attorney. 2007. Direct complaint, August 24.

Maricopa County (Arizona) Criminal Case #CR2007-154790.

Maricopa County Criminal Case #CR 2011005869001. Judge Susan Brnovich presiding.

McIlveen, Tammy, crime scene investigator. 2010. Report filed with City of Chandler Police, July 6.

Plea agreement. 2008. Prosecutor Lindsey Coates and Defense Counsel Joanne Cuccia, May 16.

Pre-sentence report dated December 22, 2011, prepared by PSI Officer Hector Ramos, adult probation officer.

Superior Courtroom of Judge Lisa Daniel Flores, East Court Building, Maricopa County (Trial July/August 7, 2011).

Testimony of Detective Nathan Moffat, Quintez Braxton, Mary Sowers, et al.

Chapter 9

THE DARKEST HOUR
Teenagers Who Kill for Love
by Amanda Lamb

T hings were starting to get fuzzy for eighteen-year-old Matt. He knew it probably had to do with the wine, the pills, and the white powder he was mixing with the alcohol and drugs. *What was it again?* He couldn't remember. Allegra had told him. *Something to do with horses?* That's right— horse tranquilizer. That's what she had told him. *Powerful stuff,* he thought. He was getting so tired. He just wanted to sleep. He steadied himself on the back of the chair and then slid down into the seat. Finally, he could relax. The anxious feelings Matt had been having started to slip away as he drifted off to sleep.

DREW LOGAN SHAW ✓

Sixteen-year-old Drew Logan Shaw was all about a good adventure. He talked a big game for a teenager. He was full of bravado and crazy ideas that came straight out of the video game world. But inside, in many ways, he was still a scared little boy. It had all been *just talk* until this night, November 30, 2008. Ryan had insisted that he go with him that night. Ryan had called Drew's house and cell phone over and over until Drew gave in to him. Ryan told Drew that "he owed him." Reluctantly, Drew had gone with Ryan without really understanding what was about to happen.

Now Drew was standing outside in the dark in front of Allegra's family's abandoned trailer, holding onto the baseball bat and keeping watch. The trailer was part of an old horse farm on Olive Branch Lane in New Hill, North Carolina—the middle of nowhere, Drew thought. It was a place you could never find if you didn't know where to look—a lush, overgrown, neglected spot with a dusty dirt drive only barely visible in the moonlight. It was so dark, other than the moon and a few small lights coming from the trailer, that Drew jumped every time he heard a twig snap or a slight rustling of the grass. He knew it was probably just a small animal or, even more likely, his imagination, but being out in the country wasn't Drew's thing.

Drew's heart was starting to flutter a bit, and his palms were starting to sweat. The bat kept slipping out of his hands as he tried to strike an imposing posture. But he didn't *feel* very imposing. His instructions had been to hit Matt if he tried to run. Drew had told Ryan he would do it, but in his mind he was still playing a video game. *It wasn't real.* At least that's what he kept telling himself, that it was still just talk. Nothing bad was going to happen to Matt. What would he really do if Matt, a dude he had nothing against, came running out of the trailer dazed and confused, and Drew was forced to make a decision? Would he really hit him? Could he?

That's when Drew decided to go inside the trailer and see for himself what was going on. Once inside, Drew saw Matt mixing some kind of white powder in a big glass of wine. Matt was also taking a handful of pills. Drew's friends—Allegra, Aadil, and Ryan—were also there, laughing and joking around. They told him they had hit Matt over the head with a hammer, and it was like nothing had happened. Matt didn't even seem fazed by the blow. He was still standing, still coherent. But Matt *was* shaking. Drew touched the back of Matt's head where there was a bloody gash from the hammer. Drew said his friends were musing over the fact of "how Matt didn't die easy."

"The plan had changed, and they convinced him to kill himself. That's what they told me," Drew said.

Drew said Matt was laughing, too, but he seemed disoriented as his friends seemed to be berating him, making him feel as though no one wanted him to live—saying things like his biological mother had tried to abort him by taking drugs when she was pregnant. Drew would later cry as he described the scene from the witness stand in court.

"For one, I'm kind of fucking scared," he said. "I don't know what anyone's thinking. I don't know how serious anyone is. I'm like, if I make any kind of move, I feel like they might have killed me or something."

Drew left the trailer that night on Olive Branch Lane before anything else happened. He didn't want to be a part of whatever was about to go down.

What he didn't know then was that no matter how fast or how far he ran, he would forever be connected to the events of that night.

MATTHEW JOSIAH SILLIMAN

Ben and Betty Silliman adopted Matthew Josiah Silliman on September 10, 1990, in Shreveport, Louisiana. He was just ten days old at the time. Ben, a college agriculture professor, and Betty, a Montessori teacher, moved their growing family around the country for Ben's work until 2001 when they arrived in Apex, North Carolina, from Wyoming and decided to finally put down some roots. The small southern town seemed just right for the Silliman family with its quality schools, active churches, and tight-knit community feel they had been looking for.

Matt's mother, Betty, said Matt was the "spice" of their self-described "very average" family that also included two biological children—younger daughter Mary and older son Jeremiah.

As he got older, Matt wasn't that different from most teenagers. He liked girls, and they liked him back. He was outgoing, friendly, and loyal to his loved ones. Matt had achieved the highly esteemed rank in scouting of Eagle Scout with thirty-one merit badges to his name. He was also very involved in his church, Peace Presbyterian in Cary, and well liked at Apex High School, where he would be a senior in the fall of 2008.

But something happened in Matt's life in the spring of 2008. He changed. Matt started to withdraw from longtime friends at church and in scouting. He started wearing all black and hanging out with a new group of friends whom his parents didn't know very well. It was also around this time that Matt was diagnosed with bipolar disorder. The doctor prescribed medication, but Matt didn't always take it. He loved his family, but he started to disappoint them. He had at one time been a young person full of promise, but now he seemed like a young man full of despair.

"He seemed down," said Matt's mother, Betty. "The spring before, he had dreams of suicide. He talked to a counselor at school about it. He started dressing differently. He started drinking and smoking. He said he had to clear his head a lot. He pierced his ears."

Matt's decline continued through the summer of 2008 and hit rock-bottom when he tried to kill himself on September 30 of that year. He cried out for help on Facebook®, posting a veiled threat online that he was going to take his life. Aadil told Matt's father, Ben, about the threat, and Ben was able to stop Matt just in time. It was then that the Sillimans knew their son was in severe pain and needed more help and support than the family could offer him. Matt was subsequently admitted to a private psychiatric hospital for treatment. When he was released, for a brief period of time, it seemed to his family that the old Matt was back.

Aadil had become one of Matt's best friends. They hung out all the time and talked about almost everything, but beneath the friendship there was jealousy because Matt seemed to get all the girls. Aadil suspected that his own girlfriend, Katherine Oliver, might have eyes for Matt. One girl who had confirmed eyes for Matt was Allegra, a classmate from Apex High School. But Allegra had a serious boyfriend named Ryan, and the spark between Allegra and Matt didn't sit well with Ryan.

Matt had no idea there was an intense storm brewing behind his back and he was about to find himself right in the middle of it.

ALLEGRA ROSE DAHLQUIST

Seventeen-year-old Allegra Rose Dahlquist met Matt through Aadil in the early summer of 2008. The petite, dark-haired girl with pale skin and forlorn eyes was immediately smitten with the tall, thin, gregarious blond boy who had an infectious smile. They started hanging out together when her boyfriend, Ryan, was at work.

"He didn't like how Matt would talk about me or look at me," Allegra said, regarding Ryan's increasing jealousy.

In October 2008, Allegra's feelings for Matt had become so strong that Allegra broke up with Ryan. But the breakup lasted just two weeks, and soon she was back under Ryan's spell again, willing to do almost anything for him. Ryan told her that a mysterious hit man named "Roger" was out to get Matt. At Ryan's insistence, Allegra started feeding Matt's growing fear about this impending danger. Matt believed wholeheartedly in what Allegra and Ryan were telling him about Roger.

"He trusted us," Allegra said of Matt.

The night they planned to kill Matt, by her own admission, Allegra had distracted him with a tarot-card reading while Ryan hit him in the back of the head with the hammer.

But it was like nothing had transpired. Matt's head must have been so deadened from all the drugs and alcohol that it seemed as though he didn't even feel the blow.

"I looked up, and Matt was just sitting there, and Ryan was holding the hammer," Allegra said. "(Ryan) said, 'You're not dead.' Matt didn't really say anything and just gave Ryan a really dirty look."

Allegra said she had to look away when Ryan hit Matt because, even though she loved Ryan more, she had feelings for Matt, too, and she knew what they were doing was wrong.

But she also had some *hard* feelings about Matt. Soon after they had ended their fling, he moved on quickly to a new girlfriend named Michelle Lippert. Even though Allegra was with Ryan again, it still hurt her heart that Matt was able to forget about her so quickly.

AADIL SHAHID KAHN

Seventeen-year-old Aadil Shahid Kahn was a guy who played all the angles. He and Matt were close, but at the same time, he was envious of Matt's ability to attract just about any girl he set his sights on—and even those that he did not.

Aadil was dating a girl named Katherine. He suspected that Matt might also be interested in her, so Aadil went to Ryan.

"Something has got to be done about Matt," Aadil said, according to Ryan's lawyer, Robert Padavano. Padavano also said that Aadil was a "manipulator" who talked Ryan into the plot to kill Matt.

RYAN PATRICK HARE

"Mastermind" was how prosecutors described Ryan Patrick Hare during his first-degree murder trial in September 2010. Ryan had an unnatural amount of power—unequaled by most teenagers—over his girlfriend, Allegra, and his friends. He also had a consuming jealousy that ran deep when it came to Allegra. With their dark hair, dark eyes, and pale skin, the couple could have passed for brother and sister. But Allegra was Ryan's soul mate and best friend, and nobody, including Matt, was going to get in the way of their relationship.

Ryan had dropped out of high school and was working at a local sandwich shop when he met Allegra. Allegra was still attending Apex High School, attending school with *Matt*. It steamed Ryan to no end that Matt was spending time with his girl at school while *he* was working hard all day long. Allegra and Matt shared their lunch period at school and bonded over their shared emotional insecurities—including how self-mutilation, known as "cutting," could relieve tension in their lives.

Ryan was not happy with the growing connection between Allegra and Matt, but despite his lack of formal education, he was smart. Ryan knew there was a solution to every problem, even one that seemed impossible to overcome, *like another guy trying to steal your girl.*

ROGER

As Ryan's jealousy grew over Matt's attention to his girlfriend, he began to get more and more angry. He told Matt a story about a mysterious hit man, Roger, who wanted Matt dead. Ryan told Matt that he needed to get out of town, out of sight, and away from places where Roger might find him. While nothing about the story was logical, Matt bought it completely and was willing to do whatever his friends told him was necessary to avoid Roger.

Allegra said Roger had given Ryan an ultimatum—kill Matt, or Roger would kill Ryan. Ryan said he was willing to sacrifice himself for Matt. But Allegra loved Ryan and said she would do anything to protect him. So, she went along with Ryan's plan to get Matt out of town. She offered up her family's trailer on a horse farm out in the country as a hideout for Matt to escape the watchful eyes of Roger.

Ryan's ex-girlfriend, Sarah Rayner, told the court that Ryan had called her out of the blue to say that Roger was back and might be out to get her, as well. During their relationship, Sarah said Ryan had talked occasionally about Roger. He told her Roger was older and was involved in criminal activity. Sarah said Ryan told her he made bombs called "hot boxes" for Roger that Roger would in turn sell and give Ryan a cut of the profits. But the further she got from the relationship, the more Sarah said she realized that there probably was no Roger.

Prosecutors in the case agreed with Sarah's suspicions that Roger didn't really exist, that he was simply a fictitious character created by Ryan to scare people when he got into difficult situations that he didn't know how to handle himself.

"I think we know who Roger is," prosecutor Jason Waller said to the jury. "It's one and the same. Ryan is Roger. I'm not talking about some split personality here. Ryan uses Roger when he gets in trouble."

FORESHADOWING

Honestly fearing for his life after what Ryan had told him about Roger being out to get him, Matt confided in his friend Victoria Thomas about his concerns.

"He said Roger was perfect," Victoria said in court. "He couldn't be caught. He was a ghost in the system."

Before heading to hide out at the trailer, Matt met his girlfriend, Michelle, in her car at the parking lot of a local shopping center to say good-bye.

"He said Roger was out to get him," Michelle testified. "I was just trying to understand what was going on. He didn't seem to know what was going on either. He told me he loved me and got out of the car."

Oleg Drozdowski was a student at Panther Creek High School who occasionally hung out and smoked pot with Drew. One Friday afternoon after school, Drew brought Ryan with him to party with him and Oleg. Oleg remembered that Ryan talked about wanting to kill someone.

"I thought it was a joke. Everybody has a bad day with somebody," Oleg testified. "He said Matt, but I didn't know it was Matt Silliman."

Oleg recalled Ryan and Drew talking about ways to kill someone—including getting the person so wasted they would pass out so that you could then easily strangle him. Little did he know how these words would later come back to haunt him.

DEATH CHAT

Computer forensics examiner Beth Whitney, with the City County Bureau of Identification (CCBI), examined a computer found in Ryan's home. The CCBI is an organization that provides crime-scene investigators to every law enforcement agency in Wake County, North Carolina.

On Ryan's computer, Whitney found excerpts of chats between Ryan (f8lessshadow) and Aadil (akhanx47).

They talked about the possibility of Matt killing himself, but Ryan said that might not be "good enough for Roger."

"A corpse is a corpse," Aadil responded.

"Sadly, I will laugh when this is over, probably," Ryan said.

"Sadly, I'll get the knives," responded Aadil.

"Just spend a good fifteen minutes laughing," Ryan added for emphasis.

Aadil admitted in the chat that there would be a part of him that would be sad when Matt was dead, "the parts that cared for him as a friend." But then he went on to muse about how Matt "has it coming."

"You take my girl," Aadil said, "I take your life. Sweet justice."

"Nice code to live by," Ryan responded.

Whitney also found another chat between Matt (M3475H31LD) and Ryan, in which the two were clearly talking about their mutual affection for Allegra and about Matt taking her away from Ryan, however briefly.

"If my entire life was to protect a girl as amazing as her for one moment, it would be worth it," Ryan said.

Matt said he understood and then added, "I hate what I did to you."

FAILED ATTEMPT

Allegra told police that she held a flashlight while Ryan and Aadil spent time over several days digging a four-foot-wide hole just twenty-five feet from the train tracks off of Old US Highway 64. This is where they had planned to put Matt's body when it was all over. When it rained, the hole filled with dark, murky runoff, creating a watery grave.

Allegra said the initial idea was for her and Ryan and Aadil to kill Matt in the car. They would drive him out on a desolate road, and at a certain point in a particular song, they would strangle him. Aadil's role was to use a stun gun on Matt, to subdue him, and then Ryan was supposed to slip a plastic zip-tie around Matt's neck and cut off his oxygen supply.

It was the perfect plan for a group of misfits who proudly considered themselves outcasts. They didn't fit in with average teenagers, but they *fit* together. In cyberspace they could be anyone they wanted to be. On social networking sites they said they were fans of the hip-hop band called the Insane Clown Posse and subscribed to the group's fantasy world know as "Dark Carnival." On MySpace®, Ryan talked about attacking a world full of love and peace because "they would never expect it." Aadil called himself an "anarchist" online who believed in "my own kind" of justice. They bonded over video games, over paintball, and over *not* fitting in.

The teens chose November 25, 2008, as the night they would kill Matt. Aadil told Matt that they needed to talk, that he needed relationship advice from Matt. Allegra told Matt that she also wanted to talk about *their* relationship. Aadil and Allegra drove to Matt's house in her Toyota 4Runner® and picked him up. Allegra drove, Matt got into the passenger seat, and Aadil moved to the backseat. As they drove off into the night, Aadil tried to shock Matt with the stun gun from the backseat as they had planned, but because Matt was wearing a hooded sweatshirt, it didn't work. Ryan, who had been hiding in the backseat, then jumped up and surprised Matt by placing a zip-tie around his neck. Matt, clawing at his neck and gasping for air, begged for help, begged his friends to stop. The thick material of the sweatshirt wasn't allowing Ryan to get the zip-tie tight enough. It became clear the plan wasn't going to work. So, Ryan eventually released Matt. When it was over, when Matt finally caught his breath and regained his composure, he wanted to know what in the world they were doing.

Aadil told Matt they needed to pretend to kill him and record it on video to make Roger believe he was really dead. This tactic, they told Matt, would keep Roger at bay, at least for the time being.

MISSING

Despite his friends' first attempt on his life, just before Thanksgiving, Matt packed a bag and left his home in Apex, North Carolina, for the trailer in New Hill, never to return again.

After not hearing from Matt for twenty-four hours, his parents called police on November 26. They had already called around to his friends, and no one had seen him. Because Matt had a history of bipolar disorder, the state issued a Silver Alert, a statewide bulletin for a person suffering from cognitive impairments who may be endangered.

But it wasn't Matt's mental state that caused him to disappear; it was the stories his friends were telling him about Roger. Matt's real enemy was not a mysterious hit man who had targeted him for some unknown reason. It was those closest to him. Danger lurked all around him disguised in the faces of people he trusted the most.

Matt believed his friends when they told him he must stay out of sight at the trailer so that Roger would be convinced he had left town. They brought him food and water, and told him when the time was right, they would smuggle him out of town. What Matt didn't know was that they never planned to allow him to leave the trailer alive.

THE KILLING

On the night of November 30, 2008, Matt was convinced more than ever that Roger was out to get him. One way or another, he knew this wasn't going to end well. Deep down inside, Matt knew that he was going to die on this night.

He hugged each one of his friends in lingering embraces—even Ryan, who reluctantly accepted the hug. The drugs and alcohol had made Matt so woozy that he could barely stand. He steadied himself against a chair and then slowly slid down into the seat. A moment later, Matt passed out. Ryan, Aadil, and Allegra carried Matt from the back porch, first to a bedroom and then into the bathroom of the trailer where there were no windows. Allegra said this was Ryan's idea, to make sure no one could see inside.

After Matt started to shake and wiggle in his unconscious state, the teens bound Matt's hands and ankles with zip-ties just like they had planned. Allegra said Aadil then covered Matt's mouth with duct tape in case he started to scream, also as planned. Then Matt started throwing up, most likely from the lethal combination of drugs and alcohol that he had taken. The teens sat Matt up so that he could throw up in the bag, but with the duct tape still on his mouth, it was going everywhere. Matt was choking on his vomit. Allegra said she and Ryan together then put the bag over Matt's head to suffocate him. The final step was a zip-tie around Matt's neck—just like the one that had been placed around his neck on November 25. But this time, no one was letting go.

"Ryan handed me a zip-tie, and I put it over his neck," Allegra said. "I pulled it, but I couldn't get it on all the way. I went outside the bathroom with Aadil. Ryan came out a few minutes later, saying he tightened it."

Matt's body was zipped up in a sleeping bag to conceal it. His so-called friends left him in the trailer, discarded like a piece of trash in the back of the bathroom underneath a pile of junk, like someone no one cared about. The problem was that many people did care about Matt and would be looking for him.

"I didn't want Matt to die, but I wanted to do what Ryan wanted me to do," Allegra said in court.

The teens lit incense to hide the smell of the vomit and then left the trailer and went to a fast-food restaurant to talk about what they had done.

"I believed [Ryan] was the only person I had in my life who cared," Allegra said of why she had participated in Matt's killing. "Ryan made me believe he was the only person who cared about me."

According to the medical examiner, Matt died from asphyxiation as a result of having the bag put over his head and tied tightly around his neck. While he did have a lethal combination of drugs and alcohol in his system, the medical examiner said this was not what killed Matt.

One day after the murder, Allegra said she came back to the trailer along with Ryan and Aadil to clean out any evidence that Matt had been there. They took out three bags of items including clothes, food containers, and water bottles and discarded them in a dumpster. Allegra said Ryan kicked Matt's body to make sure he was dead before they left.

On December 2, 2008, Wake County sheriff's investigators found Matt's body in the trailer after Drew made strange statements to his grandmother, Nancy Shaw, about Matt being dead. Drew said he had killed Matt with a baseball bat and buried him. While Drew's story was completely false, it put investigators on the right trail.

While the mystery of Matt's disappearance had been solved, the mystery of his death was just starting to unravel.

ARRESTED

Initially, Allegra answered questions from the Apex police with vague responses. She didn't know if they had found Matt's body yet, and she desperately wanted to protect Ryan. Ryan called her on her cell phone several times while she was at the police station. Finally, around four in the morning on December 3, 2008, Allegra came clean with investigators. They told her that the others had told the truth, and it was time for her to do so, as well. But Detective Benjamin Byrne said that, even in the retelling of the brutal murder, Allegra seemed strangely unaffected by it.

"She showed absolutely no emotion," Byrne testified. "There was not one tear shed throughout the entire interview."

Byrne went on to describe what Allegra said was the teens' motive for the heinous crime.

"In her words: 'We wanted to make sure that he died because we hated him. We all did,'" Byrne recalled from the interview.

Byrne then asked Allegra why they hated Matt so much, a boy with whom they professed to be such good friends on Facebook, as well as in real life.

"The answer she gave me was essentially that he was a bad person who had destroyed so many lives with his actions, that he was such an evil person that he needed to die," Byrne said.

Drew wasn't at the trailer when Matt died, so he didn't even know for sure that Matt was dead, but when he was called in for questioning by Apex police, he knew he was in trouble. He had made up some crazy stories, recounting to his grandmother that he had hit Matt in the head with a baseball bat and buried him. Drew didn't want to snitch on Ryan, but he also knew that Matt didn't deserve whatever had happened to him.

"He asked me, did I kill Matt," Drew recalled of his first interview with Apex detective Worth Brown. "And I said no. And then he asked me if I knew somebody that did. I didn't really know, but I suspected."

Police said that Drew almost immediately started crying when asked this series of questions, and that Ryan was the first person about whom he spoke.

Police also interviewed Aadil. He led them to the hole where they had planned to bury Matt, but he told investigators they had changed their minds after discovering that the hole had filled with water when it rained. They worried that if they buried Matt there, the runoff might eventually erode the dirt and bring the body to the surface.

"He was very nonchalant about it. It all struck us as very odd about how calm and collected he was, just standing there, rocking back and forth, talking about it," Detective Brown said.

Aadil also took investigators to the dumpster where they had thrown away Matt's belongings from the trailer. All the investigators testified that Aadil took them step-by-step through everything with cool detachment, as if he were narrating a murder scene from a movie, not from his own personal experience.

"It was as if it were a normal day for him," Wake County sheriff's detective Ed Blomgren said.

Ryan's videotaped interrogation with two investigators, including sheriff's detective Robert Campen, began at 3:00 a.m. on December 3. He told investigators that on December 1, he, Allegra, and Aadil went to Matt's parents' house to talk about where Matt might have gone. Ryan told police that he thought Matt had gone to Washington, DC, to see a girl named Victoria, with whom he had been involved off and on.

Ryan portrayed the visit to the Silliman home in his interview with police as a compassionate one that stemmed from his genuine concern for Matt and his whereabouts.

At times, Ryan laughed during the interview with investigators, especially when they asked him about his relationship with Matt.

"I didn't really trust him," Ryan said. "He kissed my girlfriend."

He also talked about the mysterious Roger character, saying that Roger had asked him if he wanted to work for him. Ryan told the detectives that he knew whatever Roger wanted him to do would not be legal, and so he told him no.

But when it came down to the most important question of the interview, the question that his friends had already answered truthfully, Ryan was speechless.

"Tell me what happened to Matt. It's quite obvious, but I want to hear your side of it," Campen said to Ryan during the nearly two-hour interview.

Ryan initially said nothing in response to the detective's question. But then, in a voice slightly above a whisper, Ryan said four words that convinced Campen of Ryan's involvement in Matt's murder: "He needed to die." Then, Campen said, Ryan covered his mouth with his hands.

Matt's friends were arrested on December 3, 2008, and charged with his murder. Immediately, they lawyered up and started making deals.

THE TRIAL

Ryan Hare was tried for the murder of Matt Silliman in September 2010—almost two years after Matt's body was found in the trailer. Drew Shaw and Allegra Dahlquist testified against him in return for a plea deal. Aadil Kahn was also supposed to testify in return for a lesser sentence, but as the trial date approached, prosecutors claimed that Aadil started to forget key details surrounding the events of November 30, 2008. As a result, the state asked the judge to withdraw Aadil's plea deal.

Prosecutor Melanie Shekita told jurors that although "you might think you're in the middle of a strange fiction movie," this was real life. She said the plan to kill Matt was a "sinister plot" cooked up by Ryan, because he was jealous over Matt's attention to Allegra.

On the other hand, Ryan's defense attorney, Robert Padavano, said that Matt's death was simply an assisted suicide. He said that the saddest part was that Matt's friends did nothing to stop him from killing himself. He claimed that the only reason Ryan was being tried for first-degree murder was because the others talked to police and he didn't. Investigators flipped them and made them state's witnesses against Ryan.

"Ryan Hare was singled out as the leader, the mastermind of this all for one reason," Padavano said. "Of the four, he was the one who did not go to the police and confess his role."

Prosecutors denied the assisted-suicide angle as a plausible theory.

"It's absurd to think Matt ended up like this on his own," prosecutor Jason Waller said. "What killed Matthew Silliman on the night of November 30th was that bag, was that duct tape, was that zip-tie tied tight."

Waller went on to say that the tragedy was caused by nothing more than good, old-fashioned jealousy, a love triangle, the kind of passion that has taken more men down than just about anything in history.

"Ryan did it because Matt kissed his girlfriend," Waller said. "That's it. [Matt] made him mad, and he killed him—and Matt thought he was a friend."

On September 24, 2010, Ryan was convicted of first-degree murder. Superior Court judge Paul Ridgeway sentenced him to life in prison without the possibility of parole.

Ryan addressed the court and the Silliman family at his sentencing hearing. "I would like to apologize to the Silliman family for my part in all this," he said. "I don't believe the entire truth is known, but most of it has been."

The Silliman family, in their darkest hour, somehow found a shred of light at the end of what had been a dark journey through grief and tragedy.

"At a time like this, it is hard to know what to say," Matt's father, Ben, told Ryan at his sentencing hearing. "But I can tell you, as God gives us the power, we forgive you for what you did to Matt."

But it was Matt's fifteen-year-old sister, Mary, who captured everyone's heart in the courtroom as she tearfully recalled losing her big brother. She said the hardest part was knowing that his life was taken by his friends—people he loved and trusted above all others.

"At times, my brain is so confused. All I know how to do is cry," Mary said. "Almost two years later, I miss him when we walk the dog, cook dinner, play games on Saturday night, or I play in the band we both marched with," she said, choking up briefly before continuing. "I miss the way Matt treated me like his precious sister."

Mary lamented how she would never get a chance to see her brother grow up, graduate from high school, go to college, get married, or have children.

"These things are lost to me now. I will miss his smile. I will live with this tragedy and think about my brother's death for the rest of my life, but I will be thankful for the years I had with him."

THE AFTERMATH

Allegra pleaded guilty to second-degree murder and conspiracy to commit murder prior to the trial in return for her testimony. On November 15, 2010, she was sentenced to a minimum term of thirty years in prison and up to a maximum term of just over thirty-seven years.

Prosecutors sought to have Aadil's plea deal revoked after he said he had forgotten key details of the crime and was unable to testify at trial. Wake County sheriff's detective Mariah Jarema said she interviewed Aadil for more than seven hours just after the crime took place and wrote down thirty pages of notes at that meeting. Yet, just before trial, on September 10, 2010, prosecutors said that interviewing Aadil was like "pulling teeth." But, despite Aadil's lack of cooperation, Judge Ridgeway said the plea deal would stand.

Aadil pleaded guilty to the same charges as Allegra had and received a minimum of just over thirty-two years in prison and up to a maximum of just under forty-one years—the maximum possible sentence under the law.

Drew entered an Alford plea to being an accessory after the fact to murder and was sentenced to a minimum of just under four years and to a maximum of just over five years in prison. An Alford plea is a guilty plea whereby the defendant maintains his innocence but admits that the state has enough evidence to convict him on the charge.

Prosecutors said while Drew "made a lot of stupid decisions," his decision to tell his grandmother about the crime, albeit a fictional version, was what ultimately brought the facts of the case to light. Without Drew, prosecutors said the mystery of Matt's disappearance may never have been solved.

The defendants made tearful apologies in court.

"I'm sorry for everything I caused these last two years, and I'm sorry for every word I never said to stop this," Allegra said in a quiet voice through tears.

"He was a great friend to me. I could see he loved his family and friends, and they loved him too," Aadil said. "I looked up to him at times."

"I wish he were here today," he continued. "I wish he could give more fun memories, but I know it's not going to happen because of what I did."

"I'm so deeply sorry for everything I did to Matt and everything I failed to do for Matt," Drew said. "I'm very sorry for all of this, and I pray often, sometimes many times a day, that you will find closure and God's healing."

GOD'S WILL

Again, the Silliman family exhibited grace in their darkest hour as they faced the final three teens who each took responsibility for their son's killing.

"You were created in the image of God, who even today, longs for you to know His love and forgiveness and to walk with Him in a way that makes even a prison a cathedral," Matt's father, Ben, said. "Seek Him while He may be found."

Matt had been killed by people he trusted, people he considered his friends. Throughout the trial, the Sillimans had made an effort to get to know the families of the teens. In their minds, these families had also lost a child.

"The kids and their families regret this day ever occurred," Ben said sincerely.

In the windowless courtroom, the father of a dead son turned darkness into light. Instead of lamenting the time they would not have with Matt, the Sillimans instead chose to thank God for the time they did have.

"That is our satisfaction—that for eighteen years God gave us that blessing" were the grieving father's last words.

ABOUT THE AUTHOR

AMANDA LAMB is a professional television journalist with more than twenty-two years of experience. She covers the crime beat for an award-winning CBS affiliate in the Southeast. Lamb is also the author of four books, writing in two completely different genres—true crime and parenting memoir. Lamb published her first book, a humorous anecdotal collection of essays about parenting called *Smotherhood* in 2007. Her true-crime books include *Deadly Dose* (2008); *Evil Next Door* (2010); and *Love Lies* (2011). She has also written a parenting memoir, *I Love You to God and Back* (2012), and a parenting humor book, *Girls Gone Child* (2011). The author received her undergraduate degree from Duke University and her master's degree in journalism from Northwestern University. For more details about Lamb and her writing, please visit www.alambauthor.com.

REFERENCES

The quotations contained in this story came from the first-degree murder trial of Ryan Hare in Raleigh, North Carolina, at the Wake County Courthouse. Testimony began on September 13, 2010, and Hare was convicted on September 24, 2010. The author covered the trial as a news reporter for WRAL-TV and transcribed the testimony herself. Further quotations came from the sentencing hearing of Allegra Dahlquist, Aadil Kahn, and Drew Shaw, which occurred on November 15, 2010, at the same location.

Chapter 10

INVITATION TO MURDER

The Brutal Murder of Arizona Heiress Jeanne Tovrea

by Ronald J. Watkins

Ever since the death of her husband, Jeanne Tovrea, age fifty-five, lived in the million-dollar Lincoln Hill Estates gated community. Situated on the mountainside just north of central Phoenix, the estates offered a panoramic view of the metropolis below. Barry Goldwater, long-time US senator and presidential candidate, lived not far away. The estates were secure, the nights peaceful, and, in April 1988, the searing summer heat had yet to begin.

The very wealthy widow of millionaire war hero and cattle baron, Ed Tovrea, Jeanne lived alone, though not without trepidation. A guard manned the entrance to the estates twenty-four hours a day, and her house was securely wired against intruders.

Not long after midnight that April Fools' Day, an intruder slipped past the guard and made his way unobserved to Jeanne's home. He then quietly removed the twenty-four-inch kitchen window, the only entrance to the house not wired to the security alarm system, and crawled in. He traversed the darkened house to Jeanne's bedroom. There he jerked the telephone cord from the wall, seized a pillow, placed it over the sleeping woman's head, and fired five shots at point-blank range with his .22-caliber pistol. The killer searched the room and rummaged through her jewelry box and purse but took nothing before fleeing.

Inexplicably, he bolted through the front door, triggering the alarm at 12:45 a.m. He left the estates as unobserved as when he'd arrived.

Within minutes, Phoenix police units responded to the alarm. A dog from the K-9 unit was sent into the house first. Two officers followed closely behind. When the dog began scratching at the master bedroom door, the offi-

159

cers cautiously entered. The dog immediately jumped on the bed and pawed at the covering. When the officers pulled back the bloody sheet, there lay Jeanne's dead body.

The first impression of the scene for the responding homicide detectives was that of a burglary gone awry. But close examination disclosed that nothing of significance was missing; indeed, it appeared that nothing at all had been taken. The signs of theft looked increasingly staged.

Then there was the question of how the murderer had gained entrance. He'd used the only window not wired to the security system. He was either very clever in making such a determination, or he knew about the window before he got there.

The shooting itself was also inconsistent with the burglary-gone-bad scenario. In such a situation, Jeanne would have startled the intruder and been shot while standing up or perhaps after a struggle. The fact that the intruder had placed a pillow over the head of a sleeping woman, then executed her with low-caliber bullets had all the hallmarks of a contract killing.

A rich widow living in an exclusive neighborhood, Jeanne would certainly have possessions coveted by others. More significantly, she'd married into one of the richest and best-known families in Arizona. While those outside the state might recognize the name Goldwater or perhaps Babbitt, in Arizona, the name Tovrea stood as a symbol of power and wealth.

But if this murder was a contract hit, it was an odd one. Up until the moment he'd shot Jeanne Tovrea, the killer had done everything professionally. But afterward, his actions were those of an amateur. First, he hadn't taken anything; then he'd bolted out the front door, either in ignorance or in a panic. Finally, he'd inexplicably left his fingerprints all over the window he'd so carefully removed.

However, these findings didn't make solving the case any easier. The fingerprints found on the scene matched none in the police database. The killer had never been arrested.

In 1988, Phoenix was the fastest-growing region in the fastest-growing state in America. Since the end of World War II, Arizona had experienced a nonstop economic boom. Even national recession scarcely slowed the growth fueled by tourism, construction, and the three Cs: cotton, copper, and cattle. The expansion was fueled by low taxes and modest regulation.

The influx of new residents presented a unique problem. Before the war, everyone pretty much knew everyone else. And although the state's population was increasing by more than 75,000 a year, for every four people who moved there, three people left, which resulted in nobody ever really getting to know anyone else. People lived in comfortable houses surrounded by walls. Civic participation was nonexistent. And because few people really knew anyone outside of their closest friends, it was possible to reinvent yourself. You were who you said you were, until you proved otherwise.

Twenty-nine years before Arizona became a state, Edward Tovrea moved there from Sparta, Illinois, arriving on a freight train. He settled in the booming mining town of Bisbee, where he opened a butcher shop. He quickly branched into the cattle industry, which flourished in the region. He and his first wife had five sons. The youngest, Philip—or Big Phil, as he came to be known—took over the family businesses not long after the end of World War I.

Big Phil married twice and had two sons, one by each marriage: Ed Sr. and Phil Jr. By this time, the Tovrea family was among the richest in Arizona. They owned enormous cattle ranches, vast farms to grow feed, meat-packing plants, and one of the world's largest stockyards, located just east of Phoenix beside the railroad. They also owned great stretches of valuable property in New Mexico and Arizona. Their financial and political power helped define Arizona.

Both of Big Phil's sons served in World War II. Ed Sr. was shot down over the English Channel and was held at POW camp Stalag Luft III, where he helped dig the tunnel that made possible "The Great Escape," popularized in a book and movie of the same name. After thirty-three months as a prisoner of war, he returned to the United States weak and emaciated but ready to get on with the life his father and grandfather had laid out for him and his half brother.

Two years later, Barry Goldwater, a close friend, introduced Ed to the woman who would become his first wife and with whom he had three children: Georgia, known as Cricket; Edward Jr., nicknamed Hap; and Priscilla, called

Prissy. Until 1959, the two half brothers ran the family enterprise known as the Tovrea Land and Cattle Company. Big Phil died in 1962 at the age of sixty-seven. He left his fortune in trusts to be doled out to his grandchildren over the next decades. It seemed a wise way to distribute the family legacy.

After Big Phil's death, the brothers began to scale back their operation, turning real estate in Phoenix into cash and moving most of the business to a more distant site. One intimate of the family later commented that in effect "the empire died and left a lot of money behind for the kids to play with."

There were more changes in the Tovrea family. In 1965, Ed and his wife divorced. Their oldest child was seventeen. Ed had always been a larger-than-life figure in the Phoenix area, known for his love of whiskey and the nightlife. He soon married a woman much younger than himself. The new bride sealed her fate when she reportedly turned to the gathered spectators the moment the couple were pronounced man and wife and shouted in exultation, "I'm rich! I hooked him!" Not surprisingly, they were "unhooked" in less than a year.

Ed, now fifty-one, returned to his old ways, spending his free nights at the legendary Joe Hunt's bar on Scottsdale Road and Stetson. A hard-drinking, chain-smoking man, he was the most eligible bachelor in the state. Within months, he had met and was soon dating thirty-seven-year-old Jeanne Gunter.

Jeanne was from Siloam Springs, Arkansas, and though she'd lived the life of a vagabond traveling from state to state, she retained her distinctive country accent. She'd married her first husband in 1950 and had a daughter named Deborah. The marriage didn't last long. Jeanne moved frequently, typically working as a secretary, hairdresser, or waitress. Over the years, she traveled to Oklahoma, California, Oregon, and Arizona.

While in New Mexico, she remarried, this time to a professional gambler, who was later murdered. Reports are unclear as to whether they were still married at the time of his death. She'd lived briefly in Arizona prior to that. Then she returned to Arizona with Deborah and went to work as a cocktail waitress at the Safari Restaurant on North Scottsdale Road while studying for a real-estate license.

Jeanne was lighthearted and outgoing. She loved the rodeo and considered herself to be country folk. It was in 1970 that she met Ed Tovrea. They were married three years later.

The Tovrea family moved in the best circles in the Phoenix area. Jeanne was not accepted, despite her upbeat personality and the obvious affection she and Ed shared. After all, she had a "hillbilly" accent and had worked in bars. The Tovrea children took an instant dislike to their stepmother; at least one of them reportedly called her a "gold digger."

Ten years into the happy marriage, Ed's health took a downturn. His years of heavy drinking and smoking had finally caught up with him. After Ed was diagnosed with cirrhosis of the liver and emphysema, Jeanne became his caretaker. Ed died in 1983 at age sixty-four with his wife and son, Hap, at his bedside.

Jeanne was left a very rich widow. But for the five years that remained of her life, there was never the slightest indication that she was happy to see Ed gone. In fact, with each passing year, it was more apparent that she'd been devoted to him and that her life as a widow was less than it had been as a wife.

There was no obvious reason why anyone would want to murder Jeanne; certainly no reason at all why someone would arrange to have her killed—at least not on the surface. But when detectives peeked beneath the self-evident, they uncovered a myriad of suspects.

Jeanne had recently purchased a $2.7 million life insurance policy, naming her daughter Deborah as sole beneficiary. Why would a rich widow need such a policy? It certainly made the daughter a suspect.

Then there was the murder of her second husband in nearby New Mexico. One murder in an extended family was unusual; now there were two. Was it possible they were somehow connected?

Jeanne had been dating at the time of her death. The boyfriend was married, a former rodeo champion living in Las Vegas but spending much of his time in Phoenix. He'd involved her in a business deal that had turned sour when she'd crossed someone. It had reportedly involved land speculators and mobsters.

Then police learned of a disturbing incident that took place the previous summer at the Balboa Bay Club in Newport Beach, California. Some weeks earlier, a man named Gordon Phillips had contacted Jeanne. He said he was a writer for Time Life® publications and was interested in documenting Ed's service as a war hero. Though Jeanne had disavowed much knowledge of her husband's record, Phillips was persistent. When she told him she'd be out of town in Newport Beach, he said, "What a coincidence. I'll be in Newport Beach myself. We can talk then." In the end, Jeanne agreed to meet with him in a public place accompanied by her daughter, Deborah.

It had been a troubling meeting. Not once during the half-hour conversation did Phillips ask about Ed's war record or his time as a POW, and he scarcely glanced at the memorabilia Jeanne had brought. What he did do was scare Jeanne out of her wits, and when she returned to Phoenix she made a point of saving his message on her answering machine. Then she promptly paid half a million dollars to buy the aforementioned life insurance policy. She legally took the money to buy the policy from a $4 million trust fund.

Hap, Ed's son by his first wife, suggested to police that his father had arranged to have Jeanne murdered after his death. He said their marriage had not been all that happy and that his dad had disliked Jeanne's prolific spending habits.

It was a murder with many suspects, but among homicide investigations there are certain basic assumptions. People kill out of hate and for money. The overriding question was always "Who benefited?" And if the one who benefited also hated the victim, that person moved to the top of the list.

In this case, there were several people who, if they didn't exactly hate Jeanne, certainly professed a deep dislike of her. And every one of them stood to gain from her untimely death.

Ed Tovrea had followed Big Phil's example when it came time to write what proved to be his last will and testament. At the time of his death, his assets were worth $8.7 million, of which $4 million was set up in a trust fund. He'd been furious at the way his children treated Jeanne and had told her he was cutting them out of everything. She convinced him that would not be right, so Ed compromised.

In a letter to his children to be delivered after his death, Ed reminded them that they had not earned one dime of their inheritance and that they should be grateful for every penny he gave them. He then berated them for the shabby way they'd treated their stepmother. He criticized Hap for squandering so much money, for owing everybody, and for bragging that he never intended to work. Each was given $260,000 in cash. In addition, they would collect their percentage of the trust fund, but only after Jeanne died. In the meantime, she would receive property, stocks, and bonds, as well as the interest from the trust, a total of about $400,000 a year.

Jeanne had always sought to repair relations with her stepchildren. It was one of many qualities Ed had admired. But the children had gone too far. When she went to recover the ashes of her husband, she learned the children had persuaded the mortuary to give the ashes to them. They then divvied them up, and portions were scattered at locations undisclosed to Jeanne. She received nothing of her husband. Devastated, she severed all contact with them.

The children were enraged at the terms of their inheritance. Over the next few years, they filed four lawsuits against Jeanne in a vain attempt to break their father's will. They lost them all, incurring hundreds of thousands of dollars in legal fees. They were even required to reimburse Jeanne for her legal costs.

Looking at the actions of these three children, it seemed to detectives that any one of them could have orchestrated the death of their stepmother. For the right kind of entitled mind, Ed's will had been an invitation to murder.

But these were all respected members of the community, scions to perhaps the most distinguished name in Arizona society. They were hardly murderers. Besides, two of the siblings, Cricket and Hap, had been in San Diego at the time of the murder. They'd been asked if either had ever heard of Gordon Phillips, and both denied knowing anyone by that name. All three children gave fingerprint samples, none of which matched those of the killer.

The rest of the case had likewise gone nowhere. There was no connection to the murder of Jeanne's second husband that detectives could uncover, nothing to the business deal gone bad.

But there was one troubling discovery. Time Life publications had never heard of Gordon Phillips, and detectives were unable to find anyone with that name who had a connection to the Tovreas. They had his voice on Jeanne's answering machine, and they had a physical description from the daughter who'd attended the meeting, but that was all. Odd as it was, there was no evidence to suggest he was connected to the murder.

In all, four homicide detectives worked this first phase of the investigation and interviewed more than one hundred people. They continued to grimly follow the evidence and list of suspects, but in the end, the investigation simply petered out like an Arizona frontier silver mine. They had one rock-solid lead: the fingerprints. If the day ever came when they found a match, police were certain they'd have their man.

And if someone had paid for this murder, they were certain to learn just who that someone was.

●

For three years, the trail remained cold and was consigned to the cold-case files under the direction of veteran homicide detective, Ed Reynolds. Then, in April 1992—almost four years to the day after Jeanne's brutal murder—the television show *Unsolved Mysteries* ran an episode about the Tovrea murder. The show spent time on the Gordon Phillips incident and aired a portion of a message left on Jeanne's answering machine.

Nothing significant came of this first airing, but in a subsequent airing in December 1993, an anonymous caller contacted the Phoenix police and said that he thought their murderer was a man named James C. "Butch" Harrod, age thirty-nine. The caller gave Harrod's date of birth and current address.

In September 1994, Detective Reynolds received another anonymous call. The caller claimed that Harrod had bragged about his role in Jeanne's slaying. He said that Harrod had told his ex-wife, Anne, about his involvement and that Anne had seen a letter from Hap Tovrea to Harrod, promising $50,000 for killing Jeanne. He also said that Harrod had posed as Gordon Phillips. Finally, the caller said that Harrod had been present at the murder but had not pulled the trigger. An FBI agent, he claimed, knew all about it.

Two anonymous tips were enough for Reynolds to take another hard look at the voluminous Tovrea murder files.

He began by pulling telephone records for the Tovreas and for Harrod. In the days leading up to and just after Jeanne's murder, Reynolds noticed a number of calls between Harrod and Hap Tovrea. In a relatively short time span, there had been an astounding 1,500 calls, fifty-two of them on the day before the murder.

Reynolds obtained divorce records for James "Butch" Harrod and Anne Harrod. He found Anne's last known address, which led him to Anne's mother and brother in November 1994. During his interview with Anne's mother, she mentioned that an FBI agent, Jeff Fauver, was a longtime family friend from

Albuquerque. She'd told him everything she knew, which included what her daughter had confided in her.

One of these tidbits was that Anne said that her husband had started sleeping with a loaded gun under his pillow sometime in 1990. She said that Hap Tovrea owed Harrod $50,000, but she didn't know what that was for. The mother had seen a newspaper article about a land sale relating to the Tovrea family trust and had mentioned it to her son-in-law. He'd grinned and said that meant he'd finally get the money Hap owed him.

Anne's brother had seen the *Unsolved Mysteries* episode and told Reynolds how much Gordon Phillips's voice reminded him of Harrod. Anne's mother then dropped a bombshell. Anne had told her that Harrod knew about the Tovrea murder and that Harrod claimed the killers had been in their house. Then he'd told her not to be scared, that as long as she stayed married to him, she was safe. She'd told her mother that she didn't want to live with this guilty knowledge the rest of her life. The mother promised to try to get her daughter to speak to Reynolds.

Reynolds located Jeff Fauver in Albuquerque. He was now a former FBI agent working for the Department of Defense. Fauver volunteered that he'd been the anonymous caller who had provided Phoenix police with Harrod's name and information and that he'd phoned again a few months after that.

Fauver had met Harrod and been underwhelmed. The man had bragged about Vietnam, though he'd never served in the military. He also dropped names, saying he had contacts with the wealthy and with contract killers. "Butch said he was [Hap Tovreas] right-hand man," Fauver told Reynolds. Fauver had attended Harrod's wedding to Anne and over the years had listened to repeated complaints from her family about his behavior.

In fact, Anne's mother had been so unhappy with her son-in-law that in 1992 she'd hired a private investigator to look into the background of Harrod and his friend, Hap Tovrea. Nothing beyond what was already known came of it.

Later that same year, Fauver said that Anne began meeting with him privately to express her concerns and fears. She told him that Harrod said he was the middle man between Hap and Jeanne Tovrea's killers. She'd said that her husband told her hours after the murder that the deed was done. And he said that he'd passed himself off as the elusive Gordon Phillips. Anne left Harrod in October that year just after another airing of the *Unsolved Mysteries* show.

One month later, Reynolds was ready to interview Anne, who by this time had been granted immunity from prosecution for any role she might have played in the murder. Now she unloaded the story pent up within her. According to her former husband, Butch Harrod, the three Tovrea children had despised Jeanne for spending their rightful inheritance. This included the substantial income from the trust and assets. They were enraged that she'd taken half a million dollars out of the trust to buy a life insurance policy for her own daughter.

According to Anne, Hap Tovrea had recruited Harrod, who in turn agreed to serve as "coordinator" for the murder. He was promised $100,000 for his role. She believed he'd done more than that, actually taking part in the deed, because the night of the killing she'd seen her husband leave their home dressed in camouflage, wearing hiking boots, and carrying a heavy duffle bag that she suspected was packed with weapons. After he left, she looked where his guns were normally kept, and they were gone.

She said he'd come home around two in the morning and awakened her. She asked if he "did it," and he'd answered, "Yes, it's over." That day she checked on his guns again and found them back in place. He subsequently told her that two hit men had actually done the killing and that he would pay them out of the money he'd get from Hap. Later, he was furious when he told her he'd been given just $40,000 in all.

She repeated much of what Reynolds had learned from others, but one bit of information was a surprise. Harrod "knew the window was not on the security system," she said. "He talked about the kitchen window . . . was where to gain access. . . ." That was information the police had not made public.

Anne also reported that her husband had told her Hap was supposed to call him the day after the killing. She said that Harrod telephoned the morning after the murder, going out to the patio so as not to be overheard. Phone records confirmed that such a call had taken place.

When Reynolds played the telephone recording from Gordon Phillips, Anne screamed, "Stop it, I can't take it anymore." She then began sobbing. Asked if that was Harrod's voice, she answered, "Yes. He's a bad person, bad person."

While this appeared to be the break Reynolds had been looking for, the story from a former wife was scarcely evidence. If he questioned Harrod now, there was little chance the man would break down and look for a deal. He'd just stonewall the detective and claim the whole story was a pack of lies told by a vengeful ex-wife out to make trouble for him. So, for the next year, Reynolds meticulously reexamined the mountain of evidence detectives had gathered on the murder.

Among these were the notes from the interview of Cricket and Hap, which had taken place in San Diego. According to the detective, they had said they each received $200,000 in the will, parceled out at the rate of $1,500 a month, and that they had also each received $60,000 from a life insurance policy on their father. They claimed that whatever money they'd eventually receive from the trust was of no significance. They were financially secure with trusts established by their grandfather, Big Phil, and their dad, Ed.

Considering subsequent events, Reynolds couldn't help but wonder how much truth there had been in that tale. After all, they'd engaged in a series of legal battles over the money Jeanne had received. Each of the four lawsuits had been about getting more money.

The crux of the matter was that while the Tovrea offspring knew there was a lot of money and that when Jeanne died they'd get their cut, they didn't know how much money there was. Jeanne was instructed in the will to put around half of the estate into a trust for the children. This had been about $4 million dollars, and Jeanne had been given the right to spend the considerable interest the trust produced, interest that some might say should have been rolled over and added to the inheritance.

After all the squabbling and lawsuits, the final outcome following Jeanne's murder was surely a disappointment for the children. They'd been forced to pay a million dollars in taxes when Jeanne's life insurance was paid out to her daughter. After estate taxes, more legal fees, bequests, expenses, and such, each of Ed's adult children received about $600,000 on top of what they'd been given at the time of his death. A lot of money, yes, but hardly the fortune those who knew the family were expecting. This was, after all, the Tovreas, and everyone knew they were filthy rich.

With Anne Harrod's statement and clear evidence of contact between Hap and her former husband, for the first time, this case had legs. Reynolds began to examine the connection between Harrod and Hap.

They'd apparently met in 1987 through a mutual friend. Harrod grew up in a middle-class home far from the privileged life Hap had led, but there were striking similarities between the men. Both were big talkers with a demonstrable disdain for regular work and steady employment. They'd each jumped around from one "big deal" to the next, looking to make a killing.

The year after they met—the same year Jeanne was murdered—they entered into a business venture. Hap became CEO of a company called Minerals Exploration Corporation of the Americas (MECA). It was allegedly a Chilean sulfur-mining concern, but Hap sought to expand into China. Though Harrod had no background in mining, Hap paid him considerable sums as a consultant. Hap reportedly put $225,000 into the company, just ten days after Jeanne's murder.

Harrod had been to China on business. In 1986, he'd visited the country serving as a middle man for a local attorney looking to invest in a shrimp-farming venture in Yantai Province. He'd been paid $4,000 a month for a short time. According to authorities, the attorney embezzled most of his investors' money and subsequently fled Arizona before sentencing.

Harrod apparently brought the local Chinese contact to the table, and, on the face of it, that was why he was being paid by Hap as a consultant. The three men spent three weeks in China exploring options, and the relationship between Hap and Harrod jelled.

The China mining venture went nowhere in the end, dying pretty quickly. Still, Hap was paid for fifteen months after the men returned to the United States. Investigators formed the opinion that the payments were largely unrelated to the China business, but the venture had provided a convenient vehicle for paying Harrod blood money.

Reynolds recalled the tape recordings of Gordon Phillips's phone message with fresh insight. One said, "Jeanne, this is Gordon Phillips. I'm sorry to get back with you so late. I had a little problem with Ed Jr. [Hap], which I had to go to L.A. to take care of, and I've already talked to a judge over there. Now, I'm back in Phoenix and I will try and call back this afternoon and I have the information for you."

This illusive, perhaps mythical Phillips knew Hap and had business with him? Now that was interesting.

Reynolds was satisfied that he had enough information. On September 14, 1995, Harrod was arrested outside his Ahwatukee Foothills house while working on his car. He was driven to the downtown Phoenix Police Department and placed in an interrogation room, where Reynolds soon met with him. Reynolds had two primary goals. The first was to get Harrod to confess. The second was to convince Harrod to give up whoever had hired him.

Reynolds punched the button on the tape recorder and played the telephone message from Gordon Phillips. When it was finished, he said, "That, Mr. Harrod, is your voice."

"No," Harrod said.

Reynolds continued. "There is no doubt in my mind that you organized and set up the murder of Jeanne Tovrea. I know who hired you. I know how much you were told you would be paid for it. I know how much money you actually received. . . ."

Harrod did not reply.

"Your ex-wife, Anne," Reynolds added ominously, "is gonna give you up in a heartbeat." Of course she already had, but Harrod didn't know that. Harrod suggested that he needed to talk to somebody about this. Reynolds then told him that there were eighteen matches for his fingerprints at the murder scene.

In fact, now that Harrod had been arrested, Reynolds would finally get his fingerprints. When they were compared to those taken from the Tovrea home, they matched.

Reynolds told Harrod, "This is the only opportunity you're gonna get. When those bars clang behind you, we got the consultant. . . . Only the consultant can give us number one. . . . I don't think you're the ruthless, cold-blooded killer."

"I'm not a killer," Harrod told him.

"You're the consultant, aren't you?" Reynolds asked.

"I'm nothing," Harrod said, uttering a greater truth about himself than perhaps he realized.

Reynolds pressed, but Harrod remained in denial mode. Reynolds tried getting him to admit that he was Gordon Phillips. No bite. Reynolds told him that he'd be meeting with the prosecutor on the case. "He's the top dog. And I'm gonna go to him and say [you] didn't give me squat. . . . And all the evidence points to you."

At that point, the recording of the interview was stopped. Harrod claims Reynolds leaned down and whispered, "You're gonna be living here until you give up Hap Tovrea."

Jeanne Tovrea knew what Gordon Phillips looked like, but she was dead. However, her daughter had been at the meeting. In December 1996, Deborah agreed to view a lineup at the Madison Street jail in central Phoenix. She had no problem picking out Harrod as the man who'd met with her and her mother claiming to be a reporter. Later, however, she was shown two photo lineups containing Harrod's picture, and she pointed to someone else.

Police kept a lid on Harrod's arrest for the next twenty-four hours. They wanted a shot at Hap Tovrea, now forty-five, before their information became public knowledge. Reynolds had already scheduled an interview with Hap in upscale La Jolla, California. He told Harrod he just wanted to catch up on some details, help him fill in events. Reynolds was accompanied by another homicide detective, and Hap brought his sister, Cricket, along. Everybody, it seemed, wanted a witness.

The detective with Reynolds asked if he could interview Cricket alone, and they went off to another area. When it was just the two of them, Reynolds told Hap he'd come across records held by a pawnshop owned by the Tovrea family. This was a ruse to let Hap go in the direction Reynolds really wanted to take. These "records" contained a name that appeared in the investigation records, "something like Butch, Butch Harrod."

Hap acknowledged knowing him and went on to say they'd done business in China together. Asked how long Harrod had worked with him and how much he'd been paid, Hap answered, "Oh, a few months. . . . A few thousand dollars."

Reynolds knew that it had been a lot longer than that and had involved a lot more than "a few thousand." When asked for more details, Hap came up with six or seven months at $3,000 a month. Did he have any contact with Hap after the China deal fell through? "I had no reason to talk to him anymore. There might have been one or two calls after that. . . ." Hap told Reynolds.

Reynolds pointed out the records showing Harrod calling Hap every other day during 1989, after the deal fell through. "Weird," was Hap's reply, as if this was news to him.

"Had you ever discussed the fact that you had a murder in your family or anything like that with him?" Reynolds asked.

"I wouldn't. It's something I really don't discuss," he said.

Harrod had said that he frequently discussed Jeanne's murder with Hap, the first time during a fifteen-minute telephone conversation, just eight hours after her body was found.

The other detective returned with Cricket, and Reynolds let him know he'd brought up Harrod's name. The detective reported that his name meant nothing to Cricket, even though records showed Harrod had called Cricket Tovrea's house 163 times from July through November 1991. Harrod told a reporter that he was trying to collect money he was owed, as Cricket was an officer in MECA, and he thought she might pay him.

After returning to the group and hearing Harrod's name again, Cricket suddenly recalled that she had to be somewhere else and abruptly announced she was leaving for a dental appointment.

Reynolds played the Gordon Phillips tape and asked Hap if he knew the voice. "You know that voice?" he asked.

"Maybe."

Reynolds played it again. Hap was still uncertain if he knew the voice, saying it was news to him if that was really Harrod when the caller said his name was Phillips. "But, does it sound like [Harrod]?"

"Well, it may be," Hap allowed.

Asked if there was any reason for Hap and Harrod to have had frequent contact in early 1988, Hap said there was none, "unless I don't remember stuff...."

Reynolds told Hap that Harrod had called him thirty-three times in the ten days leading up to Jeanne's murder. "Wow..." Hap said. "You're asking me to try to remember things that are a while back. I mean, don't start pointing some finger at me here."

"I am pointing the finger at you," Reynolds said.

"If this guy is a stalker weirdo, you know, I'm not part of this. But I find this all very interesting."

Reynolds told him that the police had taken Harrod's fingerprints.

"I'll bet his fingerprints were at the crime scene," Hap said.

Reynolds nodded.

"That's great," he said, but not as if it was good news.

"His prints are inside the house . . ." Reynolds told him. "He's in jail. We arrested him last night. . . . Guess what he says?"

"Oh, I can't wait to hear this. What?"

"He says you hired him to kill your stepmother," Reynolds lied.

"Oh, fuck him."

"You never hired him to kill your stepmother?"

"No. . . . You guys have a psycho on your hands here."

Reynolds laid out the story Harrod had told his wife, Anne, that he'd coordinated the murder at Hap's behest.

"So how do I know this perfect stranger is a person that can do this?" Hap wanted to know.

"He's not a perfect stranger if you're calling him thirty-three times in the ten days before this happened," Reynolds reminded him.

After more denials Hap said, "This is like a novel. . . . This has got to be some sick mind that's taking all this coincidence and blending this into some BS scenario. I feel like I've been kind of set up now."

"Will you take a polygraph?"

Hap hesitated. "Maybe."

"Are you an innocent man?"

"Yeah."

"Would you have any problem taking a polygraph today?"

"Maybe." He said his lawyer had long ago told the family not to take polygraphs. "This thing is too weird, guys. You know I had nothing to do with it."

Pressed again on any involvement in the murder, Hap answered categorically. "The answer's no and that's that."

On November 30, 1995, Phoenix police executed a search warrant on Hap in La Jolla, searching his home and office, and seizing his bank records. He was not arrested. A short time later, Hap hired one of the most prominent criminal defense lawyers in Arizona.

There was nothing left to do but proceed with the prosecution of James "Butch" Harrod.

In October 1997, nearly ten years after the brutal murder of heiress Jeanne Tovrea, and two years after his arrest, James "Butch" Harrod went to trial, alone, for the deed. All along he maintained his innocence, despite the overwhelming evidence against him. "I can't plea bargain for something I did not do," he told a reporter.

The prosecution never argued that Harrod was the single killer or alone in the house that night. "There may be other killers out there, but the evidence will support beyond all doubt that one of them is him."

The trial lasted a month and, despite a vigorous defense, there was never a moment when the verdict was in doubt. The only unanswered question was why Harrod wouldn't give up whoever hired him. In the minds of observers, the question of who that had been was not at issue.

Details of the murder were slowly revealed to a stunned, packed courtroom. Jeanne was shot twice in the face, three times in the back of her head. There were, the prosecutor said, "four million reasons" to see her dead. Technicians testified that eighteen fingerprints were found matching Harrod's. Twelve of them were on the kitchen window, where entrance was gained to the house; four were on the kitchen counter; a single print was on the outside gate; and a palm print was lifted from the kitchen-window weather stripping. There the trail of prints ended, a fact that had always given rise to the idea that Harrod may not have been the trigger man and that someone else had been in the house that night.

The best the defense could do was argue that someone had planted these prints, even though Harrod had never been fingerprinted when the murder occurred. They claimed the "real killers" had somehow obtained his fingerprints and transferred them to a rubber glove.

But a fingerprint expert testified that the prints were not forged or fabricated. They were left by Harrod himself. Prints placed in the manner argued by the defense look artificial; a technician can tell them from the original.

Jeanne's daughter, Deborah, testified to the July 1987 meeting with the man claiming to be Gordon Phillips. She said she was frightened, her mother was even more frightened, and that she'd told her mother "that something was really wrong with this man."

The defense argued she had a vivid imagination and let the jury know that while she'd picked Harrod to be Phillips from a lineup, she'd identified other men as Phillips in photographic lineups.

Harrod's former wife, Anne, testified after much legal wrangling. She'd been married to Harrod at the time of the murder and for a period afterward. Much of what she'd told police was covered by spousal privilege. The court ruled she could testify to what she actually saw and did around the time of the murder, but not to what her husband had told her. She'd done nothing to stop a murder, and the prosecutor kept his distance from her during the direct examination.

Key evidence from Anne was that FedEx® packages containing cash arrived for her husband from Hap Tovrea before and after the murder. She testified to the missing guns and what her husband wore when he left the house.

When asked about the Phillips tape, she answered, "Gordon Phillips was my husband."

This was problematic for the defense, and they seriously considered putting Harrod on the stand. Once they did, Anne could be recalled and testify about everything she'd told police. The judge ruled that "the search for truth is more important than the protection of a long-gone marriage."

In the end, the defense called Harrod to the stand, and, under direct questioning, he gave the predictable responses. No, he didn't kill anyone. No, he wasn't in the house that night. Harrod had answered these same questions during a polygraph test, and the examiner said he thought he was telling the truth, but such results are not admissible in Arizona.

One unintended consequence of Harrod's testimony was that the jurors heard his voice for themselves and could compare it to the Phillips recordings. One juror later told a reporter his reaction. "Damn! He *is* Gordon Phillips."

Harrod described his business dealings with Hap and admitted lying about serving in the military. He claimed he'd been framed and denied that Hap paid him to kill Jeanne. After listening to the Phillips tape, he denied the voice was his.

As for the night of the murder, Harrod testified that he bought cocaine for use that weekend at a bar from someone he called Carlos. The two men drank a six-pack of beer, then Harrod went home at about eleven o'clock and went to bed at around two in the morning. This version differed in details from what he'd previously told a reporter.

Under cross-examination, damning information came out. Harrod claimed all along that Hap had paid him just over $13,000 for the China venture. Now he told the jury he'd actually been paid more than $35,000.

Harrod said Anne was lying when she claimed he discussed the murder with her. "Those eighteen prints at the crime scene say she's right, don't they?" the prosecutor shot back.

Harrod tried to appear to be a normal guy while on the stand, but he came across as a schemer, and, as one alternate juror said, "He didn't have the answers to the important questions."

Anne was now recalled to the stand, and she gave a complete account of her experience, including the motive behind the contract for murder: greed for the Tovrea riches. She said she didn't call the police because she was afraid for herself and her family. Then she looked at Jeanne's daughter and blurted out, "I'm sorry, Debbie!"

She claimed she was concerned for her safety because "in my mind, Butch is not the shooter. [He] had something to do with it, but Butch is not the shooter."

The jury deliberated three and a half hours before convicting Harrod of first-degree murder and burglary. In May 1998, James "Butch" Harrod was sentenced to be executed for the murder of Jeanne Tovrea.

In 2002, the US Supreme Court ruled that defendants can only be sentenced to death by a jury that had considered all the sentencing evidence. Harrod was returned for a seven-week sentencing hearing in 2006. In the end, this jury decided he'd committed murder for hire and sentenced him to death. He currently awaits execution on Arizona's death row.

At one point during his legal ordeal, Harrod spoke to a reporter and perhaps shared insight into his wasted life. "There is no such thing as failure," he said. "Failure is when you don't try something. . . . You have to step outside of the comfort zone to do it, which means you have to step out on a limb."

Hap Tovrea has never been charged in the murder of Jeanne Tovrea.

ABOUT THE AUTHOR

RONALD J. WATKINS has written more than thirty books, including *Evil Intentions* and *Against Her Will*, both true accounts of murder. He is also the author of *Unknown Seas*, a history of the Portuguese voyages of discovery, and *Cimmerian*, a novel about the Holocaust. He is currently coauthor of the Summit Murder Mystery series, which includes *Murder on Everest*. Watkins has appeared on television shows including Dominick Dunne's *Power, Privilege and Justice*; *Now* with Tom Brokaw and Katie Couric; *Under Scrutiny* with Jane Wallace; and *Geraldo* with Geraldo Rivera. He lives in the Sonoran desert outside Phoenix, Arizona. You may visit his website at www.RonaldJWatkins.com.

REFERENCES

Bell, Rachael. Undated. "The Murder of Jeanne Tovrea." Trutv.com.

Murphy, Doug. 1998. "Harrod Sentenced to Death in Tovrea Slaying." *Ahwatukee Foothills News*, May 30.

Rubin, Paul. 1997. "Death of an Heiress." *New Times (Phoenix, AZ)*. February 27– March 5.

Chapter 11

THE WORLD'S WORST WOMAN

by Laura James

I here put up a sign warning the whole pestiferous crew of Pharisees to dive no deeper here. . . . There are women who are wantons by nature; whom no wealth, education, or moral surroundings can withhold from evil.

—Brann the Iconoclast, *The Common Courtesan*

Men who author books on female criminals sometimes cannot help but issue dire warnings (tinged with jealousy, if not possessiveness) aimed at new or casual students of the femme fatale. Those of us who can rationalize our interest in the most alluring daughters of Eve concede that studying this type of murderess is an endeavor not to be lightly undertaken. A stroll through the gallery of the world's worst women exposes the disciple to a gauntlet of sirens who come from every culture and sing in every tongue known to humankind. Legions are the fatal ladies whose strange spells grow more intoxicating with time. Their bones are dust, but they have left their portraits and in many cases reams of judicial transcripts that immortalize their sins for posterity. They are appealing and repulsive, bewitching and beastly, and if you pause too long before any one of them, she may enchant you. *Cave amantem*, as the ancients said: *Of her love, beware.*

Every collector of the stories of the femme fatale—a seductive woman who leads men to their doom—will eventually come across a lady who proves mesmeric. William Roughead (the prolific Scotsman who arguably holds the crown as Europe's finest true-crime author) may have been the most well-read man on the subject who ever lived. Of all the female killers he studied, he had five "darker favorites," including Jessie McLachlan, Florence Bravo, Adelaide Bartlett, and Florence Maybrick. Each woman was young, attractive, accused of murder, and, by many accounts (including Roughead's), morally insane. In his later years, the murder fancier stumbled on the dusty tale of a homicide involving a woman of superior social standing who was, to him, "figuratively speaking—virgin," and he was enraptured. She was Madeleine Smith, Glasgow socialite. She wrote poetic letters to her fiancé. When she found a better man, she gave her first love chocolates laced with arsenic. To Roughead, she was "matchless," his "heroine." The same murderess equally enthralled another illustrious author, American novelist Henry James. Like Roughead, James searched for years for a portrait of Madeleine. She forever eluded them both, and they had to settle for vague newspaper sketches of their heroine on trial.

But Madeleine Smith, alluring as she reportedly was, murdered only one man, and her case fell into obscurity long ago. If a woman's wickedness were measured by her social standing, the number of her victims, and the strength and longevity of her infamy, one fatal beauty would emerge as the worst femme fatale in all the recorded annals of the wickedness of womankind: Countess Marie Nicolaevna O'Rourke Tarnovska. *Cave amantem.*

She was the Russian Delilah. Like the biblical heroine, she murdered by proxy. Her only weapons were her beauty and sex. With these, she orchestrated scenes worthy of Chekhov and led at least five men to their doom. When she was arrested for murder in Italy in 1907, the case caused an international stir. A special cable to the *Washington Post* declared that the investigation alone was enough to create "a greater sensation in Europe than any episode in the criminal history of the continent," featuring an accused who "looms up as the most beautiful and captivating queen of the great criminal adventuresses of history." The *New York Times* dubbed her "a beautiful woman who wrought more harm than any other of her generation" and "one of the most beguiling and bemusing of all the daughters of Kali" (in reference to the ferocious four-armed Hindu goddess legendary for slaughtering men). Added the *Indianapolis Star*, unpatriotically yielding the palm for producing the world's worst woman to the Russians: "America, with its Cassie Chadwicks, its daring adventuresses and its feminine soldiers of fortune, has never contained such a wonderful performer upon the heartstrings of mankind as this Russian countess. In the world of love and of intrigue the woman is a genius." An editor in Jamaica called her case the Crime That Thrills the World.

What made the trial of Countess Tarnovska (often spelled Tarnowska) particularly fascinating was that she was a flagrant psychopath whose sins were exposed on cross-examination while she stood in the dock before an astonished worldwide audience. In the decades since the verdict, spellbound admirers have devoured millions of books in a dozen languages about her case. On the one hundredth anniversary of the spectacle, the lawyers of Venice re-created her legendary trial in the original courtroom at St. Mark's, overlooking the Grand Canal.

It is not coincidental that the world's worst woman would emerge from a dying autocratic class. If Marie Tarnovska merrily trampled the hearts of men until she glimpsed too late the precipice, then Imperial Russian society during the Belle Époque was guilty of letting her sins go so far unchecked. The countess was a daughter of the Silver Age. Like the perfume she wore (*L'Origan* by Coty), her culture no longer exists. She matured just as the aristocracy faced its end days. Even in the 1890s, they referred to the coming revolution and governed themselves accordingly. Waves of suicides and carnal scandals marked the waning days of the empire. Marriage as an institution collapsed, even though (or perhaps because) it was next to impossible to get a divorce in the tsar's Russia. Thus the doomed elite tried, as the historians put it, to "free themselves through exalted romantic and sexual liaisons." Russian women (already known for shocking tourists with their cigarette smoking, décolletages, and lax attitudes toward marital fidelity) forgot their scruples entirely. The last empress publicly fretted over the fact, vowing to reform the morals of married ladies. Her campaign failed, and her court called her a boor. A good half of the women from the highest aristocratic class in Russia were said to be *demimondaines*, habitually adulterous. As an American diplomat observed, "Marriage is a mere matter of convenience. The master indulges his tastes, and the mistress gratifies her whims." Countess Tarnovska would one day claim that bad company led her astray. If she had not been as deviant as she was, going far beyond what was conceivable even in the Silver Age, then her cultural defense might have succeeded.

When young, the countess was a typical Russian blue blood. She was born in 1877 as Countess Marie O'Rourke, middle daughter of Colonel Count Nicholas O'Rourke, descendant of an Irish soldier of fortune who gained a title for military service to the House of Romanov. Marie grew up on a country estate outside Kiev and matured into a tall, classical beauty with a high shape ("the best figure in Europe," an editor would one day declare). She was also known for her husky, low voice; the expressiveness of her large, heavy-lidded, Slavic eyes; the charm of her conversation; and her mastery of several languages.

With these attributes, Marie had her pick of men, and at age seventeen she met the unfortunate Count Vassili Tarnovsky. It was said that he was besotted with her from the moment his cousin Mikhail introduced them. Their families both disapproved, but the two eloped soon after meeting. Marie was lucky to marry so well and so hastily. Count Tarnovsky was, when they met, a man of enormous wealth and a notable patron of the arts and antiquities. He was the heir to several prestigious properties, including a famous country estate known as Kachanovka Palace. For a while, on the arm of a handsome man her elder and better, Marie enjoyed society life in Moscow and Kiev, devoting herself to luxuries and pleasures. When in Kiev, they resided close to the Golden Gate, and in the countryside, they enjoyed days-long parties. They had two children in quick succession, Tatjana and Vassili Vassilovich, but their marital bliss was short lived.

Marie took her first step on the path to eternal infamy as a new bride when she chose an obvious liaison. She had an affair with a sixteen-year-old student. He was also troubled, and she knew this. Moreover, he was Count Tarnovsky's younger brother, Peter Tarnovsky. For a woman who would one day become infamous for her "constantly deepening immorality," it was a fiendish beginning. It was said that she did it to fool her husband, to make him jealous, and to prove her superiority. She may well have done it just for the fun of the thing. When Peter hanged himself in 1898, some said it was because he failed his exams and feared his father. Others blamed the young enchantress for provoking him to suicide.

Her adulterous appetites grew. Marie flaunted affairs before a shocked household staff and the rest of society. "There were many scandals," the papers would report, "concerning her relations with officers in her house." As her marriage dissolved, her children were sent to live with relatives. At the same time, the countess took up with a young medical student, Baron Vladimir Stahl. A sickly alcoholic, he became her devoted servant and introduced her to two new loves, morphine and cocaine. Marie demanded that he pledge his allegiance to her in writing, expressing her desire to dominate him and feed her vanity. He complied by sending many long love letters (which, once entered into evidence, would be deemed "extraordinary epistles"). "On my word of honor," he wrote in one, "and by all that remains strong and pure within me, I, Vladimir Stahl, promise Marie Nicolaevna Tarnovska to do all that she commands of me. . . . I shall always act in the name of that pure love which has already taken up the whole of my life. . . . Keeping this promise, I declare under oath that, save with the loss of my word of honor, Countess Tarnovska shall be sacred and inviolable to me."

The countess was visiting Dr. Stahl for more of what she craved, when, in 1898, she attracted the notice of another of the doctor's visitors. He was a handsome officer named Alexis Bozevsky. Marie was haughty and ignored him. In so doing, she smited him. Both memorialized their affair in graphic correspondence. The "Marquise" de Sade tested Bozevsky as the tsar's army never had, and he proved an apt pupil. She declared him inconstant. He vowed he would prove how much he loved her. He would let her shoot him with his own weapon. He offered the palm of his hand and invited her to put a bullet through it. Marie raised the barrel, and she did it. Then she raised his bloody hand to her lips and kissed the wound.

There are many accounts of what happened next. The scene has been fictionalized in several settings. The most reliable sources indicate that Count Tarnovsky caught his wife and her lover Bozevsky in flagrante delicto: in flagrant transgression; that is, in bed. What is not disputed is that Tarnovsky retrieved a weapon and shot Alexis Bozevsky.

Marie fled their home with her wounded lover. She called on their mutual friend Vladimir Stahl to tend him. Instead, Stahl and the countess made love on a couch near the sick man's bed. When they awoke from their drug-addled play, Bozevsky was dead.

Count Tarnovsky was arrested for murder, and the mandatory punishment should he be convicted was death. When he went on trial for his life, he enriched the coffers of newspaper publishers across Russia but drained his family's assets. The Tarnovsky family was forced to sell Kachanovka Palace to fund his defense. But in the end, the Unwritten Rule—a universal legal principle positing that a man who catches his wife in the arms of another has the right to take lethal action to avenge his honor—resulted in his acquittal. After the harrowing ordeal of standing trial for his life, Tarnovsky filed for divorce. It would mean yielding another sizeable portion of his fortune to his wife. He would also lose his place in his regiment—not because he killed a man, but because divorced men were forced to resign in disgrace. At that point, neither he nor his wife had any reputation left to protect.

Alexis Bozevsky was barely cold when Marie lost another lover. Stahl took poison, penned one last love letter to the countess, and breathed his last to a woman who had already found another lover to replace him.

Donat Prilukov of Moscow was an experienced attorney and had made a fine living as an advocate of the law. He had an exceptional mind. Unlike 98 percent of Russian lawyers, Prilukov was not a nobleman but was an entirely self-made, successful man. Then he met *La Tarnovska*.

Marie called him her *mugik*, her peasant. She also called him The Scorpion. Some would say the brilliant lawyer preyed on a weak-willed woman, making her his tool. Others painted a picture of a "fond lover anxious to deliver her from her unhappy marriage." Prilukov's legal secretary, Mr. Smaiefsky, would testify that the lawyer was a model of integrity until he became violently infatuated with Countess Tarnoyska. He hired detectives to learn everything he could about her, and when she saw other men, he learned of it and, to her delight, threw jealous tantrums. Marie met in Donat a man who was her moral equal. Water seeks its own level. He left his wife and children and abandoned his law practice to devote himself completely to her. Cigarettes featured prominently in what Marie called their "love play" as she enjoyed slowly destroying him. He lavished her with his fortune. When his personal funds ran dry, Prilukov misappropriated a fortune from his clients, reported to be close to 100,000 francs.

At that point, the pair decided to embark on a whirlwind tour of the continental capitals and resorts. The countess and her lawyer spent the spring of 1906 at the Grand Hotel in Vienna, where they stayed under false names. They also traveled in France and stayed in the best hotels in Berlin. Life on the lam must have been intoxicating for them until she spent almost all of his clients' trust accounts. Even beautiful Russian countesses must pay their hotel bills. They argued over the last four thousand. Finally Countess Tarnovska gave up on her ruined lover, abandoning him in Germany and returning to Russia alone.

In Orel, near Kiev, she met Count Pavel Kamarovsky, a man of tremendous wealth who sported white linen suits and headed the Anti-Revolutionary League. They were inseparable in Orel. There she also met a friend of the count, a young, dreamy medical student named Nicholas Naumov. She learned that he enjoyed being beaten. His previous mistress let him run naked behind her carriage in the dust. An excited Marie indulged Nicholas and burned his arms and shoulders with her cigarettes. She stuck pins in his body, tattooing her name into his arm and rubbing perfume in the wounds. In his ecstasy, he forgot about his studies and his wife and children. He gave up his life to be by her side.

But Marie grew bored, and her mind returned to her attorney in exile. In a tearful reunion at a train station in Munich, the countess reunited with Prilukov. She also relayed the details of her sexual adventures during their separation. He was insane with jealousy. She left him in Germany, insistent on going back to her wealthy count. It was Kamarovsky's turn to abandon his wife, children, and career to escort Marie around Europe.

In many cities they were shadowed by Prilukov and Naumov. She juggled all three affairs dexterously, even eliciting a proposal and an engagement party from her wealthy lover, until the day came when she tired of Pavel Kamarovsky. She preferred Donat. The Scorpion had no money. She tried to extract what she could from the count, but wealthy men do not walk around with their money in their pockets. So she pleaded with him to consider the dangers to his life engendered by his politically sensitive position with the Anti-Revolutionary League. They struck a bargain: if he would insure his life for half a million francs, she would marry him on September 18, 1907, in Venice.

Kamarovsky traveled ahead to Venice to await her, taking rooms at the Campo Santa Maria del Giglio (now the Hotel Ala). Days before the wedding, he was found dying of gunshot wounds to the abdomen.

At long last, she had brought about a man's death in a manner that was specifically prohibited by the criminal codes. The law finally caught up to Marie Tarnovska when she was arrested. In her own trunk was much of the evidence against her: cocaine, pornography, love letters, telegrams, a whip made of willow branches that she used to beat Nicholas, and a collection of suicide notes from some of her dead lovers.

Almost from the moment of the countess's arrest, the experts knew that the titled beauty was an extraordinary specimen. Her case was one of the last to be the object of study and comment by world-famous Italian criminologist and author Cesare Lombroso. Though he did not live to see the trial, he perused the evidence elicited at the inquest. He believed Marie Tarnovska was perfectly sane and probably guilty. In a written report, he concluded: "If the

Countess actually conceived, planned, and carried out the tragedy . . . then she is the most remarkable criminal of modern times. Her methods show an absolute mastery of masculine sentiment, passion, and covetousness. The crimes of the Borgias and of the *Strozzi* offer no parallels. Her antecedents must have been very remarkable, for it is unusual for one of criminal proclivities to plan so rational a conspiracy. . . . She is absolutely original."

Naumov confessed almost at once. "Paul [Pavel] was a brute, and I, myself, was in love with Marie." A search of his room revealed letters from the countess and her attorney, and the entire scheme unraveled.

The trial of Marie Tarnovska, Donat Prilukov, and Nicholas Naumov for the murder of Pavel Kamarovsky was perhaps the hottest indoor ticket in the history of Venice. Reporters, lawyers, artists, world-famous actresses, and even noblemen vied for seats to witness the testimony of a bloody Muse. When pressed to explain their presence in the Venetian courtroom, they readily confessed their "fascination with Tarnovska." Sensational novelist and playwright Gabriele d'Annunzio sat next to Parisian novelist Madame Daniel Lesueur. Following with great interest, d'Annunzio announced he was writing a piece based on *La Tarnovska* (as the French called her), and some large European theaters were already asking for the finished play. Prince Luigi, Duke of Abruzzi, and Princess Odelscalchi were in the gallery. It was the first time in living memory that members of Italian royalty could be found in the audience at a murder trial. Edgar Degas, the French sculptor and painter famous for his portraits of dancers, attended with the intention of using the defendant for a model. The "Siren of the Adriatic" also drew a flock of actresses to the courthouse. Sarah Bernhardt, the great *tragedienne* and most famous actress of her age, kept her name in the headlines by attending trials in which she spotted a future dramatic role for herself. She was present for much of the Tarnovska trial, along with her Italian rival Emma Gramatica and French stage legend Gabrielle Réjane. British author Baron Corvo was another who came to hear for himself what the newspapers could not publish. He summoned only a single word to describe it: "Amazing!"

Naumov, pawn of a black-hearted queen, gave his testimony first. "She cast the spell of her terrible eyes over me and made me her slave," he stated. "I feared her, yet she fascinated me. I tried to avoid her, but wherever she went I was destined to follow. A power I could not resist drew me to her. She planned all the hideous details of murder and made me swear on her own mother's grave that I would carry the plan into action.

"Sometimes she extinguished her cigarettes by pressing them against my hand and burning the flesh. At others she ran the point of a dagger over me. But she charmed and fascinated me. I loved her, and when she ordered me to kill a man I knew to be innocent, I had to obey."

"But why," Naumov was asked, "did she want him killed?"

"It was to avenge her honor."

"Well, your honor was not concerned."

"No, but I was her slave. Also, I was jealous of the Count."

"Why was that?"

"Because an officer at Orel told me he had once seen him leaving the Countess's bedroom in very scanty attire. He said it was not the correct costume for a mere friendly visit to a lady. This displeased me."

"But—and I am compelled to put the question—did you resume your relations with her after this episode?"

"That is the case."

"You have a forgiving temperament!"

The court read a telegram Naumov had sent Marie: "I know where this man lives. I abominate and detest him. Whatever happens I will set you free."

And another: "Body and soul, I belong to my adored Marie. I weep for our broken happiness."

And the forged telegram that Donat Prilukov sent to Marie Tarnovska, which she passed on to Naumov to inflame him: "I know all. Naumov is a cad, and you are good for nothing. I regret my sentiments for you. Paul Kamarovsky."

Asked the court: "What were this woman's last words to you, as you left for Venice?"

"She said, 'Now I know that you really love me.'"

Donat Prilukov was the next to testify. He told the court he was dominated by the countess. When they met, he was a happy husband and father, respected attorney, and professional. He repeatedly tried to break with Marie, but she controlled him, he said. "She was too strong for me. There was nothing I would not have done at her command. Because she wished it, I left my wife. I robbed my clients. I sacrificed my honor. And once I even tried to kill myself."

"Yes, and you also tried to kill Count Kamarovsky. That is the matter before us at this moment."

"It was not my wish. As I have told you, I was in love with the Countess. We both considered that Naumov would be the best man to do the job."

"We have here a telegram forwarded to you in Venice by the prisoner Tarnovska. It says, 'Berta's decision to educate Adele is very serious.' What does this mean?"

"It is a code message. What it means is Naumov has decided to kill Kamarovsky."

"And this one: 'Berta prefers a hot dish.' Is that also in code?"

"Of course it is. It means Naumov will use a revolver."

Marie Tarnovska then stood in the dock. A judge ordered the blinds pulled up at the request of photographers who wanted to better illuminate her face. The countess, cloaked in black, lifted her veil and stood pale and trembling before a courtroom packed to suffocation. She noticed her father in his military uniform. Upon seeing him, she burst into tears.

The prosecuting attorney fiercely questioned her for hours about the apex of her stunning career, the murder plot that was so complex some would say she elevated the double cross to a fine art. He then went beyond the charges to ask her about her connections with other tragedies. Inside the courtroom, the questioning heightened an atmosphere already electric with excitement.

"Kamarovsky telegraphed to you twice as he was lying in the hospital dying, calling you to his side?"

"But I telegraphed." (Her message to her dying fiancé had read: "Am terribly upset at what has happened. I love you and am in despair that I cannot come to you.")

"It is said that before your divorce you excited your husband against your lovers and your lovers against your husband so as to provoke a duel and get rid of your husband."

"False—absolutely false. My husband fought a duel with Tolstoy for another woman."

"Prilukov too says that you gave yourself up to your brother-in-law, in order to excite him to remorse and urge him to suicide. Is that so? Answer!"

"Good heavens! He was only a child of sixteen." When pressed, she added bitterly, "You know I was accused of causing that suicide."

Was it true that she had a passion for Alexis Bozevsky?

"I yielded to him," she stated. "In doing so, I admit I was wrong. But I found him kind and affectionate, when the man I had married was cruel and neglectful. A woman wants love. Alexis gave it to me. Vassili withheld it."

"He was your first lover?"

"He was the only one among them all who really appealed to me."

"Prilukov has told us that you had many lovers, and that among them was a Monsieur Zolatariev."

"Then it is idiotic of him to say so."

"Why?"

"Because this man was old and ugly, and hadn't a ruble to bless himself with."

"And what about Doctor Stahl, who committed suicide for your sake?"

"Not for my sake. Please be accurate, whatever else you are. Vladimir killed himself because he quarreled with his wife."

"Listen to this letter from him," the prosecutor said. "Dear Marie Nicolaevna. Instead of at five o'clock, I arrived at the anatomical theatre at nine o'clock. I shall live for forty minutes more. All is ended. My love for you lives. I kiss you and I die."

The prosecutor asked, "Have you anything to say to that?"

"Surely I am not responsible if men do foolish things."

"How did you first meet Naumov?"

"Kamarovsky introduced me at Orel."

"Were you in love with him?"

"Yes, I was."

"And what were your relations with Kamarovsky and Prilukov at this period?"

"They were tender."

"So it would appear, Madame. What, however, is not so clear is why you should want three lovers simultaneously."

"It was because I was endeavoring to find somebody who would really love me. Instead, I was always deluded. Nobody corresponded with my ideal."

"Yet you allowed each of these three men to think you would marry him?"

"Ah, but the engagement was not official."

She could not deny what was obvious to every onlooker. Indeed, the countess herself made it clear that she was guilty of the crimes leveled against her, finally confessing to her role in many tragedies. "I am the most unfortunate woman in the world. I am a martyr to my own beauty. For any man to behold me is for him to love me. The whole pathway of my life is strewn with the bodies of those who loved me most."

Such was her hypnotic power over men that a member of the jury excused himself after her testimony. He was in love with the accused and could no longer hide it. For her remarkable ability to enchant men with looks alone, even while being publicly denounced for her crimes against men, *La Tarnovska* is absolutely unequaled as a femme fatale.

With the support of her wealthy father, the countess was able to mount an expensive defense. A score of medical experts took the stand, including surgeons, alienists, and gynecologists, many of them noted in their field: Redlich, Fenomenof, Rhein, Professor Bossi, Professor Berri, Professor Eugenio Tanzi, Dr. Mennini. For days on end, they declared that the countess was merely the victim of a feminine disorder. If it weren't for this disease, she would have been an angel of goodness. Onlookers were not convinced that Tarnovska's flaws were gynecological in nature. "That she was born with a kink in her brain is evident," as one trial observer remarked. The odds were against her in the betting on the outcome.

The jury indeed convicted the countess. But they found by a bare majority that she suffered from a "partial mental infirmity." Her sentence for inciting her lovers to murder was eight years, with two years of credit for time served. Prilukov was also convicted, but the jury found no mitigating infirmity in the case of the attorney. The judges sentenced Prilukov to ten years' imprisonment. As to the actual gunman, the jury found that Naumov intended to murder Count Kamarovsky while under mental impairment. That he was the dupe of his dangerous mistress was proven beyond a doubt. The jury found that Countess Tarnovska instigated and incited Naumov to murder. Though Naumov was found guilty of shooting the count, the judges deemed him the least accountable. He was sentenced to time served. Before he departed the courtroom, Naumov turned to the countess, bent over her hand, and kissed it. The newspapers objected, and the public was incensed with the light sentences. Per one observer, "Severe criticisms were heard on every hand." It was one final scandal to conclude one of the most shocking murder trials in history.

The lawyer who evoked the harshest punishment repeatedly tried to kill himself in prison—first by strangulation, then by poison, then by hanging. He eventually succeeded in opening his veins. He was at least the fifth man to die for the countess, if one also counted Peter Tarnovsky, Vladimir Stahl, Alexis Bozevsky, and Pavel Kamarovsky.

When the prison gates finally swung open for Marie Tarnovska in 1915, the Romanov Dynasty verged on collapse as hunger spread through Russia and millions of men died in pointless wars of empire. She never returned to her homeland. The Venus of Venice slipped into obscurity. It is not quite known where she went or when she died because the rumors disagree. Many think she passed away in Santa Fe, Argentina, in 1945.

According to some of the literature on personality disorders, psychopaths can improve with time and experience. Most experts think not. One would hope that no other man lost his life for loving the world's worst woman.

ABOUT THE AUTHOR

LAURA JAMES is a trial lawyer in private practice in Detroit, Michigan, a devotee of the historical true-crime genre, and the operator of the literary blog *CLEWS Your Home for Historic True Crime*. She has authored the book *The Love Pirate and the Bandit's Son* and provided an epilogue for Edward Keyes's *The Michigan Murders*.

REFERENCES

Books

Armandy, Anne. *Un Drame à Venise (La Tarnowska)*.
Babey, Anna Mary. 1938. *Americans in Russia, 1776–1917*. New York: Comet Press.
Bertolini, G. 1914. *Le Anime Criminali*.
Boswell, Charles, and Lewis Thompson. 1962. *Advocates of Murder*. New York: Collier Books.
Constantini, Costanzo. 1988. *Amore E Morte: I Grandi Delitti Passionali Del Secolo*. Italy: SugarCo.

Dell'Orso, Claudio. 1999. *Venezia Libertina, I Luoghi Della Memoria Erotica*. Italy: Arsenale.

———. 2004. *Nero Veneziano*. Treviso: Elzeviro.

Dell'Orso, Claudio, and Andrea Salmaso. *L'Affare Dei Russi* (ebook). http://www.hotelala.it/img/libro_contessa.pdf.

Kingston, Charles. 1921. *Remarkable Rogues*. London and New York: John Lane.

Lingua, Catherine. 1995. *Ces Anges du Bizarre: Regard sur une Aventure Esthetique de la Decadence*. Paris: Libr. Nizet.

Mondadori, Oscar. 1998. "Morire per Maria." In *Assasine: Quattro Secoli Di Delitti Al Femminile*, by Cinzia Tani. Available as downloadable PDF at http://www.scribd.com/doc/65210254/Tani-Cinzia-Assassine.

Noonan, Norma C. 2001. *Encyclopedia of Russian Women's Movements*. Westport, CT: Greenwood.

Roughead, William. 2000. *Classic Crimes*. New York: New York Review of Books.

Russell, Guy. 1931. *Guilty or Not Guilty: Stories of Fifty Sensational Crimes in Many Countries*. London: Hutchinson.

Tani, Cinzia. 1998. *Assassine: Quattro Secoli Di Delitti Al Femminile*. Available as downloadable PDF at http://www.scribd.com/doc/65210254/Tani-Cinzia-Assassine.

Wyndham, Horace. 1928. *Crime on the Continent*. London: T. Butterworth.

Newspapers

Fort Wayne (IN) News.
Indianapolis Star.
Irish Times.
Kingston Gleaner.
New York Times.
Syracuse Herald.
Washington Post.

Other Sources

Hans Habe Collection, Howard Gotlieb Archival Research Center, Boston University, Boston, Massachusetts.

Private interview with Tatjana Hine (Tarnovska).

Therapeutic Gazette. 1915.

Chapter 12

ESCAPE FROM FORT PILLOW

by Douglas E. Jones

Although they did not know each other, Ronald Freeman and James Clegg were dangerous felons, both classified as maximum-security prisoners by the Tennessee Department of Corrections (TDOC). On June 22, 1983, the inmates were transferred to Fort Pillow State Prison in isolated Lauderdale County along the banks of the Mississippi River. On the day of their arrival, the warden at Fort Pillow reclassified both men as medium security, circumventing department policies. This meant that the two inmates would be allowed to work outside the prison walls. Freeman and Clegg were stunned to learn they had been reclassified. Within days, they began working on an elaborate escape plan.

Fort Pillow Prison and its surrounding grounds occupy 5,715 acres, half of which is fertile river-bottom farmland. Behind the prison is the dangerous Hatchie swamp, made up of miles of wilderness and full of cottonmouth snakes. The prison, some seventy miles north of Memphis, is named after the nearby Fort Pillow, which was the scene of a terrible battle during the Civil War.

The treacherous swamp and mighty river form a natural boundary that forces even the toughest escapee to head in one direction: east.

On the morning of February 18, 1984, Freeman and Clegg put their escape plan into action. The escape and terrifying flight across a number of states made national news. The *New York Times* and newspapers across the country covered the story. Tom Brokaw reported the escape on *NBC Nightly News*. It would end with the deaths of three innocent people and the severe wounding of a North Carolina state trooper.

This is a horror story, not because of the existence of evil, because we are no longer shocked by evil. The horror is that those sworn to protect, the officials of the corrections system, did not protect. It is a chilling tale, because of the element of chance, which signals to us that you or I might get in the way of the next escapee. It is also a story of great pathos, because of the suffering victims. It is full of pity and fear, as there are among the cast of characters heroes and villains. However, like the best of Shakespeare's tragedies, this story contains comic relief, for there are also a number of fools in the cast.

RONALD FREEMAN

Some would call Ronald Sotka an escape artist. In 1968, he escaped from a maximum-security prison in Kentucky. This was not his first escape. He changed his name to Ronald Freeman and made his way to Knoxville, Tennessee, where he met Patricia Foster. Patricia was a divorcée and manager of a laundromat. She had an eleven-year-old daughter who was an honor-roll student. Freeman charmed Patricia into marrying him. He moved into Patricia's modest two-bedroom home in Concord, Tennessee, near Fort Loudoun Lake and convinced her to spend all her savings on a boat and trailer. Within six months, she realized that he was running around with several different women. What changed everything for Freeman was the news that Patricia Foster was pregnant. This news ate at Freeman and would not let him go.

One day in June 1970, Freeman came home around midnight to find his wife and stepdaughter asleep. He used a .7mm pistol and shot his pregnant wife and stepdaughter in the head. He wrapped their bodies in plastic then placed them in the trunk of his car. He then hooked the boat and trailer to the car and drove to Fort Loudoun Lake. He loaded the bodies into the boat and motored to a remote, hidden cove. Freeman then lashed the bodies together with rope and concrete blocks and dumped them over the side.

He returned home, showered, and called his girlfriend. Freeman then bought some beer before picking up his date. He drove her out to the boat ramp and took the boat back out to the hidden cove. He made love to her at the spot where he had disposed of his pregnant wife and stepdaughter just an hour before.

Over the next three weeks, Freeman sold his wife's furniture and other possessions, including the boat. He left Knoxville and drove to his native Ohio. He told neighbors his wife was ill and had returned home to Kentucky.

Two weeks after the murders, the bodies were found floating in Fort Loudoun Lake. Ronald Freeman immediately became the number one suspect, but he was nowhere to be found. He would later be apprehended in Ohio after fighting an intense battle with sheriff's deputies.

After Freeman was arrested, he confessed to tying the bodies and dumping them in the lake. He claimed his wife was depressed and that she killed her daughter, then committed suicide.

Freeman's statement to the police handcuffed his attorneys. His allegation of suicide made a difficult case easy for the state, for if the jury rejected the suicide defense, Freeman would have nothing to fall back on.

Even more troubling was Freeman's insistence that he be allowed to testify at the trial. His elderly mother in Cleveland, Ohio, had scraped together all her savings and hired Bill Wilson, a tough old defense attorney in Nashville. But Wilson could not persuade Freeman not to testify.

The case and trial had stunned the quiet city of Knoxville. There was wall-to-wall media coverage of the trial, and people lined up in the Knox County Courthouse parking lot to get a seat inside the courtroom.

Mr. Wilson filed a motion to prevent the gruesome photographs of the victims from being shown to the jury. The judge denied the motion and noted that since Freeman had admitted to dumping the bodies, the jury members could decide for themselves the value of the photographs in light of the state's charge of murder.

The defense suffered another major blow when the state's forensic expert testified that Patricia's head wound was not a contact wound but rather was the result of a shot fired from a distance of two to three feet. This eviscerated Freeman's "suicide claim."

In March of 1971, a Knox County jury convicted Ronald Sotka Freeman for the murders of his wife and eleven-year-old stepdaughter. There was no death penalty statute in effect at this time, so Freeman was sentenced to 198 years in prison.

After the murder trial, Freeman was placed in the Tennessee State Penitentiary in Nashville, Tennessee. His initial classification reports indicate that he was bright, with an IQ of approximately 125, but unstable, unpredictable, and criminal in attitude.

Inmate Freeman escaped from the main prison twice. The first time, in

August 1972, he got as far as the parking lot, where he was found in possession of an eight-inch dagger. The second time, in September of 1972, he eluded capture for a month and was finally found in Indiana.

Freeman continued to be a source of trouble over the years to the TDOC. In 1975, he was one of several leaders in a major hunger strike at the main prison. At that time, he was still considered a grave security risk. In 1977, his institutional file noted that he was involved in several illegal activities and, accordingly, was transferred to the maximum-security prison in Brushy Mountain, Tennessee. On June 22, 1983, Ronald Freeman was transferred from Nashville to Fort Pillow State Prison. When he left Nashville, he was rated maximum security.

JAMES CLEGG

James Clegg was born in St. Louis, Missouri, on October 7, 1947. His parents divorced when he was three years old, and he was passed from one family member to another throughout his entire childhood. He lived in Chicago, Idaho, and Pennsylvania.

Clegg finally moved in with an aunt in Bluff City, a small town in upper East Tennessee. He dropped out of school in the seventh grade and never returned. At age twenty-two, Clegg enlisted in the army and received basic training in Fort Lewis, Washington. He attended jump school in Fort Polk, Louisiana. At the Special Forces school in Fort Carson, Colorado, Clegg became a small-arms expert, an experience that would prove useful to him later in life.

Clegg completed three years of service in the army. During this time, he was arrested on numerous charges. He went AWOL, even though he had been promoted to specialist fourth class. While AWOL and hiding in the mountains of East Tennessee, Clegg was convicted of concealing a weapon, grand larceny, statutory burglary, and forced entry into a residence. In 1972, Clegg married RuthAnne Dillard. Although that marriage and the next would not last, his union to Dillard did produce one son.

In 1973, Clegg broke into a sporting-goods store in Bristol, Virginia, stealing guns, ammunition, and other weapons. He was finally arrested, received a ten-year sentence, and stayed in jail for a few years.

In December of 1980, Clegg and a friend broke into a home in Sullivan County, Tennessee. They stole hundreds of dollars' worth of guns, jewelry, and silverware. Clegg's friend received a three-year sentence. When arrested, Clegg was accused of receiving stolen property. Due to Clegg's prior record, the district attorney decided to prosecute Clegg as a habitual criminal. James Clegg's case as a habitual criminal was a first in Tennessee and resulted in a hung jury. He was later retried and found guilty. His sentence was life in a penitentiary. Despite his appearance and record, one fact remained: James Clegg was a petty thief who had never hurt anyone, yet he was sentenced to life in prison.

Clegg was transferred to Brushy Mountain State Penitentiary on September 17, 1981. He continued to hope that the court of appeals would reverse the life sentence for what amounted to a second-degree burglary. However, on June 8, 1982, the Tennessee Supreme Court of Appeals ruled that there was "no reversible error on the record and that the judgment of the trial court should be affirmed." James Clegg's conviction was upheld, and his future was reduced to a bleak life in a Tennessee prison. After another year at Brushy Mountain, Clegg was transferred to Fort Pillow State Prison in late June 1983.

THE WARDEN

Herman Davis was a tough man reared in the mountains of East Tennessee. Davis was born in 1929 in Morgan County. After finishing high school, Davis worked various local jobs. He was a logger, bulldozer operator, and machine operator. In 1949, Davis began a long career with the TDOC at Brushy Mountain State Prison. Brushy Mountain was also located in Davis's home county. He was fired from his job in 1953. In 1963, he went back to work at Brushy Mountain. Within two years, Davis was promoted to assistant deputy warden.

In March of 1969, Davis was appointed associate deputy warden for Brushy Mountain. Two years later, he was promoted to deputy warden. The warden at Brushy Mountain at that time was Stoney Lane.

Brushy Mountain was rated a "no escape" maximum-security prison, housing the most dangerous and notorious inmates in the state's system. It was isolated in the rugged Cumberland Mountains. The penitentiary was surrounded by a fourteen-foot stone wall, with heavily armed guards manning towers at each corner. A 2,300-volt cable positioned only a few inches above the wall made escape almost impossible.

◆

On Friday, June 10, 1977, Herman Davis was the acting warden at Brushy Mountain while Warden Lane was on vacation in Texas. At approximately 7:30 p.m., seven inmates using a crude ladder from broken pipes climbed over the wall at one corner of the prison yard. One of the seven inmates was James Earl Ray. The escape made international news, with newspapers from Italy to Thailand running headlines: "Slayer of King Escapes."

Initially, Warden Davis claimed that the escape had been possible due to a power failure that blocked the current from flowing through the cable. Later, Davis, through a spokesman, dropped the power-failure story. Several days after the escape, Ray was captured in the rugged mountains near a coal mine in the New River area.

After pressure from the governor's office, Herman Davis spoke to the media. As acting warden, he refused to accept any blame for the failures leading to the escape, but his final comment was "any time you have an escape from an institution; it is the fault of someone."

By 1979, Davis had worked for the Department of Corrections for almost thirty years. He had developed a reputation as a hard man, a man not to be trifled with. He did not enjoy the trust of the guards or employees of the prison, and he paid lip service to the orders and directions sent from the central office in Nashville.

Yet in March, the TDOC issued a press release announcing that Herman Davis had been appointed the warden of Brushy Mountain Prison.

◆

In January 1982, Davis was given detailed information from a prisoner about white inmates plotting to murder black inmates. Several guards also confirmed the report. Two days later, four black inmates came to Warden Davis and pleaded to be transferred because they feared for their lives. Davis denied their request.

On February 8, 1982, seven white inmates cut their bars with carbon-coated strings. They took guards hostage with semiautomatic pistols and climbed to the black inmates' housing. White inmate William Kirk then systematically shot four black inmates. Two died on the scene while the others escaped injury by hiding behind their mattresses. The white inmates were later captured without a fight.

Despite public outrage and intense media scrutiny, Davis was not fired. Herman Davis amazed the press and government officials by repeatedly stating that the shootings were not racially motivated, saying, "I was not aware of any difference between the two groups." In his aggressive style, Davis denied any wrongdoing in the matter. Yet he would not or could not offer any comment to the pointed question that the two murdered black inmates had pleaded for a transfer the week before.

Davis was transferred to Fort Pillow in March 1983.

Davis immediately set up a meeting with his new staff and guards. During this meeting, when discussing prison security and escapes, Davis declared, "If they run off, Nashville will just send some more."

The staff and guards were stunned. The new warden's philosophy was almost the opposite of the Tennessee Department of Corrections's long-standing policy that security was the number-one priority for each institution.

FORT PILLOW: JUNE 1983–FEBRUARY 18, 1984

Ronald Freeman and James Clegg arrived at Fort Pillow Prison within a day of each other. They were both immediately placed on the long-line number seven work crew.

As warden of Brushy Mountain, Herman Davis was familiar with the TDOC policies and procedures on the administration and day-to-day management of prisons across the state. The detailed policies enabled the employees to apply fair, uniform rules to all inmates.

TDOC Policy 401.05 was titled "Classification Review Process." Its purpose was to "establish a uniform procedure for the periodic review and classification status of all inmates in the custody of the Department."

Transfer to a different penitentiary was a triggering mechanism for an inmate to be reclassified. Specifically under the applicable policies, the inmate was to be interviewed by a counselor and given notice of a classification-review hearing. The classification-review committee evaluates the counselor's recommendation and then determines the status of the inmates; for example: minimum, medium, or maximum security. The committee forwards its findings to the deputy warden, who makes a final recommendation to the warden.

When Ronald Freeman arrived at Fort Pillow in June 1983, he was rated maximum security. He was immediately reclassified to medium security without any interview or classification hearing. This was done because Warden Davis had written on his job assignment form: "Resident Freeman should be assigned to long line number seven."

In effect, the entire classification procedure was ignored by Davis. Freeman's counselor had described him as "a terror" and had stated that it was against his principles that any inmate such as Freeman should ever be allowed to work outside prison walls. Also, Davis's history as the warden at Brushy Mountain Prison while Freeman and Clegg were incarcerated should have made him fully aware of their capabilities.

Fort Pillow inmates customarily worked on "long lines" of approximately twenty-five inmates per one armed guard. The long lines worked outside the prison wall, primarily chopping weeds and cutting firewood. Within two days of their arrival at Fort Pillow, Clegg and Freeman were assigned to long line number seven. Though the men had both been at Brushy Mountain and the main prison in Nashville at the same time, they did not know each other.

When Freeman and Clegg were placed on the long line, they were shocked and delighted to find that they would be allowed to work outside the prison walls and immediately began planning their escape.

During their first day working on the long line, the two inmates, in their new white coveralls, stood together chopping Johnsongrass at the edge of the prison property. Clegg noticed that Freeman was constantly staring down Highway 87 to the land outside the prison boundary. Clegg had also caught himself glancing east down the road—the road to freedom. Freeman stopped hoeing and just stood there looking. Clegg suddenly blurted out, "This is bullshit. I'm leaving this place." Freeman turned and looked at Clegg and slowly nodded in agreement.

In August 1983, long line number seven was combined with long line number three to make up a work gang of approximately fifty inmates. This aided Freeman and Clegg's plan, as the inmates on long line number three already had guns inside the prison. Freeman and Clegg bought three guns from inmates on long line number three for approximately $1,000.

Within the prison, the presence of guns was no secret. On a dark night in September 1983, an inmate met with Warden Davis in the prison recreation yard. The meeting was set up by a TDOC internal-affairs officer who was investigating guns inside the prison. The inmate told Davis and the internal-affairs officer details about the escape plans and the fact that there were guns in the prison. To establish credibility, the inmate gave Davis a sock full of .22-caliber bullets. Within a matter of days, the internal-affairs officer at Fort Pillow Prison was advised by another reliable inmate that the guard for long line number three was selling guns to the inmates. The internal-affairs officer advised Warden Davis of this fact, as well.

Among the information given to the warden was the fact that two particular inmates on long line three, Sevars and Fortner, were going to escape. On January 6, 1984, these two inmates did escape. That same day, a gun was fired in Unit C of Fort Pillow Prison. Nevertheless, no complete search of Unit C was performed for several days. On January 16, 1984, an inmate turned in a .25-caliber pistol to Warden Davis.

In late January 1984, Freeman and Clegg joined the Black Muslims of Fort Pillow Prison. This was the first time in the history of the prison that white inmates had joined the Black Muslims. At this particular time, the Black Muslims did not work on Fridays because it was considered their holy day. Instead, Black Muslims' long-line crews went out on Saturdays. Since Freeman and Clegg had joined the Black Muslims, they did not have to work Fridays and, accordingly, went out on Saturdays.

Only one armed guard worked outside the prison walls on Saturdays, supervising the long line. For that reason, Freeman and Clegg had joined the Black Muslims. On Saturday, February 4, 1984, according to Clegg, the men had a practice run wherein they rehearsed the details of their escape, except for actually pulling their guns on the guards.

The following Saturday, it rained and the Black Muslims' long line did not go out.

On Saturday morning, February 18, 1984, Ronald Freeman, James Clegg, and Riley Arzeneaux carried a .32-caliber pistol, a .25-caliber pistol, and a .22-caliber pistol out of the prison with the long line. They also had extra ammunition, rope, razor blades, granola bars, and plastic bags to cover their feet in case they had to swim a river.

The inmates were able to come and go with weapons easily because Warden Davis had dramatically relaxed security and search requirements at the prison. During a staff meeting, Davis gave a specific order that the metal detectors not be used on inmates entering or leaving the prison grounds. He stated that making the inmates pass through the metal detectors "took too much time."

The long line marched through the prison gates and down Highway 87 to the warden's home. They turned left and walked to a field still within sight of the warden's house. They started chain saws and began cutting brush along a ditch. At approximately 10:15 a.m., it began to rain, and guard Norman Hooper radioed the prison for permission to bring the long line back.

"It's raining. Do you want me to bring them back in or stay and see if it stops?" Norman Hooper spoke into the radio.

There was a pause. Then the radio signaled, "Bring 'em in."

"Ten-four, over." Hooper snapped his radio back on his belt. As he looked back up, Clegg was pointing a pistol at him. He also saw Freeman and Arzeneaux pointing pistols at his partner, Long.

"Drop 'em," Clegg said, "Don't do nothing stupid. Drop your gun."

Long just stood there, facing the gun pointed directly at him. He had no real choice and dropped his shotgun.

After the three armed men had subdued the two guards on the work detail, Sylvester Alexander and Randolph Oliver, two other inmates, joined the escape party. The fugitives threw the guards into a silage pit. Freeman put on one of their uniforms and climbed out of the pit. Meanwhile, a car approached, heading west on Highway 87, which runs through the prison complex. In the small automobile were David Demps, his wife, and their two young daughters on their way to Fort Pillow State Park, where Mr. Demps was planning to run in a 5K race.

Freeman, now in a guard's uniform, flagged them down, and as Demps lowered the window, Freeman said to him, "Sir, we've got a little problem. Some prisoners have escaped."

"Oh, goodness, that is not good," replied Demps.

"Yeah, and I'm one of them," snarled Freeman as he jammed his gun into Demps's face.

Riley Arzeneaux stared at guard Norman Hooper. Arzeneaux, well built at six-foot-three, towered over the diminutive Hooper. It was well known that Arzeneaux despised all the guards. The inmate held a razor blade in his right hand and stared at Hooper's throat.

Just as Arzeneaux started toward Hooper with his blade, Freeman yelled, "Let's go! Let's go!"

Arzeneaux and the others turned and jumped out of the pit. They ran up the rise to the road. The five men then piled into the car with the Demps family, with Clegg driving. The escapees had brought with them the guards' prison radio, which would enable them to monitor all conversations about tracking down the missing men. Oddly, the prison did not change the frequency, which would have prevented such monitoring. Embarrassingly, this was only one error in a number of glaring mistakes on the part of the authorities.

As the group was driving, Wayne Douglas, a teacher at the prison, happened to drive by and recognize Arzeneaux, who had been his student. Douglas immediately drove to the prison headquarters and notified officials of the escape. Then, in an act of unbelievable boldness, Douglas sped down Highway 87 after the convicts. He found the inmates and the hapless Demps family, who were now pulled over at the New Salem Baptist Church. When Douglas whipped his car in front of the escape vehicle, the armed men jumped out and blasted Douglas's vehicle with the shotgun. Miraculously, Douglas remained unscathed.

Another car, driven by the wife of a prison employee, came along, but sped away as bullets sprayed around her car. Then two elderly black gentlemen drove down the road in a new Oldsmobile®. Clegg stepped out into the highway and stopped them. One of the old men quickly got out of the way, but Clegg threw the other into a ditch and fired a shot, which barely missed the man's head. The fugitives then fled in the roomier and more luxurious new automobile, swerving past the horrified Demps family as they sat shocked in their car.

The inmates continued east on Highway 87 to Henning, Tennessee. Just south of Henning, Alexander and Oliver were forced out of the car. They had not been part of the original escape plan and were liabilities to Freeman and Clegg.

An hour later, Deputy Warden of Security Marvin Smith drove a Fort Pillow Prison flatbed truck down a country road near Henning. Two Fort Pillow guards rode in the cab with Smith as they searched for the escapees.

Smith pulled over and stopped the truck when he saw Alexander and Oliver walking down the road. The two men looked at Smith and, without a word, hopped onto the bed of the truck. It is part of the unwritten protocol of the prison that, if an inmate is apprehended after an escape and quietly surrenders to his captors, the punishment will be significantly reduced. In Fort Pillow terms, the two inmates would not be beaten.

After a half mile or so, Smith stopped the truck, leaned out the window, and asked the men, "Where do you boys live?"

Alexander and Oliver looked at each other, muttered something in reply, and pointed down the road. Deputy Warden Smith cautioned them, "You need to be careful. We've got some escaped inmates. Be sure to call Fort Pillow if you see them."

The two bewildered men jumped off the truck and continued on their way. Oliver would be picked up shortly thereafter for hitchhiking, just outside Brownsville—the first of the five men to be captured. Alexander would travel all the way to California and establish himself there with a job and an apartment. He would be the last of the five to be apprehended.

Meanwhile, Freeman, Clegg, and Arzeneaux abandoned the Oldsmobile, stole another car, and hid for several hours in Haywood County, while taking over the Parker household at gunpoint and forcing the family to feed them. Later, the three stole the Parker's old truck and went into Brownsville, where police chased them around the square and exchanged gunfire with them, finally forcing them to abandon the truck on a dead-end road.

Now on foot, Freeman and Clegg split from Arzeneaux. They eluded the Brownsville police and made their way to the farm of Paul and Elizabeth Windrow in south Haywood County.

Riley Arzeneaux would soon give himself up at the request of an elderly lady in Mason, into whose home he had forced entry. The remarkable account of Arzeneaux's surrender was eventually published in *Guideposts Magazine*.

On Sunday, February 19, at about 5:30 a.m., Freeman and Clegg arrived at the Windrow farm. In the middle of a cotton field, they found a hole with a log over it. The weather was mild, and they were able to remain in this hidden place until Tuesday evening. During this time, there was an intensive manhunt on the Windrow farm by state corrections officials, the highway patrol, and the Haywood County sheriff's department. Helicopters swarmed overhead while bloodhounds sniffed the ground. Guards even walked within ten feet of the hole where the fugitives hid—a hole so small that the feet of both men protruded from it.

The following Tuesday, authorities mistakenly concluded that the men were not on the Windrow property and moved their search to Braden, Tennessee, some twenty-five miles from Brownsville. It is possible that the rivalry between Haywood County sheriff James Sullivan and Brownsville police chief Jerry Wyatt figured in the decision to move the search. For whatever reason, Freeman and Clegg, aware of the calm that had descended on their surroundings, came out of the hole and walked toward the Windrow house that evening.

Earlier Tuesday afternoon, Paul Windrow, a tough and savvy tire dealer who had been a decorated hero in World War II, had thought it was time to celebrate the end of the siege of terror brought about by the manhunt. Paul trusted the judgment of the officials who had declared that the inmates were nowhere near his home. He had bought steaks and had begun grilling them at about 6:15 p.m., while his wife, Elizabeth, a social worker, prepared salad and potatoes in the kitchen. At 6:30 p.m., he walked into the house and told Elizabeth to finish up her preparations because the steaks were about ready. When he walked back out onto his porch, he was confronted by Ronald Freeman and James Clegg.

As soon as Paul Windrow walked through the back door, Elizabeth heard a shot, followed by other shots. Within a matter of seconds, Freeman kicked the door in and entered with his pistol drawn, screaming for her to drop to the floor.

Clegg came in a few seconds later covered with blood. He ran to the bathroom mirror and patted himself as he cried out, "I can't believe he missed me! I can't believe he missed me!"

The men began searching the house for ammunition and guns. They disabled the telephones while Elizabeth pleaded with them to let her go to her husband. After about thirty minutes, they allowed her to see him. He was still alive and breathing. After she had knelt briefly by her husband, Freeman grabbed her shoulder and pushed her into the car and ordered her to drive them to Nashville.

Along the route to Nashville, the escapees ordered Mrs. Windrow to stop several times to buy gas and make telephone calls. The two men repeatedly vowed not to be taken alive, and they told their hostage that she would certainly be killed should she try to escape. Freeman kept his pistol pointed at Elizabeth the entire trip. They refused to allow her to call an ambulance for her husband.

The three arrived in Nashville at about 9:30 p.m. Freeman telephoned a number of friends requesting help but was unsuccessful. Freeman had been incarcerated for such a long time that he was surprised when Mrs. Windrow informed them that they could obtain food from a drive-through window at McDonald's, for he was unaware of such a modern development.

When they went through the drive-through, there were a number of police cars around them but only by coincidence—perhaps a shift change—for they were only a few blocks away from the police precinct station. At any rate, nothing came of it. As they parked on a westbound Nashville street, waiting for a contact that never appeared, Elizabeth suggested to her captors that they might leave her there, sitting on a park bench. Ironically, the two men who had shot her husband protested that the neighborhood was too dangerous and that someone might harm her there. After eating and buying gas, they resumed their journey at about midnight, heading toward Knoxville.

They pulled off the interstate at the Dandridge exit east of Knoxville, and Freeman told Mrs. Windrow to get on the floorboard and count to five hundred. He said that if she rose up, he would have to hurt her.

While she lay on the floor, she heard a car drive up and doors shut. She then heard the car drive away. She continued to count, and when she finally got up she saw that the other vehicle was gone. She then managed to start her car and drive to Knoxville, where she found a telephone and called the Haywood County sheriff and the ambulance service back in Brownsville. When they got to Paul Windrow at 6:00 a.m., he had bled to death.

Meanwhile, Freeman and Clegg had been whisked away by Bernice Blevins, a friend of Clegg's old cellmate at Brushy Mountain Prison. They would stay with Bernice in her trailer in Unicoi County, hidden in the mountains of East Tennessee until things cooled down a bit. They would then move to Cleveland, Ohio, to spend some time visiting with Freeman's relatives. Freeman had shed his Polish surname of Sotka, but had not cut all ties with his family.

Eventually, the pair headed south again to North Carolina. Around 1:30 a.m. on March 6, 1984, the fugitives were speeding down Interstate 40 when they were stopped by North Carolina trooper L. H. Rector. As the trooper approached the two men, Freeman shot Rector in the abdomen and chest four times. Trooper Rector was severely injured, but he managed to survive the attack.

The two men, now in a state of panic, fled at high speed, swerving off the interstate at the next exit and landing in a ditch where they abandoned their car and headed down the railroad tracks to Marion, North Carolina. There they holed up in a shed by the tracks. The next morning, Freeman left, and Clegg remained hiding under a pile of plywood.

Freeman walked up to a hillside cemetery. He sat beneath a tree and studied the graves. He knew the entire area would be swarming with law enforcement eager to claim justice for the shooting of the trooper. He spotted a sunken grave and made a snap decision. He stepped down inside the grave. There he lay all day like a monk contemplating his last end. He began thinking about the house that he had seen down the hollow.

The white frame house was the home of an elderly couple, the Harveys. Rossie Harvey was blind, and his wife, Molly, also legally blind, was a diabetic with a bad heart. Because of the shooting of Trooper Rector and the ensuing manhunt, Ronnie Harvey, the son of Rossie and Molly Harvey, had brought his wife, Peggy, and their two young daughters to his parents' home. That evening, he left them all there and went to work at a North Carolina correctional facility nearby. Molly Harvey and the girls settled down and fell asleep in the back bedroom. Peggy Harvey, unable to sleep, paced around the small kitchen.

In the early hours of March 7, 1984, Freeman arose from the grave and walked down to the Harveys' house, where he hid in the basement. Then, at around 2:00 a.m., he kicked in the door of the house and encountered Peggy.

This strong woman, perhaps partially because of her training as a nurse, seemed to know how to deal with Freeman. She offered him a cheese sandwich. The children and their grandmother, in the next room, were awakened by the talking. The little girls began to cry. Molly Harvey walked out of the bedroom and came face-to-face with the convict. She vomited and passed out. Peggy, aware of Molly's fragile condition, feared the worst, and screamed at Freeman, "I don't care if you shoot me. I'm calling an ambulance."

"Go ahead," said Freeman, and he went on down the hall and lay down in the back bedroom. There are many paradoxes in Ronald Freeman's behavior. Perhaps he had a soft spot for elderly ladies, or perhaps by now he was disoriented and confused. Whatever the case, the exhausted man went to sleep, while the ambulance came and took the unconscious Molly Harvey away to the hospital on the last journey of her life.

At 7:30 a.m., Ronnie Harvey returned from third shift at the prison. Peggy whispered to him that one of the escapees was asleep in the back bedroom. He summoned the local authorities and waited outside with a shotgun.

An hour later, near the railroad tracks, a deputy searching for the escapees noticed something strange about a pile of plywood. He walked over for a closer look. James Clegg came out, hands up, from under the plywood and was captured without a single shot being fired.

When the sheriff and his men arrived at the Harvey home, they entered and politely knocked on the bedroom door, requesting that Freeman give himself up. He shouted an oath and jumped out the bedroom window to find Ronnie Harvey waiting for him. What followed was like an episode from one of those movies about a monster who would not die. Harvey shot Freeman in the leg, and Freeman returned fire. Harvey shot him a second time, again in the leg, and Freeman fell but got up and shot at him again. The third time, Harvey shot Freeman in the eye, and he did not fall but continued to fire back.

A wounded Ronald Freeman, blazing with his pistol, staggered up to an abandoned farmhouse. He hid in the front room behind a broken door. A North Carolina game warden, who happened to be just down the road from the Harvey home, arrived on the scene. He joined the local law enforcement surrounding the farmhouse. Freeman was trapped. He was running out of choices, out of time.

Each time Freeman fired, a volley of bullets would rip through the house.

"Give it up. It's over," a state trooper hollered.

Then it was quiet.

"Maybe he has had enough," an officer said to himself.

They did not know Ronald Freeman. He reloaded his pistol and began firing again. This brought a storm of return fire. The game warden finally spotted Freeman behind the broken door. He gently squeezed the trigger of his powerful 3.06 rifle. The heavy round exploded directly into Freeman's chest.

When they entered the house, the men found Ronald Freeman still clutching his gun; his face angry in death, as he had been in life.

A Tennessee grand jury indicted James Clegg for unlawful escape, kidnapping, assault, and first-degree murder. At that point, James Clegg was headed to the electric chair. During the drive to Nashville, Freeman had repeatedly threatened to kill Mrs. Windrow, but James Clegg stopped him each time. After Clegg was captured, Elizabeth Windrow asked the district attorney to seek a life sentence rather than the death penalty. James Clegg's life was spared.

Mrs. Windrow sued the Tennessee Department of Corrections for negligence in security at Fort Pillow State Prison. She specifically alleged negligence in the reclassification of Freeman and Clegg from maximum to medium security, as well as for allowing weapons in the prison. Three weeks before the trial, the state settled the case.

Protecting the public is the Department's number one priority.
—Tennessee Department of Corrections, Policy & Procedure 1983

How could this happen? Why would a monster like Ronald Freeman be allowed to work outside prison walls? Like the fog of the Mississippi River, the answers are shrouded in mystery.

What is clear is that the checks and balances of the high-risk penitentiary did not work. The officials' negligence caused a complete breakdown of security and unleashed a reign of terror on an unsuspecting public, resulting in the needless loss of innocent lives.

ABOUT THE AUTHOR

DOUGLAS E. JONES is an attorney and partner at the law firm of Schulman, LeRoy & Bennett, PC. He has practiced law in Nashville, Tennessee, for thirty-six years. An accomplished litigator, Jones has tried lawsuits throughout the South. He has also led several cases of national significance and has authored legal articles on antitrust law. In 1994, Tennessee governor Ned McWherter appointed Jones to serve as chairman of TRICOR, the Tennessee prison industry program, a position he held for nine years. In 2010, Jones coauthored a book with Phyllis Gobbell, *A Season of Darkness*, which told the story of the kidnapping and murder of a Girl Scout in Nashville, Tennessee. The case was considered the leading murder mystery in the history of the city. In 1984, Jones was retained by Elisabeth Windrow to file a complaint against the Tennessee Department of Corrections and the warden of Fort Pillow Prison for negligence in allowing dangerous inmates to escape and murder her husband, Paul Windrow. The escape and subsequent murders garnered national headlines. The Tennessee Department of Corrections eventually settled weeks before the trial.

REFERENCES

Davis, Herman. 1977. *Tennessean*, June 13.
———. 1982. *Tennessean*, April.
Guideposts. 1985. May.
Minutes of Fort Pillow Prison Staff Meeting. 1983 (March and May).
Tennessee Department of Corrections Non-Transfer Request Form, p. 62283.

The latter two references were not public records but were produced in response to the author's subpoena duces tecum in representing Mrs. Windrow in the lawsuit against the warden and Tennessee Department of Corrections, and was used in depositions in the case in 1984.

Chapter 13

MATCHBOOK

by Michele McPhee

The fluorescent bulbs in the bathroom of the DoubleTree® Hotel gave the tattoos scrawled across Joey Torres's sinewy boxer's frame a sickly green hue, exactly the color of the frozen peas the prison cafeteria mutts served him nearly every goddamn day. He stared at the permanent graffiti scrawled across his bantamweight torso in the mirror and thought back to the jailhouse artists who pricked his skin with makeshift tattoo needles and filled the bleeding holes with black ink. He was so numb then he barely felt the pain.

Twenty-three years. Twenty-three fucking years.

As his manager bound his warped knuckles with yellow wraps, Torres sucked in sharp breaths and exhaled forcefully, trying to get rid of the anxiety, the panic that rose every time he thought about the time lost, decades as faded and blurred as the ink on his body. He pulled on his gloves and hurtled punches at the mirror, murky with splattered toothpaste stains. Each jab thrown with such force, it was as if the rapid-fire thrusts would pound down the memory of that night in 1979, when his life ended, the night he shot a man dead in a gas-station parking lot, a murder he still contends was committed in self-defense against an abusive boxing manager during a cocaine-fueled fury. The facts, eventually, would catch up to him. His story of self-defense would unravel. But, right now, the man who grew up with the nickname "Boxer" had a fight to think about. He continued to throw punches at his past. When the careful flailing finally stopped, he wiped at the sweat collected on his face, jumped from foot to foot, and turned his stare to his manager, Sean Gibbons.

"You sure this is going to work?" Torres asked Gibbons, a rising star at Top Rank, the nation's largest boxing promotion company, a sports racket rivaled only by Don King Productions. Top Rank was promoting Torres's first fight since he was released from prison, a card at Anaheim Pond in California featuring the ex-con and a virtual unknown, Perry Williams. The April 27,

2002, bout had sold out the stadium weeks before, but his managers did not seem all that concerned that Torres was overweight, taking medication for highly contagious hepatitis C, and very close to legally blind.

"They're going to take my blood, find it, the hepatitis," Torres spat, thinking about the medical records California prison officials collected on him, documents citing his "severe neurological problem," impaired vision, hepatitis, and liver disorders. "I can't even see. My vision is shot. No one is going to let me take this fight."

"Not to worry," Gibbons said reassuringly. "I'll take the tests for you. Anyway, it's all taken care of. The fight is fixed. You can't lose."

It would not be the first time Gibbons orchestrated a victory before the opponents even stepped into the ring. Over the years, his boxers—Top Rank's carefully picked talent—seemed to have extraordinary winning streaks.

A grin crossed Torres's face.

Fuck the past.

He was forty-one years old, a free man. Joey Torres was about to make a comeback. And, in the process, he had made a deal, a deal that would ensure that he would never land behind bars again. As Gibbons talked about fixing the fight, Torres was not the only one listening. By then, the ex-con was at the center of a federal undercover investigation aimed at cleaning up an industry so notorious for its scandals that fifty years ago, boxing writer Jimmy Cannon termed it "the red light district of sports." Every word being uttered in the shabby hotel room that afternoon was recorded and entered into evidence as part of "Operation Matchbook"—the name the secret investigation was given by the FBI in early 2002. Law-enforcement sources told *Stuff* magazine that the FBI case was sparked by pressure from former presidential hopeful, Arizona senator John McCain.

For years, McCain tried to sway Congress to approve the Professional Boxing Amendments Act, which would appoint a federal czar, of sorts, to oversee what he calls the most corrupt sport in the nation. The government would be responsible for protecting fighters and for strengthening safety measures, and it would oversee medical histories—making it increasingly difficult for rich promoters like Don King and Bob Arum to control the sport. "Boxing is incestuous, it's corrupt, and it has to be fixed," McCain, who boxed while attending the Naval Academy, told the author. "The only way it can be fixed is with a federal boxing commission."

Ten years after Operation Matchbook was begun, the case is as dead as Torres's career. The case that was expected to topple the professional boxing world and land dozens of the sport's major players behind bars is now a story of a failed multimillion sting thwarted by politics and powerful men.

Torres, the informant at the heart of the case, thought Operation Matchbook would be his get-out-of-jail-free card. It wasn't. He is back behind prison walls at a California correctional facility, railing against the government that he says used him to infiltrate Top Rank's hierarchy, then abandoned him when the case against the company began to gain momentum. "I made a deal with the devil. The devil being the FBI who did in fact promise me the greatest gift to any man: his freedom," Torres told the author in a collect call from Mule Creek State Prison in Iona, California. "They told me, 'If we can prove your fight is fixed, and you help work with us to clean up boxing, there's no way you are going back to prison.' Well, here I am back in this living hell I call home."

In 1979, Torres was known simply as "Boxer," just another sleekly built teenage gangbanger who slept in the ring at Main Street Gym in downtown Los Angeles and swept the floor to keep up with his training. He was nineteen then and was already one of the country's best amateur boxers and a full-contact karate fighter. But cops knew him by his birth name, Kim Joseph Torrey, by his prominent position in Los Angeles's 18th Street Gang, and by his addiction to cocaine—the combination of which made him more than familiar with the local jail system than the boxing ring. But hard state-prison time is an altogether different animal, as Torres found out that year after pleading guilty to the shooting death of the man he called his longtime manager, Jose Luis Ramirez. On June 18, 1979, Torres allegedly confronted Ramirez about monies skimmed off the top of amateur karate matches and boxing bouts during a cocaine-fueled fury. To this day, Torres insists he fired a single bullet into Ramirez's chest in self-defense. But Los Angeles prosecutors didn't see it that way. Their case proved the motive was much simpler: $335 in cash stolen from Ramirez's office. In fact, the victim didn't know Torres at all.

Torres convinced a lot of people, prominent people, that he took the rap, pleading guilty to first-degree murder charges because he was promised six years in a California youth facility. He was hit with twenty-five to life in a maximum-security state prison instead. That sentence was imposed by a judge who read a letter Torres had penned to a girlfriend while in jail, telling her to buy a gun. Within months of his incarceration, a teenage Torres was housed in the cell next to mass murderer Charles Manson.

"They had nothing on me then, and they have nothing on me now," Torres said, reading from the piles of court documentation he has accumulated over the years. "They had no gun, no witnesses, no evidence. I was a scared street kid. They played me. They are still playing me."

Torres could barely read, but his cell quickly became bustling with activity. He read law books voraciously—when he wasn't taking bets on major sporting events. He also created a chapter of Boxers against Drugs and wrote to baseball stars such as Darryl Strawberry and Paul Molitor, and to former World Boxing Council welterweight champion Carlos Palomino to convince them to mentor prisoners.

The relationships he forged from behind prison walls opened doors for him when he was granted a temporary reprieve from prison on January 6, 2002. He had uncovered a trial error that temporarily vacated his 1979 murder conviction on something called writ of error *coram nobis*, which meant that Torres pleaded guilty without having full awareness of the consequences. A judge vacated Torres's conviction on December 19, 2001, and Molitor, a future Hall of Famer who is now the Mariner's pitching coach, put up a $100,000 cash bail and bought Torres a car.

The quick-fisted welterweight title holder was now a thickly set, forty-one-year-old cruiserweight, but Torres had enough juice to get back in the game, and Carlos Palomino was all too happy to help him. Palomino was tight with a well-respected matchmaker named Bruce Trampler, a loyal employee at Top Rank. Trampler brought Torres to Top Rank's Las Vegas headquarters and introduced him to the company's owner, Bob Arum.

By then, Arum—a charismatic Brooklyn native who worked as a Department of Justice attorney under Robert Kennedy—had emerged as one of the most powerful promoters in the sport. Arum took a chance on Torres, gave him an apartment, a cell phone, and an advance on a four-fight contract, billing the ex-con as the comeback kid. "I'm not under any illusions that this guy is going to be a great fighter or have a long career. We're just delighted that we're the ones to help him realize his ambitions," Arum told reporters after signing Torres. "Here was a kid who looked like he needed a break and been screwed out of twenty. He deserved a shot at a fight."

Torres, who is five-foot-six and built like a swarthy model, was overweight when he stepped into the ring with Perry Williams, who investigators believe was trained on how to take a dive that night. "Mr. Gibbons, with Top Rank associates, directed my opponent how and when to go down," Torres says. "He moved furniture around the room to make it look like a ring, and taught Perry how to fall and make it look real."

Still, within minutes of the first round, Torres was hurtled to the canvas with a single punch to the face. Williams looked alarmed and swung his head toward the ringside seats while waiting for Torres to sway back to his feet. In the second round, Williams went down as the crowd began to boo and chant "WWF! WWF!" The judges were so disturbed by the match, they withheld Williams's purse until the completion of an investigation into the fight.

But there was another shadowy figure in the Torres corner that night: a heavyset, raven-haired man swathed in an expensive suit. He did not say much, but when he spoke, he did so with a Brooklyn accent thick as concrete. His name was "Big Frankie" Manzione, and he had been introduced to Top Rank bigwigs as Torres's cousin from New York City.

The whispers around Las Vegas were that Big Frankie was a made guy in New York City's Genovese crime family, who was in town to sell stolen goods known as swag. Within weeks of his arrival, he opened a warehouse on an industrial strip stocked with mink coats, stolen cars, expensive motorcycles, and boxes of wholesale booze—a business he called "YGJ & Company." He traveled with a muscled, goateed driver named Ari, who wore a permanent scowl and acted as Big Frankie's muscle. Where Big Frankie went, Ari went. And each time either of the men handed out a card for YGJ & Company, they could not help but smirk.

Big Frankie was really an undercover New York City detective working with the FBI on Operation Matchbook. His driver was an FBI special agent. They had chosen the company's name carefully.

The acronym stood for "You're Going to Jail."

Big Frankie Manzione was no stranger to dangerous detective work as an undercover with the NYPD's Organized Crime Investigation Division. He was such an astute undercover that the FBI asked Police Commissioner Raymond Kelly if the agency could "borrow him" for Operation Matchbook. The investigation was going to be costly, and the Department of Justice wanted long-reaching results—namely, Arizona senator John McCain's goal of creating a federally controlled commission to oversee the entire sport. Big Frankie Manzione had proven himself to the FBI during a federal case dubbed "Steel Fences." Then, Big Frankie posed as the mobbed-up owner of a Virginia trucking company while collecting hundreds of hours of secretly recorded tapes against gangsters like Genovese capo Patsy Parello and high-earning soldier Carmine Russo. He even planned a payroll heist at the *New York Times* with the assistance of a *New York Post* driver.

As that case came to trial, Big Frankie testified without revealing his identity. Still, there were threats on his life. The government acted swiftly, moving the cop's entire family out of state. His father had to quit his job, his mother had to leave the house she loved, and his wife began praying every night that her husband would make it home from court alive. "Big Frankie was one of the best undercovers we had," said retired NYPD chief William Morange, who was in charge of the Organized Crime Investigation Division. "The guy was absolutely fearless." He was a perfect fit for Matchbook, and Police Commissioner Kelly was as passionate as Senator McCain in bringing drastic change to stem the bloodletting, both financially and in the ring. Kelly was once the New York State boxing commissioner and had heard countless stories about boxers who suffered brain damage by participating in mismatched bouts and fighters robbed blind by their handlers. Bribery was rampant, and fixed fights were the norm. "This is a sport full of danger," Kelly said. "The most legitimate thing you see in boxing is the heart and soul of the boxers."

Once the FBI tapped Big Frankie, the cop moved to Vegas and rented a posh apartment near the Strip. The FBI introduced him to Joey Torres for the first time at the pool in his complex, a hot spot for topless hookers and strippers who make the city their home. The two hit it off immediately. "It was like we really were cousins," Torres says.

It was relatively easy to spread rumors that Torres's "cousin" was a made guy from Red Hook—a hardscrabble Brooklyn neighborhood ironically made famous by the Marlon Brando boxing film *On the Waterfront*—who was tight with imprisoned Genovese family *capo dei capi* Vincent (The Chin) Gigante. The detective quickly became friendly with Top Rank executives, especially Sean Gibbons.

Together, the undercover cop and the boxing matchmaker hit the nightlife scene along the Las Vegas Strip, flashing knots of cash at posh restaurants like Charlie Palmer's Steakhouse and ultra-exclusive hot spots, including the Foundation Room atop Mandalay Bay, Nine at the Palms, and A. J.'s at the Hard Rock. Big Frankie threw his muscle around right down to the smallest of details. One night, Torres remembered, Big Frankie harangued his driver in front of a dozen people at Charlie Palmer's and sent him home to change his shoes because he didn't like the sound of them squeaking on the restaurant's floor. "That made everything more believable," Torres says. "Ari carried his suitcases and everything."

As Big Frankie's clout grew during the twenty-month undercover operation, so did the mounting evidence against the boxing industry. Big Frankie began traveling with Top Rank promoters, working ringside at major bouts all over the country as a company scout. The entire time he was wearing a "kel," cop parlance for hidden listening devices. "Everyone thought Frankie was God in Las Vegas. Frankie was hanging out with everyone," Torres said. "If the FBI didn't pull him out, he would have been the Godfather of Vegas. They thought he was the king."

Torres had a lot to do with Big Frankie being pulled out of Vegas. In September 2003, Los Angeles County deputy district attorney Pamela Froheich tracked down Torres's lawyer and said his client was expected at a court hearing that would likely send him back to prison immediately. "I remember I was sitting by the pool and Big Frankie came up to me and said, 'She fucked you, Joey. That bitch fucked you,'" Torres said. "I wasn't going back."

Sending Torres back to jail was an unusual move, considering his role as government informant. Historically, moles and criminal turncoats are given a free pass. Terrified of returning to prison, he jumped bail and fled to Costa Rica, which made the government's task of getting him off on murder charges nearly impossible. It would take months for investigators to catch Torres, and when they finally did, it was in the very place where he had tried to reinvent himself: Las Vegas.

By then, Torres had become a liability to the case, making unreasonable demands for money and relocation all while threatening to blow Big Frankie's cover to his pals at Top Rank. "He was like a Judas," said one investigator with direct knowledge of the case. "He was playing both sides, Top Rank against us."

Within weeks of Torres's return to prison, Operation Matchbook was detonated. In January of 2004, while seventy-three-year-old Bob Arum was vacationing in South Africa, FBI agents swarmed into the Las Vegas headquarters of Top Rank and began seizing evidence: computers, medical records, financial statements, and files on boxers. Days later, Sean Gibbons, then the company's top matchmaker, was fired. He has repeatedly denied any wrongdoing. As the case became public, Mitchell Rose, who knocked out the undefeated Eric "Butterbean" Esch at Madison Square Garden in 1995, began cooperating with the FBI. Rose told the author he was offered thousands by Top Rank officials to throw the fight, a claim the portly pugilist denied. Arum has repeatedly refused to talk about the case against his company. He issued a written statement after the FBI raid that said: "Top Rank has done nothing wrong. Top Rank does not know the scope of the government's investigation. Top Rank is cooperating with that investigation."

The investigation was expected to land dozens of boxing industry players behind bars by the end of 2011, but the Department of Justice pulled the plug. No celebrity boxers are expected to be listed on the pending indictments, and Arum is not expected to be charged. But it is likely that his company could be destroyed as some of his top management—including Bruce Trampler, the very man who brought Joey Torres in—face jail time. The case was described by one investigator this way: "There is a long laundry list of fights that are in question. There are hundreds of hours of tapes from Top Rank fights that are going to end the careers of more than a few people. The reputations of some big-name boxers are going to be ruined. It's a very detailed case."

Even if Arum does not join the ranks of celebrities in pinstripes, his reputation will become increasingly sullied. Investigators are quick to point to a statement Arum made more than a decade ago, when his career was blemished after admitting to making an improper payment to okay the famous George

Foreman and Axel Schulz bout in Atlantic City. "Yesterday I was lying," Arum said then. "Today I am telling the truth."

Torres, too, insists he is telling the truth. He is trying an old tactic to weasel his way out of prison, writing letters to the NYPD, FBI, federal prose-cutors, the media, and old pals, begging for help. This time, no one is listening. He has been labeled a rat by the investigators who used him in the case and by the people who helped him regain his freedom. "I used to ask Frankie all the time, 'How am I doing, champ?' He would say, 'Great, Joey. Great.' Everyone going to jail on this case are my friends," Torres says. "Why would I do that? So I can go right back to prison? I wanted to clean up boxing, and now I am going to do more time than a mass murderer."

And, so far, Torres has done just that. Time. Hard time, in fact. He has a plate in his head after another inmate—furious that he had stepped in to stop an assault on a female guard at a maximum-security prison in California—bludgeoned him with a metal pipe. He has been called a snitch and a rat, and has been shuttled from one prison wing to another to avoid retaliation. Gone are the long hours on a prison pay phone plying good will and cash from sports stars. The favors have dried up. The lies have ensnared him. His rough-and-tumble reputation followed Joey Torres around and helped catapult him, albeit briefly, back into the ring. But it was an old probation report written after his arrest on the murder charges that would become so ironic. The telling report quoted Torres's parents as saying he was a "skillful fabricator of stories who can weave fantasy and fiction together in a most convincing fashion."

ABOUT THE AUTHOR

MICHELE R. McPHEE is the bestselling author of *A Professor's Rage*; *A Mob Story*; *A Date with Death*; *Heartless*; and *When Evil Rules*. McPhee is an investigative reporter for ABC affiliate WCVB Newscenter 5 in Boston. The former award-winning police bureau chief for the *New York Daily News*, McPhee was also the courts and crime reporter for the *Boston Herald*. *A Date with Death* was the basis for a 2011 Lifetime television movie, *The Craigslist Killer*. McPhee's true-crime stories have appeared in more than a dozen national magazines, including *Maxim*, *Stuff*, *Cosmopolitan*, *New York*, *ESPN* *the Magazine*, *Gotham*, *Manhattan File*, and other international publications. She was the host of two Court TV *Mugshot* specials, and her reporting is also featured on the A&E television special *Crime Ink* and on the Discovery series *Rats*. Her journalism has taken her to crime scenes across the country and has made her a commentator on breaking news for CNN, MSNBC, and the Fox News Network. She lives in Boston, Massachusetts.

REFERENCE

Quoted material was obtained from interviews with the subjects conducted by the author.

Chapter 14

MURDER ON MINOR AVENUE

by Lee Lofland

Charity Ruppert's forty-one-year-old son, James, sat in his tiny upstairs bedroom, waiting patiently to set his plan in motion. It was a simple plan, actually. Kill everyone, including the children—all eight of them. There could be no survivors.

Closing his eyes, James went over the layout of the house, picturing where they'd be standing. Yes, killing them would be like shooting fish in a barrel, and he had exactly what he needed to get the job done—plenty of guns and plenty of ammunition. Easy money. The corners of his mouth slowly crept upward into a slight smile. In a couple of hours, his problems would be over.

Charity's oldest son, Leonard, his wife, Alma, and their eight children had gathered at her home around 4:00 p.m. to enjoy the remainder of a busy Easter Sunday. Leonard Ruppert worked at the General Electric office on Victory Parkway in nearby Cincinnati, so having the holiday weekend off to spend time with his family was a welcome change of pace.

Leonard and his family had already spent the bulk of the day with Alma's parents, where they'd stuffed themselves on a huge lunch. So, for dinner, they'd decided to have a light snack of sloppy joes and whatever else Charity managed to throw together. Before sitting down to eat, the younger children braved the cold March weather and spent an hour or so in the yard hunting for brightly colored Easter eggs. As usual, during that time of the year in the Buckeye State, the day was cloudy and the mercury never went above the thirties.

Inside, Charity Ruppert and her daughter-in-law, Alma, were hard at work preparing the evening snack. The house was warm, and the odor of frying meat, spicy tomato sauce, and hot bean soup filled the air. Leonard stood at the sink finishing a cup of coffee, chatting with three of his kids who were a bit "too grown" to hunt for eggs. The older children relaxed in the living room, just down the narrow hallway from the kitchen.

Upstairs, James listened to the sounds below. He heard the kids outside, their playful squeals plucking at his nerves. The smells emanating from the kitchen sickened him. And the mere thought that his brother and his wife received so much of his mother's attention and love filled him with rage. After all, why should his brother have it all?

James had thought about this day for a long time. He was out of work, with no real source of income. And his mother never let him forget it either, accusing him of being lazy. And that other accusation, the one about him being a homosexual, well, that one really pushed him to the edge. But it was the family's life insurance money that weighed on his mind the most. He wanted it bad. All $300,000 of it.

It was dinnertime when James heard the front door slam shut, a sign that the younger kids had finally come inside, bringing their annoying squeals and laughter with them. James took it as a sign to make his move, so he calmly gathered a few weapons and extra ammunition and began his descent down the stairs.

Once at the bottom, he turned and walked toward the sound of his brother's voice in the kitchen. Leonard saw James standing in the doorway and spoke to him, asking his younger brother about his car. Innocent babble to break the ice with his moody sibling. James responded to his brother's question by immediately shooting him to death. No hesitation. No brief thoughts of the "good old days." No moment of brotherly love. Nothing. Just a couple of rapid trigger pulls, and his brother was dead. Then James quickly fired a round at Alma and another at Charity, his own mother. When their bodies hit the floor, he quickly blasted a round, point-blank, into each of their skulls.

James then killed two of the kids in the kitchen in the same manner, first a round or two to drop them, and then one to the head to be sure they were dead.

The third child made a futile attempt to escape through the back door but was gunned down before she could reach the safety of outdoors. Her body came to rest backed up to a full-length mirror hanging beside a bathroom door in the narrow hallway. The grisly reflection clearly showed an exit wound in the little girl's back. It also doubled the appearance of the large pool of blood surrounding her head, oozing its way along the baseboard.

Charity Ruppert, the family matriarch, lay dead on the cold linoleum floor—her midsection a mangled mess. Her right hand rested above her right breast. The left stretched above her head, as if reaching for something just out of her grasp. Her slacks and dress shoes were painted in blood spatter. Her eyeglasses lay beside her on the floor, tangled in her wavy hair. The expression frozen on her face was one of surprise and disbelief. Her eyes stared blankly skyward.

Alma almost appeared to be sleeping, lying partially on her right side with her cheek against the cool floor. Her glasses were still in place. Her right leg was curled gently beneath her, and her left leg was extended straight to where her foot rested in one of her dead children's blood-matted hair. Her husband's face was a few inches away, in a puddle of their daughter's blood.

James reloaded his guns and calmly made his way to the living room, where he began firing at each of the five remaining kids, as if he were in a field taking target practice at a row of tin cans. And to be certain that no one but him would ever receive a dime of the insurance money, he walked around the crumpled bodies of the dying children and fired a single shot to each of their heads.

Standing in the center of the living room, James surveyed the aftermath of his actions. An overturned wastebasket with its contents—wadded papers and cigarette butts—scattered across the space. The corner of a *TV Guide* rested against the black tennis shoe of one of the dead boys. A caricature of Bea Arthur's face stared back at James from the cover of the magazine.

A child's Disney® book lay in the center of the carpet. Mickey Mouse's wide smile and trademark ears were out of place among the carnage. A little girl's body lay in a corner, her feet clad in black-and-white saddle oxfords, tangled in a heap of boxes that had once been stacked neatly against the wall. She'd apparently been trying to escape but had backed into the corner, trapped, where her uncle took aim and shot her. Her body fell to the floor, face-up beside a bouquet of fresh Easter flowers. Her head was a bloody mess.

Charity Ruppert's once neat-as-a-pin living room was now cluttered with the corpses of her precious grandchildren.

With his entire family now out of the way, James was ready for the final stage of his plan: to prove he was mentally incapable to stand trial for the murders, the only way that he could legally claim the inheritance.

James moved around the house, carefully positioning each of his guns on various pieces of furniture. Two revolvers on the coffee table and another on the arm of the couch, along with a box of bullets. A rifle beside the refrigerator, and four boxes of bullets as well as several loose rounds of ammunition on the kitchen table. Yes, everything was just right. Perfect, actually. Only a person not fit to stand trial would do what he'd just done.

It was time to call the police.

Bob Minor worked the 3:00 p.m. to 11:00 p.m. shift that Easter Sunday in 1975, assigned to work the Lindenwald beat alone, driving a typical Hamilton PD patrol vehicle, a station wagon that served double-duty as an ambulance.

At 9:15 p.m., the outside temperature was brisk and getting colder. And, like all patrol officers, Minor was certainly hoping to make it to the end of his shift without having to answer a lot of outdoor calls.

The night had been fairly quiet—no fights and no drunks to arrest, just the usual he-said-she-saids, when the radio in his patrol car crackled. It was 9:35 p.m. "A man's been shot at 635 Minor Avenue. Male caller is standing by at the residence. Another unit is en route to assist."

A left off Pleasant Avenue toward Lindenwald Park put the white shotgun-style house on Minor Avenue on his right. The house was well lit, and a man stood at the entrance behind an aluminum and glass storm door, waiting. Minor pulled his patrol car to the curb and switched off the ignition. When he stepped from the vehicle, he first looked at the man's hands. Empty. No weapons. Probably the caller, and probably another false alarm.

The officer was cautious, though, as he made his way up the short walkway, never taking his eyes off the man. But there was nothing alarming about him. In fact, he appeared to be quite timid—small stature, dress pants and shirt, large-rimmed glasses, and thick, wavy hair that was oily and in desperate need of washing. However, when Minor placed his foot on the bottom concrete step leading to the front door, the hairs on the back of his neck immediately stood on end. Something didn't feel right. He paused.

The wiry little man at the top of the three steps was extremely calm, with his lips split into an odd smile. He was too calm, actually. When Minor looked past the man into the brightly lit living room, he could not believe what he saw before him.

Several children lay dead, sprawled at various angles across the living-room floor. Plum-colored puddles of congealing blood, along with specks of human tissue and bone, marred the wall-to-wall area rug.

Officer Minor quickly handcuffed James Ruppert and turned him over to Officer Terry Roberts, who'd just arrived as backup. Roberts placed the suspected killer inside his cruiser and waited at the curb, guarding the prisoner while Bob Minor stepped inside the house.

Minor was no rookie. He'd been with the Hamilton Police Department for six years, and he'd seen his share of gruesome murders, but nothing could've prepared him for the next few hours of his life.

With his weapon drawn, Minor made his way through the living room. He stepped slowly around the dead children, taking care not to disturb the evidence. He had to be certain that James Ruppert, if he was indeed the killer, had acted alone. Satisfied that the first room, the stairwell, and the hall were clear, the officer headed slowly toward the rear of the house, hoping to find at least one survivor. But there were none.

In the kitchen, there were so many lifeless bodies that Officer Minor couldn't make his way inside without stepping on an arm, a leg, or a torso. More blood, two inches deep in some places, had begun to seep through the floorboards into the basement. Anxious for fresh air, and for some assistance, Minor went back through the house and out the front door, where he used his radio to call the shift commander, Lieutenant Sam Duley.

"I've got a bad one, here, Lieutenant. You need to come on down," Minor said.

The next hours were a blur. Officers hauling bodies out on cots, placing them in the back of their station wagons. Detectives in and out of the house. Lieutenant Duley was on the phone with police chief George McNally, briefing him on the current situation.

The Butler County coroner, Dr. Garrett Boone, had arrived and was busy supervising the removal of the bodies, including the remains of four-year-old John Ruppert. The little fellow, dressed in kid's corduroy pants, black sneakers, and a football-patterned knit shirt, reminded many of the officers that they, too, had children around the same age. But no one experienced the heartbreak more than former Hamilton police chief Simon Fluckiger, who had the unpleasant task of hauling the four-year-old's body to the morgue in the back of his station-wagon cruiser.

A collection of media trucks had parked along the curb, and the street and walkways were filled with people trying to get a glimpse inside the "Ruppert House," a name that would forever be attached to the dwelling.

Twenty years later, James Ruppert sat in his prison cell in Lima, Ohio, well into serving the two consecutive life sentences he'd received for his unimaginable crimes. He'd recently seen his sixty-second birthday come and go. His first parole hearing had also come and gone within the past year. Naturally, the parole board's denial had not come as a surprise to the man who'd shocked a nation by committing the largest family mass murder in the history of the United States. But even James Ruppert, one of the worst killers on record, couldn't imagine the horror that was about to occur again on Minor Avenue, almost directly across the street from where he'd murdered his entire family two decades earlier.

Tina Mott had never wanted to move to Hamilton, Ohio. But Hamilton was where the father of her baby, Tim Bradford, wanted to live. Besides, the couple really didn't have anywhere else to go. Neither of them were working full-time jobs, and, after all, Tim's parents, who lived in Hamilton, had offered to help out, especially since the young couple had a baby on the way.

Tim's mother was one of the reasons Tina was so apprehensive about the move to Ohio. She feared that Mrs. Bradford would take the baby away from her once the child was born. There was no basis for her fears, just an internal gnawing that wouldn't go away. Something just didn't feel right about Hamilton, and she didn't have good feelings about the Bradford family. Still, ignoring the advice of her best friends and her own instincts, Tina packed her belongings and moved with Tim to the mostly blue-collar city just outside of Cincinnati. She was so head-over-heels in love with Tim, she'd have followed him to the moon.

Tina should have listened to her friends and to her intuition.

Howard and Elizabeth Bradford, Tim's adoptive parents, had wanted children quite badly but weren't physically able to have them. Before Tim came along, they'd tried adopting the traditional way, but the state wouldn't approve their application because Howard was a construction worker who moved around a lot—a job that didn't offer much in the way of stability. So, with no other options available, the couple contacted a private individual to assist them with finding a newborn. It was through that person that they connected with a twenty-year-old drug addict from Tulsa, Oklahoma, who was about to give birth and would gladly give up the child to them or anyone else who wanted it.

The Bradfords were standing by in the hospital waiting room the night the woman delivered the baby boy. But there were problems. The infant came into the world malnourished, weighing a mere four pounds, thirteen ounces. His skull had not completely formed, and he was experiencing severe respiratory troubles. The baby's chances for survival were extremely slim.

The doctor left the delivery room to convey the devastating news to the waiting couple: the little boy they'd wanted and waited for so long was not expected to live through the night.

Minutes turned into hours, and hours turned into days. Doctors were amazed. Against all odds, the baby was slowly gaining strength. Then, one week later, the Bradfords were finally able to take their son, Tim, home with them to their modest home on Laurel Avenue in Hamilton.

Tim's childhood was a good one, and the Bradfords did all they could for him. Especially Howard, who'd always wanted a son. He and Tim were practically inseparable.

Howard taught the boy everything he knew about hunting, fishing, and camping. He even took little Tim along on outdoor survivalist adventures, like the wintertime trip to a remote area near Rifle, Colorado, where the boy first learned how to track (in the snow), hunt, skin, butcher, and cook wild deer on an open campfire. Tim was five years old at the time of the outing.

Howard taught Tim the importance of gun and knife safety, and he taught him how to live off the land. Survival was the name of the game, and

Howard was an expert. After all, he'd been a long-standing member of Living History, a group that educates the public about life in pioneer times.

Out of everything the group taught and had to offer, knives were the thing that caught Tim's fancy. He was good with them, and he kept one with or near him at all times. He could easily turn a block of scrap wood into a perfect replica of an eagle, a bear, or even a small statue of a Native American chief with a full headdress. His specialty, though, was making flutes from ordinary tree branches. The tone of Tim's handcrafted musical instruments was clear and pure, like something precision made in a factory. Yes, knives and carving were a big part of Tim's life.

However, in spite of all the love and attention from his parents, Tim still had his share of problems, feeling very much like an outsider, even in his own home. He was a mixed-race child living with white parents, and that was a situation that begged for teasing and bullying from the kids at Tim's school.

Determined to overcome the mockery, Tim set out on his own, answering a help-wanted ad to sell magazines and books with a company that employed a group of young people like himself. That's where he met a striking young woman from Buffalo, New York, named Tina Mott.

Certainly, Tim was drawn to Tina's good looks—her blonde shoulder-length hair, full lips, model's cheekbones, and nearly perfect smile. But Tina's bubbly personality is what most people noticed first. She was an absolute joy to be around.

Behind the wide smile and cheerful personality was a very unhappy young woman. Tina's childhood was, in fact, very traumatic. Her parents were divorced, and her mother spent quite a bit of time in a mental institution. And, according to neighbors, her natural father was a little on the quirky side. Proof of his eccentricities, they'd said, was that he kept goats in the family basement.

Tina's stepfather, Steven Mott, was charged with raping Tina when she was fourteen years old. He later pleaded guilty to reduced charges of sexual abuse and endangering the welfare of a child. He was sentenced to six months in prison.

After the rape, authorities separated Tina from her family. She spent the next few years moving from foster home to foster home. During her brief stay with one of her foster families, she was sexually assaulted again—this time by two boys who grabbed her and pulled her into a wooded area as she walked home from school one afternoon.

Afterward, the boys ran away, leaving her lying in the dirt and grass. When she was sure they wouldn't return, Tina got up, collected her things, and finished her walk home. She had become so accustomed to assaults that she'd begun to think of the attacks as a way of life, the way it was for all young women. She didn't report the incident with the two boys.

Tina and Tim had been together for only a short time when Tina learned she was pregnant. Realizing that a baby wouldn't fit into their current lifestyle, Tim suggested that they move in with his parents in Hamilton, Ohio. Tina reluctantly agreed, and the two headed to the Midwest.

Tim's parents were good to Tina, treating her like the daughter they never had. Still, it wasn't long before Tina felt like she was living in a foster home all over again with no privacy and having to abide by someone else's rules. So, when the baby was born, Tina put her foot down. She wanted a place of her own to raise their child.

Tim reluctantly agreed and began searching for an apartment. It wasn't long before he came home with the good news. He'd found a nice little upstairs unit in a duplex just a couple of blocks away, which meant they could have their privacy while still being close enough that the Bradfords could spend time with their new grandchild. Tim and Tina even hit it off with their new neighbors. Finally, life had dealt Tina Mott a new set of cards. For the first time in a very long time, she felt as if the world was smiling at her.

Things were going great for the couple until Tim started having trouble holding down a full-time job. He was unemployed and spent most of his days smoking pot, fishing, and using his knives to create his ornate wood carvings. Tim's carefree attitude toward bill paying and accountability placed the burden of supporting the family squarely on Tina's shoulders. It was a lot of pressure for someone who had already been through so much in such a brief time.

Tina's short-lived happy life soon morphed into the mundane. Every day was the same. She worked while Tim was busy getting high with his friends. He'd even started abusing the prescription drug Ritalin®. He'd grown his hair into long dreadlocks, and when he wasn't firing up a joint, he was puffing away on menthol cigarettes—another expense they couldn't afford on one salary.

Tina's life had begun to darken again, and she was regretting the move to Hamilton. She and Tim were arguing almost every day. She wished he would just help around the house instead of hanging out with his dope-smoking buddies all day, every day.

Tina was a dependable worker. She was always on time and never missed a day. Her coworkers said she was a responsible go-getter who would do anything for anyone. She was a beautiful girl with a beautiful smile and personality who never had a cross word for anybody.

It was a real shock to the Thriftway employees when Tina failed to show up for work on the morning of June 4, 1996. They were even more mystified when days and weeks passed, and she never returned to pick up her last two paychecks.

Seven days after Tina missed work, Elizabeth Bradford showed up at the Hamilton Police Department to report her common-law daughter-in-law as missing. Officer R. Horton took the report, and it was a story he'd heard many times. Tina had had a fight with her boyfriend, left home angry, and hadn't returned.

The next day, the Mott report made its way back to the detective division, where it was picked up by Detective Jim Nugent, a hardworking, tough-as-nails, old-school detective well known for his attention to detail and for his ability to solve murder cases with very little evidence.

On June 11, 1996, Detective Nugent sat at his desk reading the Mott missing-persons report. He made a few phone calls to the woman's friends and family in Buffalo. Nothing. No one had seen or heard from her in weeks, if not longer. And she'd disappeared without taking her child with her. Nugent had a feeling that something bad had happened to Tina.

Eight days later, Tina Mott was still missing. Not a sign of her anywhere.

She still hadn't called or gone by work to pick up her paychecks. Nugent called Mrs. Bradford. No, she hadn't heard from her. Yes, the baby was still with her. No, please don't tell my son that I've contacted the police. He has a very bad temper. *Really* bad.

On August 9, Detective Nugent decided to drop by the Bradford home unannounced. He spoke to Elizabeth Bradford and Tim. Tim said that on the day Tina left, they'd gone fishing at Linden Lake, near the sewage treatment plant, and, after returning home, they had played a game of Monopoly®. That's when the quarrel started. Things got out of hand, there was yelling and screaming, and she left. And that, Tim said, was the last time he'd seen her. He seemed quite calm.

However, Tim's statements weren't very convincing. The only thing Detective Nugent was convinced of was that Tim had something to do with Tina Mott's disappearance. So he started following Tim around town, watching him. Trying to make him nervous. Rattle his cage.

Nugent brought Tim Bradford to the police department a couple of times, hoping to hear a confession. But the young man had no intention of confessing to anything. He was as cool as a cucumber and stuck to his story about the argument and that Tina had gotten angry and left.

The detective kept digging into Tina's past. He spoke to officials with the traveling magazine sales company where Tim and Tina had met. He learned that Tina had once been struck by a vehicle while making door-to-door sales calls near Omaha, Nebraska. She was transported to an area hospital, where x-rays revealed that she'd suffered an injury to her skull. Nugent filed the appropriate paperwork and obtained the Nebraska hospital records.

Somehow he knew that Tim Bradford would slip up. He had to have left some evidence behind somewhere. All Detective Nugent had to do was find it. He also needed a little bit of luck to come his way.

On August 7, 1996, two twelve-year-old boys, T. J. DeJohn and his friend Tim Lyons, had been fishing all day in Linden Lake just five blocks from where Howard and Elizabeth Bradford lived on Laurel Avenue. Tina Mott was still missing, and Tim Bradford still lived around the corner from his parents in the small duplex apartment on Minor Avenue.

Having had no luck at any of their normal fishing spots, DeJohn and Lyons decided to make one last attempt before dark at catching one of the lake's monster catfish. They wanted to try a spot on the other side of the water, so they gathered their gear and made their way back to the apartment complex, fishing poles and tackle boxes in hand. They turned back toward the water at the crest of a long, grassy hill.

The boys kidded and joked until they reached the bottom of the slope, where they headed for a partially hidden passageway in the thick brush, the entrance to a well-worn footpath that meanders around the sandy edge of Linden Lake.

Linden Lake is a serene, secluded place where local kids often go to hang out, drink beer, and smoke cigarettes and pot. It's also private property surrounded by a six-foot-high chain-link fence. But the barrier had not succeeded in keeping anyone out. Vandals had cut access holes in the wire at a number of places around the perimeter.

The boys slipped through the small opening and followed the narrow path around the lake, in some places wading in almost knee-deep water. The area at the edge of the water was thick with undergrowth and darkened by a mass of tree canopies. Even though poison ivy and poison oak made up a large portion of the tangled groundcover, the trek had been worth it. They'd finally reached the best spot on the whole lake to fish.

They cast their weighted lines out as far as they could and waited for the "big one" to strike. After several minutes without even a nibble, the boys decided to call it quits and head home. Besides, it was nearly dark.

Lyons had wound his line about halfway in when he felt a sudden pull. He slowly reeled in the line, hoping not to lose what would have been the only catch of the day. When his "fish" finally broke the surface, disappointment quickly set in. He hadn't caught a fish after all. Instead, he'd dredged up what appeared to be an old Halloween decoration—a plastic skull.

Lyons pulled in the head and decided that it was an old, discarded Halloween ornament. DeJohn agreed and watched his friend toss the skull high up on the bank, away from the receding water. Then they headed out of the woods, retracing their earlier footsteps.

That night, the boys couldn't get the image of the skull out of their minds. Curiosity got the best of them, so they went back to the lake the next afternoon. They found the skull lying exactly where they'd left it. A full day of sunshine had dried it, giving it a bleached look. It looked even more genuine this time than it had before. No doubt about it. It was a real human head. Someone had been murdered.

Lyons went straight home and told his parents about their find. His mother immediately called the police.

Hamilton police officer Kevin Flannery was the officer who caught the call. Thinking this was probably going to be an unfounded call, he met the boys at the apartments, where they led him to their find. Officer Flannery looked at the skull for a second, picked up a small stone, and tossed it at the head.

"The cop was irritated. He really acted like a prick, like we had caused him a bunch of work or something," said Tim Lyons. "He just chucked a rock at it."

The rock struck with a clunk that didn't sound like it had hit plastic. Officer Flannery knew immediately that the skull was real.

Tim Lyons and his friend T. J. were soon forgotten in the frenzy of activity that had suddenly erupted around the lake. The news of finding a body, or even a piece of a body, brought every available cop to the scene.

Detectives summoned the local coroner's on-call investigator, Andy Willis. Willis, a brand-new investigator, was at home when the call came in. It was his first case. Thinking this could be a big deal, Willis called his boss, Butler County coroner Richard Burkhardt. He located the doctor at the New Miami High School, where he'd been conducting physicals for the football team. Dr. Burkhardt immediately postponed the remaining exams and headed for Linden Lake. Detectives also called the Butler County sheriff's office, asking for the assistance of its dive team. Cadaver dogs were quickly brought to the scene.

The search was on for the rest of the body.

Within twenty minutes of receiving the call, Detective Jim Nugent arrived at the scene. He spoke to Dr. Burkhardt, who said he thought the skull belonged to a female. He also pointed out that it had been stripped clean by the constantly moving waters and the wildlife in the lake. At first glance, Nugent figured dental records wouldn't help in this case, because the teeth were missing. In fact, the entire mandible was gone.

However, Dr. Burkhardt had noticed the presence of a couple of upper wisdom teeth that probably had not erupted prior to the time of death. They were slightly visible at this time because the soft tissue that normally surrounds them had either decomposed or had been eaten by scavengers. Nugent saw a little daylight at the end of the tunnel. He knew that scientists might be able to recover DNA from the molars.

Nugent watched the wet-suited divers break the surface one at a time, shaking their heads from side-to-side, indicating they'd not had any luck. Finally, when they reported that they'd found nothing of interest on the lake bottom—the water was simply too dark and murky—Nugent told them to pack it in and then called off the underwater search.

The cadaver dogs had come up short as well. There were no human remains in the water or in the area surrounding the lake. Gradually, all the searchers and other officers packed up their gear and left the area. Nugent remained behind, standing at the edge of the water, staring out at the lake and dredging up memories of police reports he'd read. Missing-persons cases. And one case in particular stood out above the rest.

He hadn't needed Dr. Burkhardt to tell him the skull belonged to a female. In fact, he was pretty sure he already knew the victim's name—Tina Mott. He also thought he knew the name of her killer—Timothy Allen Bradford. Now, all he had to do was prove it.

Nugent sought out Tim Bradford, asking him to come to the police station. There, he again questioned him about Tina's disappearance. Tim was again adamant that he didn't know anything about her whereabouts. Nugent told him about the skull, wanting to see Tim's reaction. Nothing.

So Detective Nugent started over, in case he'd missed something the first time around—questioning neighbors, friends, coworkers, Mrs. Bradford, Tina's New York friends, her mother, and anyone who might have come into contact with Tina. Again, he came up empty-handed. No one had heard a thing. And months passed.

In the meantime, Detective Nugent contacted forensic anthropologist Dr. Beth Murray from the College of Mount St. Joseph in Cincinnati to see if she could shed some light on the strange markings found on the skull. Dr. Murray agreed to help and quickly discovered several tool marks in the bone, including a large chop mark, possibly made by a hatchet.

Many of the other marks observed by Dr. Murray appeared to have been made by an instrument with a serrated edge, like the blade of a steak knife or something very similar. There was a great deal of fracturing around the tooth sockets, indicating that the teeth had been forcibly removed. In fact, when viewing the fractures from a right angle, Dr. Murray was able to clearly see the imprint of the ends of a pair of needle-nose pliers.

Dr. Murray was then firmly convinced that someone had killed this young woman and had attempted to hide the victim's identity by removing her teeth.

Armed with Dr. Murray's findings and a favorable comparison of the skull to the x-rays taken of Tina Mott during her hospital stay in Nebraska, Detective Nugent was able to secure a search warrant for the home of Tim Bradford. He also obtained a second warrant for a U-Haul® storage unit rented by Bradford.

Nugent and his team of detectives then raided both locations, simultaneously. At the house, officers searched the kitchen and seized a set of black-handled knives they found in a matching butcher block. They also seized a large meat cleaver. Investigators searching the U-Haul storage building recovered a cutlery set containing nineteen knives.

Detective Nugent was sure that he finally had the evidence he needed to tie Tim Bradford to the skull. But before he could make the arrest, he still needed to identify the skull and then positively tie the knives to the murder. He took the items to Dr. Murray's lab.

Dr. Murray sent core samples of the skull, two molars taken from it, and a blood sample from Tina and Tim's two-year-old son to LabCorp in Raleigh, North Carolina, for DNA testing.

A couple of months later, while vacationing in Florida, Dr. Murray received a call from Detective Nugent. It was the call she'd been anticipating, and she waited anxiously for the detective to read the LabCorp findings to her.

Nugent began to read. "No comparisons could be made between the tooth samples and the blood samples submitted. Nuclear DNA testing was also attempted on the tooth sample, however, insufficient DNA was recovered to yield reportable results through Polymerase Chain Reaction analysis.... However, the results were indicative of maternal relationship between the blood donor ... and the bone ... from the skull."

They had a match. The skull belonged to Tina Mott.

The DNA match meant that Detective Nugent finally had his killer. Tim Bradford did murder Tina Mott. And he'd tried to cover his tracks by removing her teeth and then tossing her head into Linden Lake. Where was the rest of her body?

Once again, Nugent brought Tim in for questioning. This time, faced with the overwhelming evidence against him, Tim agreed to tell everything, including where they could find the rest of Tina's body. But there was a catch. He'd tell them where they could find Tina's remains only if prosecutor Robin Piper would agree to his terms: no murder charge that would force him to serve a lengthy prison sentence with no hope of ever getting out.

Piper and Nugent both wanted Tina to have a proper burial, so, after giving the case a lot of thought, and, bothered by the fact that Tina's remains were lying out in some deserted location, Piper agreed to Bradford's terms. There would be no murder charge as long as Tim's information proved to be truthful and that he led them to Tina's remains. Instead, he'd plead guilty to voluntary manslaughter and abuse of a corpse. But first, a signed confession was needed.

Even though Tim had already reached a deal with the prosecutor, Nugent advised him of his rights, reading from a preprinted form. When he finished, he slid the paper across the table to Tim.

Bradford pulled the page closer, examining it for a second or two, and then scrawled his signature beside a small X. He pushed the paper away and leaned back in his chair.

Nugent pulled out a camera, telling Tim he needed a photograph for the record. The killer looked at the camera and cocked his head slightly to the left. The corners of his mouth turned up slightly, a tiny hint of a smile, just as the flash lit up the room. Was Tim Bradford proud of himself? Pleased that, in a way, he'd beaten the system and had literally gotten away with murder and could now sit face-to-face with a police detective and tell his story without fear of going to prison for the rest of his life?

After Detective Nugent returned the camera to his desk drawer, he said, "Tell me what happened, Tim."

"Tina Mott, who was my girlfriend and the mother of my child, had been fishing by the sewage treatment plant [the plant is adjacent to Linden Lake]," Tim said. "After we got home, Tina and I started arguing, like we did, a lot. It was about my friends, who she did not like, and that she wanted to go home, back to New York."

Tim then told about the two of them playing a game of Monopoly, that Tina continued to argue, and that at some point she ran toward him. Tim said he hit her on the nose, and she started to bleed, so she ran into the bathroom to clean up. When Tina returned, she was crying, and she immediately began to pack her clothes, saying she was going back to New York.

Tim was in the living room, picking up the scattered game pieces and putting away the fishing tackle. He'd just picked up a filleting knife to put it away when Tina suddenly came charging at him. As a reflex action, Tim said, he swung at her with the hand that held the knife. His judgment was off—Tina was closer to him that he realized, and the knife blade cut her. Tina fell to the floor.

"I really don't know what happened then. I just ran. I ran down to the park," Tim told Nugent. "After a little while, I came back. I don't remember how Tina got in the bathtub. She was dead. That night I had been doing Ritalin. I was on speed."

He claimed that all he could think about was that Tina was dead and that he would go to prison for the rest of his life. He was worried that he'd never see his son again. He knew he had to do something to keep from going to prison, so he grabbed the cutlery set. He also picked up a meat cleaver and hacksaw before walking into the bathroom.

Tim looked at Nugent and calmly said, "That's when I started taking her apart. I cut off her head, her arms, her hands, everything. I skinned her whole body while it was in the bathtub. Some of the skin and stuff I flushed down toilet."

Tim told of placing Tina's internal organs inside plastic garbage bags. Then he picked up Tina's head and started hacking it with the meat cleaver, trying to split it in half. When that was unsuccessful, he reached for a hacksaw and began sawing the longer limbs and bones into smaller, more manageable pieces.

"Oh, yeah," Tim said. "I know Tina was dead when I pulled her teeth because I'd already cut off her head. I used a pair of pliers to pull her teeth out. Then I put them in a bag with some of the other body parts."

He glanced down toward the floor. "All my life," he said, "I have wanted somebody to love, and with Tina I thought I had found that person."

A pause. Then he looked back to the detective. His voice returned to the strong, in-charge tone. "I skinned her body and put the skin mostly in the bag with other body parts. Then I put everything into a duffle bag and a backpack and walked to the sewage treatment plant. I put them in a field near a row of trees. Then I walked home."

Tim rubbed his face with both hands. "When I got back home, I found Tina's head still there. I carried it to the lake and threw it in along with the hacksaw, the pliers, and the filleting knife. Then I went home and started cleaning up, using bleach and ammonia. I threw away the clothes I had on when I cut up Tina. It was trash night, so the garbage was picked up the next day."

A pause. Tim crossed his arms in front of his chest. "I did not talk to anybody while I was doing this. I did everything myself."

Tim slumped back into the seat. He was done.

Detective Nugent and Dr. Murray were never able to recover all of Tina's remains. Due to the months of exposure to the elements and animal scavengers, many of them are lost forever. However, a memorial service was finally held for Tina Mott at the Greenwood Cemetery in Hamilton. Her remains were laid to rest inside a small cardboard box in grave number forty-nine of the Babyland section of the cemetery. The cost of her burial was $150, paid for by Elizabeth Bradford, the only person to attend the graveside service.

Detective Jim Nugent still visits Tina's gravesite, regularly placing flowers at the base of her small memorial stone.

When asked about the bizarre murders on Minor Avenue in Hamilton, Ohio, investigative medium Laine Crosby had this to say: "I remote viewed the inside of the house next door to the one with the brick front porch, the one where the man murdered his girlfriend. There may be a number of spirits there, maybe across the street? However, I see three very strong energies. One is a male in his late teens or twenties, and another is a girl about the same age.

"The other spirit is an older woman, and I see her watching from the main-floor kitchen in the back of the house. The older woman may have crossed over, and she may be there for the younger woman—to protect her and see if she can help her cross. The younger man and woman see each other, but I'm not sure if they know of the older woman."

Crosby had never been to Hamilton, nor was she given any background information about either of the cases. Interestingly, Charity Ruppert's body, the oldest female victim of her son's murderous rampage, was found lying on the kitchen floor. And the house directly next to Tina's former apartment does indeed have a large brick front porch.

Tina Mott's former neighbors say they sometimes see Tina late at night, passing by the windows of her old apartment. Tina's former landlord eventually moved into Tina's upstairs home. He says he still sees Tina or feels her presence in the apartment from time to time. But she moves on after he acknowledges her existence.

A former next-door neighbor said Tina once told her that she never liked living across the street from the "Ruppert House" because people had been murdered there. And the thought of being murdered gave her the creeps. . . .

ABOUT THE AUTHOR

LEE LOFLAND is the author of the bestselling book *Police Procedure and Investigation*, a 2008 Macavity Award nominee for best nonfiction mystery. He has written numerous articles for newspapers and magazines across the country, including the *Writer* magazine. He writes and edits the popular blog the *Graveyard Shift* and is the founder and host of the Writers' Police Academy. Lofland is a former police detective and nationally acclaimed expert on police procedure and crime-scene investigation, appearing on BBC Television and on national television and radio programs such as NPR's *Talk of the Nation*. He is a recipient of the esteemed Virginia Association of Chiefs of Police Award for Valor.

REFERENCES

Bradford, Timothy A. 1997. Quotations from signed confession dated August 14, at 4:10 p.m.

Lyons, Tim. 2002. "Skin of Her Teeth," *Forensic Files*. Season 2, episode 43. October 23.

Minor, Bob. 2011. E-mail correspondence with the author, July 2.

Nugent, James A. 2008. Interview in Butler County prosecutor's office. Hamilton, Ohio, June 16.

Piper, Robin N. 2008. Interview in Butler County prosecutor's office. Hamilton, Ohio, June 16.

Chapter 15

LOST INNOCENCE
The Murder of a Girl Scout
by Phyllis Gobbell

It happened in 1975, but Nashvillians still want to talk about it. I remember the evening Marcia Trimble disappeared. I helped with the search. I will never forget the day her body was found. The Marcia Trimble story is part of the fabric of Nashville.

The nine-year-old Girl Scout lived with her parents and brother on Copeland Drive in the area of the city known as Green Hills. Copeland was a quiet, attractive street with large trees, where most of the residents of the modest, red-brick houses knew each other. In neighborhoods like Marcia's, Nashville appeared much as it had in the sixties. The unrest in other cities and other parts of the world didn't seem to touch Copeland Drive. Marcia and her friends played outdoors, up and down the street, rode bikes, and returned home in the evenings when the streetlights came on.

Some of the mothers worked, like Virginia Trimble, who was a kindergarten teacher, but many of the women were stay-at-home moms. Marie Maxwell, mother of two small children, lived across the street from the Trimbles. Marie had ordered Girl Scout cookies from Marcia. On the bright, springlike afternoon of Tuesday, February 25, 1975, Marcia had delivered cookies with her friend March Egerton, who lived a few houses up and across from the Trimbles. Marie Maxwell and her children had gone to a birthday party, so Marcia came home without making her delivery.

At about 5:20 p.m. that afternoon, Marcia told her mother she was going back out to Mrs. Maxwell's.

"Put your coat on, honey," Virginia said.

"Oh, Mom, I won't need my coat," Marcia said. "I'll be right back."

But she never came back.

The search that followed, the discovery of Marcia's body, the murder investigation, and the conviction of her killer that finally came in 2009 have captivated Nashville as no other crime has done. In a way, Marcia Trimble belonged to the entire city. Even today, Nashvillians ponder how a thing like that could have happened in such a nice neighborhood, in that more innocent era. And they talk about all the lives that were damaged. And they talk about how the Marcia Trimble murder changed Nashville. It's a common saying now: Nashville lost its innocence, too.

Virginia Trimble went outside and began to call for Marcia, sometime between 5:45 and 6:00 p.m. The sun had set, and it was getting cold. February was like that in Nashville. Warm, sun-filled days brought a promise of spring, but it was still winter. Marcia had said she'd come right back, but she'd been gone about thirty minutes, and supper was ready. Her father, Charles, who was a salesman for an industrial supply company, was supposed to attend a meeting with the Boy Scouts that night.

Up the street, a group of boys were playing basketball in the Egertons' yard with March's older brother. Marcia's friends, the Harris girls, came by asking for Marcia. They hadn't seen her. Virginia spotted the family dogs, Popcorn and Princess, across the street. The dogs followed Marcia everywhere, so Virginia was concerned, seeing them without her daughter. The streetlights had come on. Virginia called some of the neighbors. She said she was worried because Marcia always came home at dark.

Since Marcia had said she was going to Mrs. Maxwell's house, Virginia's first call was to Marie Maxwell. Marie related the story that she would tell many times again in the years to follow. She'd arrived home at about 5:30 p.m., pulled to the back of her house, and was getting her baby out of the station wagon when she saw Marcia in Mrs. Howard's driveway. The Maxwells' driveway was separated from Mrs. Howard's driveway by a privet hedge, but Marie was sure she'd seen Marcia talking with two other individuals. She later described a taller figure and a shorter one. Marie told Virginia that she had gone inside to get her checkbook because she thought Marcia would be there soon with her cookies. "But she never came over," Marie said. "I think she went through Mrs. Howard's backyard, toward Estes."

Estes, a main road through Green Hills, ran parallel to Copeland Drive. The Thorpe family lived on Estes Road. Virginia called them, but they hadn't seen Marcia.

Charles Trimble went out in the car with his son, twelve-year-old Chuck, to look around the neighborhood. Virginia continued to make calls. Charles passed Geddes-Douglas Nursery on the corner of Hobbs and Estes, where landscapers were preparing for spring planting. Sometimes Marcia and her friends went to the nursery to buy soft drinks. He drove by Harpeth Hall, the prestigious school for girls. A few minutes later, he returned home. No sign of Marcia. It was as if she'd just vanished.

Charles and Virginia didn't know where else to look, who else to call, except the police. At 7:15 p.m., Charles called the home of their good friend, Metro Intelligence sergeant Sherman Nickens. Sergeant Nickens left for the Trimble house after making two calls: one to the police dispatcher, requesting a youth-guidance officer, and one to Sergeant R. C. Jackson in homicide. Nickens knew Marcia. He knew this was not a case of a runaway or a child who'd lost track of time.

That was Major George Currey's assessment as well. Currey, commander of youth guidance, came to the scene as soon as he received word about the missing child. He called in his lieutenant, sergeant, and others from youth guidance. Other divisions of the police and civil-defense workers arrived at the scene. "When a child was missing, all stops were pulled," Major Currey recalls. But no one could have imagined how this particular search would escalate. Cars lined Copeland Drive and adjacent streets. Neighbors and other volunteers joined the search. Two police helicopters shone spotlights into wooded areas and a nearby rock quarry. The television stations sent news teams, and reports of the missing child made the ten o'clock news. Searchers continued to arrive, bringing the number to more than two hundred before the night was over.

Police set up a command post in Charles and Virginia's bedroom. They tapped the phone line and installed their own line. If Marcia had been abducted, perhaps a ransom call would come soon. Virginia Trimble, a deeply religious woman and devout member of the Lord's Chapel, went into Marcia's bedroom and prayed. Friends from the interdenominational church came to offer their support. Youth-guidance officers worked the neighborhood, asking questions and answering calls that came in reporting sightings of Marcia. Excitement mounted with each call, but each led to a dead end.

Jeffrey Womack, a fifteen-year-old boy who also lived on Copeland, came to the Trimbles' house at about 9:45 p.m. He said he'd heard police were looking for him. His name had come up during interviews with the neighbors. When Marcia went to the Womack house that afternoon, Mrs. Womack was not there, and Jeffrey said he didn't have money to pay for the cookies. Virginia told the authorities that Marcia was expecting Jeffrey to bring the money. Detective Tommy Jacobs and Sergeant Jackson from homicide, along with the Trimbles' friend, Sergeant Nickens, interviewed Jeffrey in one of the bedrooms at the Trimble house. Jeffrey had long hair and "Fuck you" written on his shoes. Some neighbors who remember the teenager describe him as a "punk." He agreed to empty his pockets. He was carrying a five-dollar bill and some change, including a partial roll of pennies in a red wrapper and a package of condoms. Jeffrey said he hadn't seen Marcia since she came to his house to deliver cookies.

His mother also came to the Trimble house, arriving with Peggy Morgan. Peggy was a divorced woman in her early thirties who owned a daycare center on Copeland. Jeffrey, a student at Hillsboro High School, worked part-time for her. Peggy spoke up: "He couldn't have done it. He's been with me." Police found it odd that Peggy so quickly provided an alibi for Jeffrey, especially when they learned that she and Amy Norvell, another worker in her daycare center, had gone bowling that evening and left Jeffrey at Peggy's house with nine children.

Some of the officials who were part of the search that night have described the scene as chaotic and have pointed to the "turf wars" that were in place among the various police divisions. It is fair to say that everyone wanted to find Marcia, and they wanted to find her alive. Major Currey described the situation as "fairly controlled," but already it had the making of the most massive search Nashville would ever know. Searchers left millions of footprints in the ground that was soggy from recent rains. Given what we know today about working crime scenes, one can only imagine how evidence was compromised that night and during the days to follow.

As the clock ticked the minutes away and the night grew colder under a clear, moonlit sky, Marcia was still missing, and there were no viable leads.

The next morning, the missing nine-year-old Girl Scout dominated the Nashville news. Police, rescue workers, reporters, television cameras, volunteers, and spectators filled the yard and street around the Trimbles' house. Portable toilets had been set up on the lawn. As the day went on, more than one thousand people searched for Marcia. Search teams went out to remote areas, including Percy Priest Lake, east of Nashville, and the 2,500 acres of mostly wooded land in Edwin Warner and Percy Warner Parks. Joining the Davidson County Civil Defense were rescue squads from thirteen other counties. Each police division had its own command structure. Logistically, communication was difficult because the police department had no central database in 1975, but the spirit of cooperation among divisions did not improve as the search intensified. Later in the day, FBI agents appeared on the scene and began conducting their own interviews with the Trimble family and their neighbors.

Visitors to the Trimbles' house during the next few days included the wife of Governor Ray Blanton, Nashville mayor Beverly Briley, and the director of Metro Schools. Chief of Police Joe Casey, who had arrived early on and spent the next few days involved in the search, still hoped for a ransom call. If Marcia had been kidnapped, she might still be alive. A $30,000 reward was announced: $10,000 raised by the family; $10,000 offered by the evening newspaper, the *Nashville Banner*, through its "Secret Witness" program; and $10,000 offered by Governor Blanton on behalf of the state of Tennessee. A sorrowful and fatigued Charles Trimble made a public appeal that was published in the *Nashville Banner*. More than forty recruits from the police academy were brought to Copeland Drive on Friday to join the search that now extended to a thirty-mile radius. Reported sightings of Marcia led nowhere, and the week ended on a somber note.

A mix of rain and snow hindered the search on Saturday. For the first time, Virginia Trimble appeared on her front steps before a small crowd. She was composed, smiling a brave smile, as she quoted Marcia's favorite scripture. Her deep faith was encouraging to some, but to others who expected a more emotional reaction, her stoic demeanor was disturbing. Virginia became a controversial figure in the public eye.

On Sunday morning, the Trimbles attended church at the Lord's Chapel, where the congregation prayed for Marcia's safe return. Though officials insisted they were not giving up, police began moving their command post from the house. Civil Defense also moved its operations, taking its panel truck from the Trimbles' yard, now churned into mud. The streets around Copeland that had been blocked were opened, and spectators returned. The missing Girl Scout was still headline news.

The next week, two tracking dogs and their trainer, Tom McGinn, were flown in from Philadelphia to search the neighborhood. McGinn had trained the dogs that participated in the search for kidnapped heiress Patty Hearst. One of his German shepherds had helped to trace more than five hundred people. Though it had been more than a week since Marcia disappeared, hopes were high that the dogs would find her trail. The dogs sniffed through the streets around the Trimble house but showed no positive reading past Mrs. Howard's driveway, the last place Marcia was seen by Marie Maxwell.

Chief Casey told reporters, "The neighborhood holds the key." Neighbors were interviewed and reinterviewed and given polygraphs. At the top of the suspect list was Jeffrey Womack. Police had focused on Jeffrey since the night Marcia disappeared, February 25, when he'd showed up at the Trimble house. FBI agent Dick Knudsen sent a teletype to the FBI director on February 26, saying, "Metro PD has developed a possible suspect, Jeffrey Womack." Police held to the theory that Jeffrey was a good candidate for the taller individual Marie Maxwell had seen in Mrs. Howard's driveway, and Marcia's classmate and friend, March Egerton, was a good candidate for the shorter one. The Womacks had hired an attorney because, according to the newspapers, police were "leaning too heavily on the youth." Jeffrey passed two polygraphs. Still, police kept digging, trying to place him in Mrs. Howard's driveway.

Meanwhile, other crimes had occurred within five miles of Copeland Drive, but they were overshadowed by the search for Marcia. On February 2, a Vanderbilt University coed, daughter of a prominent Vanderbilt physician, had been murdered in her apartment near the campus. Sarah Des Prez's murder was the first in a series of vicious crimes that took place in February and

March. On February 16, on the nearby Belmont College campus, Judy Porter was brutally raped and robbed. The victim described a black man who repeatedly called her a "white bitch" and remained in her dorm room for an hour. Twenty-four-year-old Charlotte Shatzen was attacked by a black man in a dark overcoat outside her apartment on Fairfax Avenue in Hillsboro Village, an area bordering both the Vanderbilt and Belmont campuses. Charlotte fought, and the attacker ran away after slashing her neck three times, sending her to the hospital. The Shatzen attack occurred on February 23, two days before Marcia disappeared.

Around 2:00 a.m. on March 9, Dianna McMillan left her apartment on Acklen Park to drive her husband home from work. A black man in a dark overcoat accosted her outside the apartment, forced her to go inside, and raped and terrorized her, calling her a "white bitch," over and over. The attacker's luck ran out on March 12 when he tried to break in the Bransford House Apartments. Judy Ladd, whose boyfriend was a policeman, held his gun up to the window, showing the man in a stocking cap that Judy was not defenseless. She called police, and when they arrived at the apartment complex, they found the man breaking into the laundry room. The intruder was taken into custody.

A young detective named Diane Vaughn was assigned to the Sarah Des Prez murder case, then to the Porter and McMillan rape cases. In 1975, there were only a handful of female detectives in the Nashville Police Department. The "good ol' boys" dominated. But Detective Vaughn was smart, hardworking, and professional. When she learned that police had arrested a black man in a dark overcoat and stocking cap, her thoughts turned quickly to statements given by Judy Porter and Dianna McMillan. Her thorough police work uncovered incriminating evidence in the suspect's apartment—rings and other articles that Judy Porter had described. The suspect confessed to the Belmont rape and robbery, stating he was a messenger of the Nation of Islam who was ordered to do what he did. He said he was always looking for an unlocked door or open window.

The twenty-six-year-old man was Jerome Barrett, an angry Vietnam vet who had grown up in Memphis. A bare-fisted street fighter who clashed with police before and after his military service, he'd finally been convicted of several sex crimes. He served eighteen months in the main prison in Nashville before he was released in August 1974, just a few months before he went on his vicious crime spree.

Barrett was identified by Dianna McMillan and also by Charlotte Shatzen. He was charged in those cases, as well. It was a good day's work for Detective Vaughn, but she had not yet solved the murder of Sarah Des Prez. She requested that hair samples from Jerome Barrett be sent to the FBI lab to be used in the Des Prez case. The district attorney filed a motion, based on Vaughn's affidavit, but then the search for Marcia Trimble snowballed. Detective Vaughn joined the many other officers and detectives on the Marcia Trimble case. Jerome Barrett would eventually be convicted in the Judy Porter rape case and would serve twenty-six years in prison.

In 1990–91, Captain Mickey Miller and Lieutenant Tommy Jacobs, two detectives who followed the Marcia Trimble case for years, prepared a review of the investigation. The document stated, "It should be pointed out that there were no unsolved crimes of this nature around the time or area that Marcia was raped and killed. There was no indication of a multiple rapist loose on the community." But Jerome Barrett was, indeed, on the loose, committing brutal crimes, at the time Marcia was murdered.

In 2010, Demetria Kalodimos, news anchor at WSMV-Channel 4 in Nashville, was searching through the archives of the *Nashville Banner*. In the March 18, 1975, issue of the *Banner*, two stories ran on the same page. "Trimbles' Lives Go On, But. . . ." with photos of Marcia from the missing person's flyer appearing in the middle of the page. Above, accompanying the story, "Confessed Rapist-Robber Faces Four Counts," was a photo of Jerome Barrett. No one made a connection.

●

Easter Sunday, March 30, marked thirty-three days since Marcia's disappearance. The Thorpes on Estes Road had weekend guests, Marie's sisters, and their families. While some of the group were at church, Marie's brother-in-law, Harry Moffatt, from Memphis, went into a cluttered garage without doors behind the Thorpes' house to look for a boat motor. As he rummaged around in the junk of the outbuilding, Harry discovered the body of a girl in a blue-checked blouse, crumpled in the back left corner, partially concealed by a shower curtain and other items.

Harry rushed to the house and brought his brother-in-law back to the garage. "Please tell me that's not that girl's body over there in the corner," he said.

"I think it's a doll," his brother-in-law said.

But it was no doll. The girl in the blue-checked blouse was Marcia Trimble.

The Thorpes' garage was less than two hundred yards from the Trimbles' house.

Shockwaves reverberated throughout the city. A statement by Captain Mickey Miller best expressed what Marcia's death meant to Nashville: "In that moment, Nashville lost its innocence. Our city has never been, and never will be, the same again. Every man, woman, and child knew that if something that horrific could happen to that little girl, it could happen to anyone."

As Marcia's family grieved for their child, the Nashville Police Department was faced with grueling questions. Had the body been in the Thorpes' garage for the entire thirty-three days? Why wasn't she found during the extensive search? Had police simply bungled the case? Adding to the confusion, the state medical examiner, Dr. Jerry Francisco, first estimated that the time of death was sometime between March 20 and March 27, leaving police to try to explain where she had been before that time. At first, police said there was no evidence of sexual molestation. Marcia had been strangled, and robbery was considered a motive. The envelope that had contained money from her Girl Scout cookie sales was empty. Later, the medical examiner found traces of sperm. The newspapers reported that sex was now considered a motive.

By the time Dr. Francisco gave his official autopsy findings—setting the time of death at about the time Marcia disappeared, stating that her body had not been moved but had remained in the garage from that evening on, and reporting the presence of sperm on her body and clothing—many discounted his work. Police were under tremendous pressure to bring the investigation back on track and find Marcia's killer.

Lieutenant Tom Cathey, now in charge of the murder investigation, continued to echo earlier sentiments: the answer was in the neighborhood. The boys in the neighborhood were withholding vital information, and if pressed hard enough, they would provide the key to solve Marcia's murder. Jeffrey

Womack, represented by attorney John Hollins, wasn't talking to police. March Egerton's father, prominent writer John Egerton, had first cooperated with authorities in hopes of finding Marcia, but after her body was discovered, Egerton retained counsel and refused any further questioning of his son. Neighborhood residents were reinterviewed. Stories emerged involving neighborhood children playing what police referred to as "sex games." Marcia's murder and the investigation took a devastating toll on the neighborhood. Over the next few years, many of the residents would move away.

The suffering endured by Virginia and Charles Trimble over the loss of their child was exacerbated by rumors that targeted Virginia, accusations that she had killed Marcia. Angry callers on radio talk shows denounced her for the lack of feeling she displayed for her missing—and then murdered—child. She received threatening phone calls, even a bomb threat. Virginia turned more and more to spiritual consolation, as Charles turned to alcohol.

Police questioning focused largely on Jeffrey Womack. Amy Norvell, who had worked for Peggy Morgan in the daycare facility until they had a falling-out, revealed to police that thirty-two-year-old Peggy and fifteen-year-old Jeffrey were having an affair. Statements by some of the boys in the neighborhood contradicted Jeffrey's statement about his activities during the afternoon that Marcia disappeared. Police had no physical evidence to place Jeffrey at the scene of the crime, but they pointed out that he couldn't keep his stories straight. He'd had five dollars and change, including a partial roll of pennies, in his pockets the night he came to the Trimble house, but earlier he'd told Marcia he couldn't pay for the Girl Scout cookies. One of the neighbors had given Marcia a roll of pennies when she delivered the woman's cookies. At one point Jeffrey told police that Peggy Morgan had given him the money when he and Amy Norvell went to McDonald's to buy hamburgers for the daycare children, but Amy stated that Peggy had given *her* the money to pay at McDonald's. Most serious were statements from several classmates and coworkers, over the next months and years, that Jeffrey had admitted to killing Marcia. Jeffrey Womack did not do himself any good.

In the summer of 1979, an aggressive assistant district attorney, Pat Apel, believed he could finally convict the young man police had targeted for four and a half years. Jeffrey had dropped out of high school and worked at a series of low-paying jobs. Detective Terry McElroy went undercover at the Jolly Ox and became acquainted with Jeffrey, who was also employed at the popular restaurant. McElroy worked and socialized with Jeffrey for a few weeks and then filed his report: "It is my opinion after being on assignment and closely associated with Jeffrey Womack that he should be considered a prime suspect in the case." He listed several reasons: Jeffrey's attitude toward females; his "heavy use of drugs and liquor"; his unstable mental condition, including the desire to stay "high" all the time; the fact that he became nervous when Detective Tommy Jacobs showed up at the restaurant; and his mention of the "tarp" that had covered Marcia. Police went back to the shower curtain that had partially covered Marcia's body and discovered that it had paint on it. The paint was similar to paint in Peggy Morgan's house, where Jeffrey spent a lot of time, but still there was no definitive evidence connecting him to Marcia's death. Nevertheless, Assistant District Attorney Apel arranged for Jeffrey's arrest.

The arrest came in the middle of the night. Once again, the Trimble murder made the headline news. A hearing was set to determine whether Jeffrey should be tried as an adult or as a juvenile, since he was fifteen at the time of Marcia's murder. For months, the prosecution and defense battled, until the hearing finally occurred. What was supposed to be a preliminary hearing took on the overtones of a murder trial, with both sides showing their hands. In the end, the prosecution realized there was not enough evidence for a conviction, and the case against Jeffrey Womack was dropped.

A decade passed. Though police continued to believe in Jeffrey Womack's guilt, it appeared that the Marcia Trimble murder investigation was at a dead end.

In 1990, DNA analysis had come into the spotlight as an effective forensic tool. Detective Jacobs, who in 1976 had replaced Lt. Tom Cathey as lead detective in the Trimble case, and Captain Mickey Miller, commander of personal crimes of criminal investigation, decided to review the Marcia Trimble investigation in hopes of using DNA to at last find her killer. They began to round up the young men who had lived in Marcia's neighborhood in 1975. Locating them and obtaining DNA samples proved to be a formidable task. Many had left Nashville. Some of the children from the neighborhood had suffered psychological and mental problems, and a few were incarcerated.

Jeffrey Womack had remained under police scrutiny. Jacobs and Miller confronted Jeffrey at his place of work, a Burger King in Green Hills, and with grudging permission of his attorney, John Hollins, Jeffrey went to General Hospital where the doctor took three vials of blood and thirty hair samples. March Egerton, now living in Seattle, came home to Nashville in the fall, and police requested samples from him. The Egertons, angered by the way police had handled the investigation, were not eager to comply. In a dramatic scene that John Egerton described for the *Tennessean*, "carloads of police" came to the Egerton home and took March to General Hospital for blood and hair samples. The incident incited a new round of criticism of police tactics in the Trimble case. DNA from Jeffrey, March, and dozens of other young men was analyzed at the FBI lab in Washington and compared to hairs and fibers on Marcia's clothing. No match was found.

Throughout the 1990s, Nashville police continued to obtain and submit samples for comparison, using various labs across the country whose work represented advancing DNA technology. From 1990 to 1996, DNA analysis of approximately seventy young men who were boys in the Trimbles' neighborhood in 1975 yielded no matches. Detective Jacobs retired from the police force in 1996, but Captain Miller continued to search for a DNA match that would reveal Marcia's killer. The century came to an end without a resolution of the case. By 2004, police had submitted approximately one hundred DNA samples for analysis. Many Nashvillians believed the Trimble case would never be solved.

❦

Nashville's Cold Case Unit was established in 2002 as a unique team of investigators charged with working on old, unsolved homicide cases. During 2002 and 2003, the new squad solved nine cases. Detective Bill Pridemore and Sergeant Pat Postiglione worked together on several high-profile cold cases that resulted in convictions obtained by Deputy District Attorney Tom Thurman. Publicity about the cases always generated calls from family members of other victims, requesting that the Cold Case Unit take another look at a particular case.

In April 2007, Sergeant Postiglione set a large black three-ring binder on Detective Pridemore's office desk. It was the Sarah Des Prez file. Someone had called the unit about the case, which was now thirty-two years old. Pridemore and Postiglione decided it was time to take another look at the Vanderbilt coed's murder.

The two detectives drove to the Metro Property Room and found an old, dust-covered box with evidence from the Des Prez case, each piece packaged separately. Pridemore checked out the evidence and took it to his office. Over a period of time, he worked his way through each item, until one afternoon he came upon a court order dated March 26, 1975, based on an affidavit by Detective Diane Vaughn. She had requested that hair samples from Jerome Barrett be sent to the FBI lab. Pridemore also found a property receipt, listing Vaughn as the officer who deposited three articles of clothing that had belonged to Jerome Barrett. Detective Vaughn had died in the 1990s. She'd had a lead on Barrett in 1975. Pridemore wished he knew more about her investigation. He contacted the FBI lab in Washington, DC, asking about other evidence that Nashville police had submitted for testing and was disappointed to learn that records in the Des Prez case had been destroyed.

But Pridemore was not one to give up easily. When he came upon obstacles, he looked for other ways around them. Some of the evidence he'd obtained from the property room had never been examined for DNA. The crime occurred before the onset of DNA analysis. Pridemore took several items from the victim's bed, along with her blouse, to the Tennessee Bureau of Investigation (TBI) Lab to be tested for DNA evidence. "If positive, examine for possible profile," he requested.

The first breakthrough in the cold case occurred when the TBI was able to establish a profile from the evidence. The male contributor's DNA profile was added to the CODIS database, the FBI's DNA index system. A profile was like a fingerprint. The unknown male might eventually be identified—or might not. Pridemore's job now was to locate suspects and obtain DNA samples. Again, he immersed himself in the Des Prez files, looking for males who were connected with Sarah Des Prez.

A few weeks went by before Detective Pridemore received more news. TBI agents informed him that they had a CODIS match on the Des Prez case. Not only that, but the profile of the unknown perpetrator matched evidence in another unsolved case. Pridemore was stunned when he heard the name associated with Nashville's most infamous murder mystery: Marcia Trimble. He immediately shared the information with Postiglione, and then with

Deputy DA Tom Thurman and Captain Mickey Miller, who had followed the Trimble case for so many years. More than a decade of DNA testing, mostly targeting young men who'd lived in the Trimbles' neighborhood, had not resulted in finding the Girl Scout's killer. But DNA might be the key to the mystery after all.

The progress thus far indicated that Pridemore was on the right track to solve not just one but two cold cases. Continuing his work on the Des Prez case, he obtained DNA samples from some of the males he had identified from the Des Prez file and sent them to the TBI Lab. Jerome Barrett, one of the men on the list, was living in Memphis. Barrett had been paroled in 2002 after serving twenty-six years for the rape of Belmont College student Judy Porter. Pridemore discovered that Barrett's DNA was not in the CODIS database. Because he was sent to prison before 1996, he'd never been required to supply a DNA sample.

Detective Pridemore and Sergeant Postiglione went to Memphis to follow up on the person Diane Vaughn had been investigating in 1975. With the help of the Memphis police, they obtained a search warrant and located Jerome Barrett, now nearly sixty years old. Barrett read the search warrant. "That's not me," he said, but he did not protest when Detective Pridemore swabbed the inside of his cheek.

"If they don't match, you'll never see us again," Pridemore said.

The next day he submitted the DNA samples to the TBI Lab.

On October 30, 2007, six months after Pridemore had started reviewing the Des Prez file, he received a call asking him to come in for a meeting at the TBI headquarters. One of the agents met him and took him to a conference room adjacent to the TBI director's office. Pridemore had not expected to see the director, assistant director, and several agents around the conference table. He could feel the energy and anticipation in the room. It was in this setting that the TBI director reported a match between Jerome Barrett's DNA and the evidence from the Des Prez crime scene. Before Pridemore could respond to the exciting information, the director added: "We also have a match in another one of your unsolved murder cases." Jerome Barrett's DNA matched the evidence in the Marcia Trimble case,

Pridemore allowed himself to savor the news briefly before he began to think about what the next move would be. As word of the DNA match in both cases spread through the police department, many of the veteran detectives were skeptical. How could a black man have roamed in the Trimbles' neighborhood in 1975 without being noticed by one of the white neighbors? What was he doing in that part of town? Evidence connected him to attacks on college-age and young adult women in the area within five miles of Copeland Drive, but unlike those victims, Marcia Trimble had been just nine years old. Some of the detectives insisted that even if Barrett's DNA was at the crime scene, Jeffrey Womack was surely involved.

Pridemore and Postiglione transported Jerome Barrett from Memphis to the Criminal Justice Center in Nashville, and in November 2007, he was charged in the Sarah Des Prez murder. The media had been quick to pick up the scent and report that there was also a link to the Marcia Trimble case. Sergeant Postiglione told reporters that it was "routine for investigators to look at cases with similar circumstances," but the public wouldn't let it go. The Marcia Trimble murder came back into the city's consciousness. Blogs were posted in which Nashvillians recalled the massive search for Marcia and the horrible Easter Sunday that her body was found. The media reported that John Hollins, Jeffrey Womack's lawyer, had heard from reliable sources that Barrett's DNA matched evidence in the Trimble case. Nashvillians were anxious for an indictment in Marcia's murder, but months passed with no announcement.

Meanwhile, Detective Pridemore was reviewing every page of the Des Prez and Trimble files, reexamining evidence, and interviewing potential witnesses. His investigative work was essential to the process, to reinforce the DNA evidence. By the end of spring, Deputy District Attorney Thurman believed he had a body of evidence sufficient to convict Marcia's killer.

In June 2008, a grand jury handed down an indictment of Jerome Barrett in the Marcia Trimble homicide. Police had been accused of bungling the Trimble case in 1975. This time was different.

Detective Bill Pridemore had been planning for retirement for many months, even before he'd started reviewing the Des Prez case. The time came at the end of September 2008. He would continue to consult on the Des Prez and Trimble cases, but now that there was a shift from investigative work to preparation for trial, that responsibility fell on Deputy District Attorney Thurman. Thurman, known by his colleagues as "The Thurmanator," had spent twenty-five years prosecuting rape and murder cases. He had won a conviction in 2006 in a case where the body had never been found, a rare accomplishment. But until the discovery of Barrett's DNA, the oldest case in which the TBI had found a DNA match was from the early 1990s. Would DNA evidence from 1975 hold up in court? The burden was on Thurman's shoulders.

The Des Prez case went to trial in January 2009. The jurors came from Chattanooga, two hours southeast of Nashville. Barrett's lawyer had requested a change of venue, but Judge Steve Dozier had ordered that an out-of-town jury be brought to Nashville. One of the more dramatic moments of the trial occurred when a TBI agent testified about the DNA found in the victim's fingernail clippings. He said, "There was more of Barrett's DNA under Sarah Des Prez's fingernails than her own."

The jury was out just ninety minutes before finding Jerome Barrett guilty of first-degree murder. He was sentenced to life in prison.

Deputy District Attorney Thurman was gratified by the guilty verdict, demonstrating the strength of DNA evidence, but he recognized that the Marcia Trimble case, set to go to trial in July, presented its own challenges in regard to DNA. In the 1990s, as DNA technology advanced, slides made from vaginal swabs during the Trimble autopsy had been analyzed. The lab results came back reporting multiple profiles on the slides. Nashville police at that time had speculated that three or four males from the neighborhood must have been involved in a sexual encounter that "got out of hand." The explanation given by the medical examiner's office was that the multiple profiles had occurred due to "touch contamination." In 1975, before the advent of DNA testing, it was not standard practice for the medical examiner's staff to wear gloves, so those particular slides had been contaminated during the autopsy. Thurman knew the defense would use this issue to cast doubt in the jurors' minds about the validity of DNA testing, though other evidence had been analyzed using the strictest protocol.

Thurman recognized that in prosecuting the case that had once again caught Nashville in its grip, he must address the question: What was Jerome Barrett doing in the Trimbles' neighborhood? Geddes-Douglas, the tree and garden nursery once located at the corner of Hobbs and Estes, had employed parolees as day workers in 1975, but no records existed regarding those workers. There was no evidence that Barrett was connected with the nursery.

Thurman had another theory: Barrett might have been looking for Charlotte Shatzen, the young woman he had attacked two nights before Marcia's death. Her parents lived on Dorcas Drive. Their property backed up to the Trimbles' yard. Maybe Barrett had returned to Charlotte's apartment on Fairfax and found her name on the mailbox. He wouldn't have known she was in the hospital, recovering from the knife wounds he'd inflicted. Trying to find her, he could have wound up in the Copeland neighborhood because Charlotte's parents were the only Shatzens in the telephone directory.

In a preliminary hearing just days before the trial, Judge Dozier ruled that the state could not present its theory. "There's just no proof," Judge Dozier said. Another blow to Thurman's team came with the ruling that the prosecution could not bring in evidence from the other "bad acts" that might prejudice the jury.

Jury selection began on July 13, 2008. Barrett had not wanted another jury from Chattanooga. He believed he'd get a better outcome with a Nashville jury. Some from the pool of potential jurors admitted they could not be impartial, but after an intense two days, a jury was in place. The trial would begin on Wednesday. Ken Whitehouse from the *City Paper* wrote that "the sights and sounds, fears and suspicions of 1975 that changed how Nashvillians forever lived their lives will resonate once again."

Virginia Trimble was the state's first witness.

Many in the courtroom had followed Virginia's story. Some would remember her statement to reporters the week before Easter 1975. "It is a time of miracles," she'd said. "And who knows what may happen?" Her words, spoken with a serene smile, came back to haunt her after Marcia's body was discovered on Easter Sunday. Virginia and Charles had divorced in 1989, and Charles died shortly after. Often, on the date of February 25, the media would contact Virginia for a quote. Her strong religious beliefs had sustained her through sorrow and loss, but the mystery of Marcia's murder had remained a dark cloud for Virginia Trimble.

The year 2000 had seen a bright lining to the cloud. A *Tennessean* reporter named Frank Ritter did a feature on the Trimble murder, twenty-five years after it occurred. Virginia and Frank became friends, and a few years later, they married. They now lived in Kentucky, not far from Virginia's son, Chuck, and his family.

On the witness stand, Virginia related the events of the evening of February 25, 1975. At one point during her testimony she was asked to identify the blue-checked blouse, which she had not seen since Marcia left their kitchen to go across the street to Marie Maxwell's house. At first she was speechless. Then, as she'd always done in the face of shock and grief, she regained her composure. The defense could not do much with Virginia Trimble's heartfelt testimony.

Marie Maxwell, having seen Marcia in Mrs. Howard's driveway just moments before she vanished, had been interviewed more than twenty times over the years. Marie had also submitted to hypnosis, trying to help police with identification of the individuals she'd seen with Marcia. Police had used her statements to target Jeffrey Womack and March Egerton. But when Detective Bill Pridemore took on the cold case, he'd approached the facts without a bias toward the neighborhood boys. Now testifying in court, Marie admitted, "I've always been concerned about the reliability of my descriptions."

The state laid out its case, showing how carefully evidence was collected from the Thorpes' garage, how advancing technology had been used in the investigation, leading up to the connection with Jerome Barrett. One witness, an inmate from the Criminal Justice Center, testified that he'd heard Barrett admit to killing Marcia. But the prosecution's case relied heavily on DNA evidence, and Thurman had saved Jennifer Luttman, chief of the FBI's CODIS unit, as his last witness. Her testimony was lengthy and technical, though she described in a clear and precise manner how scientists had calculated the match between Jerome Barrett's DNA profile and the DNA in the stain on Marcia's blouse. Then she was asked the question "What can you say about the calculated probability of the match?"

She stated that the match was "rarer than one in six trillion." Given that "the world population is six to eight billion," she explained, "I, therefore, can say with a reasonable degree of science certainty that Jerome Barrett was the source of the DNA found in semen on Marcia Trimble's blouse."

With that definitive statement resonating in the courtroom, Deputy District Attorney Thurman rested his case.

Public defenders James McNamara and Laura Dykes presented the argument that the state could not reconcile all the facts in the case. In her opening statement, Dykes had asked a string of questions that she believed the prosecution would not be able to answer, and she had told the jury, "When you have heard all the evidence, you will have more questions than answers."

The jury deliberated Friday afternoon and through the evening. Recalling the jury's forty-five minutes of deliberation in the Des Prez case, reporters speculated that if the state had made its case, surely the jury would reach a decision at some point Friday night. But no announcement came. At 8:30 p.m., Judge Dozier sent them to their hotel. The media reported that the jurors looked "exhausted."

Late Saturday morning, the jury announced its verdict: Jerome Barrett was guilty of second-degree murder. Under 1975 law, the jury was allowed to set the sentence; this jury attached a sentence of forty-four years. In coming weeks, Judge Dozier would rule that the sentence should run consecutively to the life sentence set in the Des Prez case. There was virtually no chance Jerome Barrett would ever leave prison.

Following the verdict, the prosecutors, detectives, Virginia Trimble, and a host of her family and friends gathered for a press conference. It was a day that many in the room had imagined for thirty-four years. The long path to justice was complicated by twists and turns. Tom Thurman best expressed the public's sentiments when he said, "There were many victims in this case."

Virginia Trimble spoke into the microphone for nearly an hour. Clearly, her heart was full of memories but also full of gratitude to those who worked so diligently through the years to find her daughter's killer. In a poignant moment, Virginia said she would like to ask Jerome Barrett exactly what happened and exactly when it happened. "Was it when I was calling her to come to supper?" she said.

Barrett, who did not take the stand at his trial, is not likely to provide any further information about the events of February 25, 1975. People still wonder about the two individuals Marie Maxwell saw in Mrs. Howard's driveway. If Barrett was the taller of the two, who was the shorter one? Some are not satisfied with proposed explanations for Barrett's presence in the Trimbles' neighborhood. There are those who insist Marcia's body was not in the Thorpes' garage when they searched it. There are a few veteran detectives who still say Jeffrey Womack was involved somehow.

The questions that remain unanswered make for lively speculation but do not change the fact that justice has been served.

As the press conference was coming to an end, Virginia Trimble was asked if she had closure now. "I don't know about closure. I'm on the other side of pain," she said. "I can go to Marcia's grave and say, 'Now I know.'"

In that, there is some measure of comfort—for Marcia's family and for the city that will not forget the nine-year-old Girl Scout.

ABOUT THE AUTHOR

PHYLLIS GOBBELL coauthored *An Unfinished Canvas* with Michael Glasgow and *A Season of Darkness* with Douglas Jones. In addition, she has been published in literary journals and has received awards in both fiction and nonfiction, including Tennessee's Individual Artist Literary Award. Gobbell is an associate professor of English at Nashville State Community College, where she teaches creative writing and serves as editor of the college's literary journal.

REFERENCE

Quotations used by the author were obtained from a book she coauthored with Douglas Jones, *A Season of Darkness* (New York: Berkley Books, 2010), about the Marcia Trimble case.

Chapter 16

HERBERT BLITZSTEIN AND THE MICKEY MOUSE MAFIA

by Cathy Scott

T wo men, lying in wait for an aging gangster to return home, jump from the shadows with their guns drawn. "Why me?" a stunned Herbert Blitzstein asks as the gunmen surprise him in his own home. It is a moment of reckoning for sixty-two-year-old "Fat Herbie" Blitzstein.

His life flashed before him. And in the flick of a second, Herbie, once a feared Mob enforcer, was reduced to the little boy pressured to earn cash on the streets of Chicago so his family could eat. From the time he was five years old, people not only asked him for money; they depended on him for it. Even as a kid, Herbie knew how to make cash, hustling corner craps games with older boys and peddling fruits and vegetables to neighbors. He continued to earn big when he became a juice collector and bookie in the Windy City, then as a high-interest moneylender for *La Cosa Nostra*, and again as a fence for the infamous Hole in the Wall Gang's band of burglars in the Mojave Desert. Finally, he became an unexpected partner with Los Angeles's Mickey Mouse Mafia operatives.

Herbie's life had started out uneventful enough. He was born into the modest suburb of Lakeview—an area marked by overcrowded living quarters that was linked to other parts of the city by streetcars and elevated trains—a gateway community for new immigrants. Herbie, the youngest of three children, was born to poor Jewish immigrant parents, Samuel Blitzstein and Helen Holtzman. Herbie's father was from Russia, and his mother arrived in America from Poland. Most new immigrants were unskilled workers. They found work in steel mills, stockyards, and factories.

When Herbert was five, his father, who had found it increasingly difficult to support the family, abandoned them after he was unable to pick up a shift in nearby stockyards. It was devastating, emotionally and financially, for his mother, Helen. Blitzstein's father provided no support, and the family lived in abject poverty. Herbie's mother worked long hours for a leather company, sewing professional boxing gloves. It paid very little. The living conditions had a profound effect on Herbie, who once described his mother's wages as "pitiful." She took whatever sewing jobs she could for work at home, but that also paid very little.

To help cover the rent for the family's small cottage-style bungalow, Herbie at age five, soon after his father left, began working on a dairy route, helping deliver bottles door-to-door. It meant rising before dawn at 4:00 a.m. Then, on weekends and after school, Herbie made deliveries for the neighborhood fruit peddler.

The streets became a classroom for the impressionable young Herbie, who quickly learned survival techniques. He was evolving into a street-tough kid in 1930s Chicagoland. It wasn't long before Herbie graduated to collecting money from both the milk and produce deliveries, which served as yet another training ground for later in life, when he would become a juice collector for the Mob.

He was an above-average student at Von Steuben High, one of two senior high schools in the Albany area that Jewish kids attended. It was located on the Northwest Side, east of Cicero Avenue on the north branch of the Chicago River. But at sixteen, Herbie dropped out so he could work full-time for the Cook County morgue (a few years later, he would earn his diploma at night school). At the morgue, he helped the coroner's staff pick up bodies and take them either to the examiner's office or to their respective funeral homes. In those days, the deadhouse was located inside the Cook County Hospital at Polk and Lincoln Streets, close to his home. When other boys his age were starting to date girls and still playing kick-the-can on street corners, Herbie was picking up bodies for the coroner. While working his various jobs, Herbie graduated from playing corner craps to placing small-time bets that he later developed into heavy sports betting. He was always looking to make a big score.

Next, Herbie joined the army and was stationed at Fort Wayne, Indiana, until he was honorably discharged in 1961. He returned to Chicago.

Shortly after his release from the military, Herbie met Tony Spilotro.

"While they grew up in different neighborhoods in Chicago," a court profile of Blitzstein says, "Mr. Blitzstein had friends living in other areas and often was in the neighborhood in which Mr. Spilotro lived."

The same thing motivated both Herbie and Tony: they never wanted to be poor again. In actuality, Tony was grooming Herbie as a Mob associate. Herbie was rubbing elbows with wiseguys. From that point on, all he wanted was to be a mobster. Poverty had carved a deep mark in his psyche. He was determined to put that behind him. Herbie and Tony, a fellow high school dropout, became almost inseparable. They were at each other's homes nearly every day. Herbie was regularly invited to swimming parties at Tony's house.

Tony's parents, Pasquale and Antoinette, ran Antoinette's Restaurant at West Grand and North Ogden Avenues, where notorious mobsters like Paul Ricca, Sam Giancana, and Frank Nitti regularly dined. Tony and Herbie traveled together on vacation, they went to movies together, and they did "what friends do," the court profile says, palling around together. But their growing list of associates knew better. Wiseguys don't have best friends. They learn to trust no one. They do, however, count on each other. But it would not be until the two were partners in Las Vegas that they learned to trust each other. Beginning in those early days, Tony and Herbie had a business relationship.

Herbie's mother, worn out from the poverty in which the family had lived for so long, was naive about her son's increasing illegal activities after he returned from the service. For a few months, he lived at home. When she would ask Herbie where he was going, her son would tell her, "To see my friends, Ma."

"Be a good boy, Herbert," she would tell him, even though he was an adult by then.

"Don't worry, Ma," he'd answer and then head out the door.

What she did not know was that her youngest son was already a tough guy, one of the boys running numbers on the street.

While Herbie and Tony had a lot in common—they both grew up in inner-city Chicago—they also had disparate backgrounds. Tough Tony engaged in petty crimes, including shoplifting and purse snatching from elderly women, which landed Tony his first arrest for robbery at age sixteen.

Conversely, Herbie started out working legitimate part-time jobs and innocent craps games, gradually working up to bookmaking. Where Tony was the senior-high bully and a poor student at Steinmetz High on the far South Side of the city, Herbie had good grades and was well liked at Northwest Side's Von Steuben High.

But Herbie's formal induction into "The Outfit" was not through Tony. It instead happened when he met Moe Shapiro, a bookie who was connected to the Rush Street Group that hung out at the old North Side cabaret businesses. Moe's main hangout was the Playboy Club, a swank key club on East Walton Street where he took bets. It was also where Herbie and Moe partnered up.

Herbie, Moe, and their fellow gangsters were nicknamed the Jewish Mob because most of the bookies and gamblers in the group were Jews. By the late 1960s, Herbie became a top soldier—albeit an unmade one—for The Outfit. Herbie was partners with Moe, working for Sam Giancana. One of his first assignments for The Outfit was the shakedown of Myron and Phil's delicatessen in Lincolnwood. Herbie collected $500 a month from the owners.

"This guy testified in court that Herbie was the collector," said Blitzstein's long-time attorney, Gerald Werksman. "It shocked everybody, even me. I had no idea," he said, adding that he felt badly for the storeowners. "We all regularly ate at Myron and Phil's. They were nice people," he said.

Police reforms in the 1960s and subsequent federal law-enforcement activity—including the Operation Greylord probe—discouraged juice collecting or corrupt protection arrangements. Even though Herbie was fingered when a man testified against him, Blitzstein was never charged with strongarming the owners of Myron and Phil's.

Still, Herbie Blitzstein's early rise in Chicago came at the expense of others. In 1967, Arthur "Boodie" Cowan, a bookmaker and an associate of Blitzstein, was found dead in the trunk of his car with a bullet in his head. It was believed that Spilotro killed him because Cowan had been withholding street tax monies. Blitzstein took over Cowan's clients, as well as those of Henry Kushner, another bookie, after Kushner was sent to the federal pen. Blitzstein, who still lived on the far Northwest Side of Chicago, but now with his third wife, was one of the mobsters the FBI tested during the early days of the FBI's Top Hoodlum Program.

During Blitzstein's first years in the life, the FBI would not acknowledge that the Mob existed. The Top Hoodlum Program targeting mobsters first began in the 1950s when FBI director J. Edgar Hoover focused his investigations on Mafia and other gangland groups. The Top Hoodlum Program marked the first formation of organized crime squads in FBI bureaus across the country. Blitzstein was one of those tailed under Hoover's program. At that time, according to FBI reports, Herbie lived with his third wife on the far Northwest Side of town in the suburbs of Lincolnwood, ten miles from the city and just three miles from Myron and Phil's, where Herbie went each month to collect the Mob's share in exchange for protection. At the same time, he became a seasoned bookmaker. In Chicago, Herbie, nicknamed "The Buffalo," was considered one of the top Jewish bookmakers on the North Side.

"Joe Glickner, Mike Posner, Herbie and his partner Moe Shapiro, they were the top bookmakers at the time," said attorney Gerald Werksman. In Las Vegas, Herbie was the guy to see whenever anyone connected to the Mob was in town. He could put things together—meetings, deals, money, people. "Whatever they wanted, he could get it done," one Mob source said. "He didn't have to say it was for Tony. That was understood. The boys knew that Herbie would handle it."

The feds caught up with Herbie in the early 1970s. Before the US Attorney prosecuted him on illegal gambling charges, Herbie was pressured to turn on his associates. But Herbie never ratted anyone out. He was considered a stand-up guy and did not snitch out anyone, no matter how much law enforcement threatened him, no matter what deal they offered. Ultimately, a jury convicted the close-mouthed Herbie, and he went to the federal pen in Marion, Illinois. After Herbie's release from the pen, his Mob bosses moved him to the Mohave Desert to help oversee the casino skim with Tony Spilotro.

Blitzstein was a monster of a man with a gut and a goatee. Because of his ominous presence, Spilotro was rarely seen without him. Few people in Las Vegas, however, viewed Herbie as a brutal man. Instead, they described him as a "warm, stand-up guy" who shunned the gangster image. The police nicknamed him "Fat Herbie," a moniker Herbie despised. But before he teamed up with Spilotro, in Chicago Herbie was called "The Buffalo" when his Chicagoland partner was bookie Moe Shapiro. "Everybody called Herbie 'The Buffalo,'" Werksman said. "I called him 'Buff.' And we called Moe 'The Spider.'"

In Vegas, Tony, his brother John Spilotro, and Herbie ran the Gold Rush Jewelry Store, a front near the Las Vegas Strip for the Hole in the Wall Gang's burglary ring, so named because they punched holes through walls and ceilings to grab the loot and run. Blitzstein also worked as a fence for stolen goods at the Gold Rush's combination jewelry store and electronics factory.

On July 4, 1981, FBI agents caught Hole in the Wall Gang members red-handed in the act of committing a burglary. Blitzstein, in the meantime, was indicted along with Spilotro on federal racketeering charges. Before that, Herbie had spent several months in jail on contempt of court charges for failing to provide handwriting samples to a federal grand jury that was investigating Spilotro.

Spilotro and Blitzstein were prosecuted, but the court declared a mistrial after one of the jurors informed the judge that she had heard two fellow jurors discussing a bribe they'd been offered. Before the second trial could begin in mid-June of 1986, Spilotro and his brother Michael were beaten, buried alive, and left to die in an Indiana cornfield.

After Spilotro's death, Blitzstein still faced charges and a retrial. The prosecutor in the case described Blitzstein as "an important crime figure in Las Vegas." The charges included using counterfeit credit cards, receiving stolen government postage stamps, and income tax evasion. In 1987, instead of going to trial, he pleaded guilty to receiving stolen government property—postage stamps—and using counterfeit credit cards. In prison, the ravages of time, dietary problems, and illness took their toll, and Blitzstein's health deteriorated. He suffered from diabetes and a heart condition. In addition to two heart bypass surgeries, doctors removed several toes on Herbie's right foot. Herbie received an eight-year sentence but got an early medical release in 1991 after five years in a federal penitentiary near Oklahoma City.

After his release from the federal pen, Herbie returned to Las Vegas and the rackets. He had business and family ties in Vegas, plus his son and daughter-in-law were there, as was his on-again, off-again girlfriend Kathleen Delaney. For Herbie, it was home.

By 1991, however, new gaming laws and the death of the Spilotro brothers had diminished the Chicago Mob's control in the city, and Herbie had to start from scratch. He needed seed money to pick up where he had left off. He and Spilotro had been on good business terms with Benny Binion, owner of the Horseshoe Club downtown. Binion, who in the 1940s opened the Horseshoe Club in Las Vegas' Glitter Gulch, had always had a good relationship with the

Mob. Benny died in 1989 while Herbie was incarcerated, so after Herbie got out of prison, he reached out to Benny's youngest son, Ted, who had been running the Horseshoe with his brother Jack.

Ted continued his father's tradition of being friendly with Mafia members by fronting Herbie $200,000 for his loan-sharking business. Ted also authorized a cashier at the Horseshoe in 1995 to cash $11,500 in checks for Herbie.

But, unlike during Benny Binion's time, it was a different era, and the association with a known mobster hurt Ted's standing in the community and his business. Because he'd done favors for Herbie, the Nevada State Gaming Commission suspended Ted's license, citing as the reason that he hung out with "unsavory characters," namely, Herbie Blitzstein.

At a commission meeting, board member Steve DuCharme said of Binion's association with Blitzstein, "Every time we unroll a rock, we get some notorious creature stumbling out from under it." These were interesting statements from DuCharme, considering DuCharme had publicly admitted taking $800 in bribes from Blitzstein a decade earlier when DuCharme was an undercover officer for Las Vegas police. Even though the accusation was made, an investigation into the claim was never launched against Blitzstein allegedly bribing an official. DuCharme later said he turned in the money to the Las Vegas Metropolitan Police Department's evidence vault.

Ted Binion, who originally got his gaming license in 1964, worked the Horseshoe casino floor as his father Benny had—greeting big shots, dealing with troublemakers, and trying to keep everybody happy. But because of Ted's association with Herbie, Gaming Control Board members took away Ted's gaming license, which meant he could not be allowed to work at his family's casino.

In the meantime, Herbie had reestablished his large loan-shark business and some prostitution rackets. He had also gotten involved in a fraudulent auto insurance scam, which he operated with Joe DeLuca out of Any Auto Repair, selling phantom insurance to naive Americans who wanted to lead a high-roller lifestyle. By the mid-1990s, Blitzstein's rackets were earning him a more than decent living.

In the winter of 1996, Las Vegas resident Carmen Milano, the underboss of the crime family in Los Angeles, avoided what was to be a lengthy trial by pleading guilty to a federal racketeering charge. Milano was one of several named in a series of indictments stemming from the two-year investigation of organized crime in southern Nevada. Once in court on trial, Milano admitted to being part of a fraudulent diamond scheme in the winter of 1996 with Herbert Blitzstein.

A second defendant in the diamond scheme, then-sixty-three-year-old Dominic Spinale, who moved to Las Vegas in 1984, also pleaded guilty. Spinale, an aging mobster on the periphery who had served an earlier sentence for running an illegal gambling business, pleaded guilty to a conspiracy charge.

Spinale—who was added in 1994 to Nevada's Black Book of unsavory people forever barred from entering a Nevada casino—also admitted his participation in the diamond-fraud scheme with Blitzstein and others, as well as a separate plan involving auto insurance fraud. According to court records, those involved in the diamond scheme offered a genuine diamond for sale and then planned to switch it with a fake diamond. The conspirators attempted to defraud each potential victim out of around $36,000.

On January 7, 1997, DeLuca went to Blitzstein's home after Blitzstein failed to show up at work for a business appointment with attorney John Momot. Momot was at Any Auto to buy a car for his son. Finding Herbie slumped face-first into an easy chair, DeLuca called 911, saying to the dispatch operator that he thought Blitzstein had suffered a heart attack. Paramedics arrived and found that Blitzstein's heart had indeed stopped, but not because of heart failure. It was because of slugs in the back of Blitzstein's head, fired the night before.

"I went to work," DeLuca told the author in an interview a few days later, before his name surfaced as a suspect connected to the case. "Herbie didn't show up. That wasn't like him."

"I was worried about him," DeLuca continued, "so I drove to his house. I went inside and found him dead."

DeLuca acted innocent, but he knew better because he'd been part of the plan to take down Blitzstein. He'd known all along that Blitzstein was going to be killed and had helped plan Herbie's demise. DeLuca had provided the burglars and killers with the key to Blitzstein's house. When Blitzstein got home that night, the hit men greeted him.

"What'd I do?" Herbie had asked, staring at his assassins' guns with a genuine look of disbelief. They were the last words Herbie would ever utter. He got his answer soon enough.

Antone Davi and Richard Friedman, the two gunman hired by the gang planning to take over Blitzstein's rackets, had gone into Blitzstein's home that January 6 and, using the key provided by DeLuca, waited inside for six hours for Herbie to return home from dropping off his girlfriend Kathleen after dinner. They shot Herbie in the back of his head with a .22-caliber revolver and a .38 pistol. After the shooting, the pair emptied Herbie's floor safe of jewelry and cash, left the townhouse, and went to a nearby Outback Steakhouse® restaurant to eat a casual dinner.

On that cool January night, after Herbie's killers squeezed off three slugs, nearby FBI agents, tipped off that the hit against Blitzstein would happen, passively sat by. Herbie had been under investigation as well by the FBI because Los Angeles–area Mob informant and ex-convict Johnny Branco had named Herbie as running rackets in Las Vegas. Talk of the hit against Herbie was in the audiotapes handed over to the FBI by Branco, who had been wearing a wire.

His death marked the end of an era. Fat Herbie, a top lieutenant to Mob enforcer Tony "The Ant" Spilotro and a soldier and high earner for The Outfit for two decades, was executed gangland style in a contract killing in his own living room. Blitzstein had gotten a taste of his own medicine, the same kind he administered to others over the years. It was the risk of being one of the boys.

Blitzstein's death also marked the last Mob execution in Las Vegas. The front-page headlines blared, "Reputed Mobster Slain" and "Mob Figure Found Dead." His murder also prompted the premature and sudden end to a two-year undercover federal investigation, code-named Operation Thin Crust, a RICO (Racketeer Influenced and Corrupt Organizations Act) investigation.

Running simultaneously to Thin Crust was Operation Button Down, the FBI's long-term national campaign, which was originated to eliminate *La Cosa Nostra* as a significant crime factor in the United States. In Los Angeles, agents had the Milano crime family—commonly known as the Mickey Mouse Mafia—in their sights during the Thin Crust investigation. Because low-level Los Angeles–area Mob associates ended up suspects in Herbert Blitzstein's death, it forced the Southern California side of the probe to come to a screeching halt.

Operation Thin Crust took off in October 1995 after Anthony Angioletti, a convicted felon whom agents said had ties to New York's Genovese crime family, leased office space using FBI money at an industrial complex at

South Valley View Boulevard on the west side of Las Vegas. The location quickly turned it into a social club for local underworld associates.

In late 1995, Blitzstein met Joe DeLuca, a smalltime player, and they soon collaborated and opened the auto shop as a front for Herbie's street rackets. Herbie introduced Joe to Peter Caruso, who had ties to the Buffalo, Chicago, and Los Angeles crime families. The introduction turned out to be the beginning of the end for Fat Herbie.

In May 1996, Herbie arrived at Club Paradise, a topless joint he frequented with his friend Ted Binion, only to find that Peter Caruso and his associates were sitting in Herbie's favorite booth. So Herbie had a bouncer chase them out of the joint.

In the fall of that year, Caruso was able to convince DeLuca that Blitzstein was cheating him out of his share of the business. Caruso wanted to take over Blitzstein's lucrative business, which included loan-sharking and prostitution rackets. Caruso had not told DeLuca that he owed Blitzstein $50,000, which was a large part of Caruso's motivation for getting Blitzstein out of the way.

Then, in December 1996, the same Gaming Control Board that stripped Ted Binion of his gaming license because of his ties to Blitzstein recommended that Herbert Blitzstein's name be added to the infamous Black Book. Board members were unhappy with Herbie for befriending Ted, a casino part-owner, and wanted to put an end to the association between the two.

Blitzstein's name was to be added to the other twenty-seven underworld figures and casino cheaters already in the book at the time. The list was created in 1960 to protect the integrity of the casino industry. As Nevada Deputy Attorney General Charlotte Matanane told gaming agents, quoting the Illinois Crime Commission, Herbie was "a Mob enforcer" and "a juice collector," strong-arming people into paying high-interest loans. She also called Blitzstein a "notorious and unsavory" person who had associated with known mobsters Chris Patti, Frank Rosenthal, and Dominic Spinale (an Angelo family associate), all of whom were already included in the Black Book.

Nevada gaming board member Steve Duchamp, once a sergeant with the Las Vegas Police Department, said that Blitzstein, as a member of Spoleto's Hole in the Wall Gang of burglars, had not only corrupted Las Vegas police but had also "preyed on the people of Nevada." He commented that Herbie's life story "reads like a crime novel." Ted Binion admitted to commission members that he was with Herbie at least a dozen times in one year. The commission also confirmed that Ted had cashed insurance checks for Blitzstein totaling $11,000.

Herbie's nemesis, Tony Spilotro, had been included in the Black Book in the 1970s. So Herbie's question to the control board, through his attorney, was: Why now? If he was so God-awful, why hadn't they included him years earlier when Spilotro was added to the Black Book of unsavory characters? It's because Blitzstein would not testify against Ted Binion, and, some say, that gaming commission members punished Herbie by voting him into the Black Book in the autumn of his gangster career.

In March 1996, Herbert Blitzstein, sticking to his roots as a stand-up guy, refused to answer questions in a deposition with State Gaming Control Board's investigators about suspended Horseshoe Club executive Ted Binion.

"The scheme never was carried out, but there was the concept," Carmen Milano told US district judge Philip Pro. Milano, a disbarred attorney, also admitted laundering $50,000 worth of proceeds from food stamps. The case, while investigated along with the Blitzstein murder case, was independent of Blitzstein's murder. Still, Milano, the brother of reputed Los Angeles Mafia boss Peter Milano, was implicated in Blitzstein's death.

With Herbie Blitzstein cut off from the Chicago Mob, he was skating on thin ice with new associates both in his loan-sharking rackets and in the diamond scheme—and, most important, without the physical and financial protection he once enjoyed under the Chicago outfit. Unbeknownst to Blitzstein, newly transplanted low-level members of both the Southern California–based Mickey Mouse Mafia and the Buffalo crime family were eyeing his street interests with envy.

Another thing Blitzstein did not know was that his partner, Joe DeLuca, was working with Mickey Mouse Mafia associates, including Carmen Milano. Ultimately, the associate who sold Herbie out was DeLuca himself. A few days before the hit, DeLuca met with low-level Los Angeles Mob members Stephen Cino and Peter Vincent Caruso and alleged Buffalo mafioso Robert Panaro, as well as federal informant Johnny Branco, at a Denny's® restaurant outside Las Vegas. At the meeting, they divided Fat Herbie's assets and decided who would take what.

Some have said that the federal agents' delay in informing Blitzstein of the proposed contract on his life was due to an effort to cover up their own lack of action. Others say agents wanted to look for Herbie's "Shylock" book, which Blitzstein used to keep track of loans as well as payoffs. It included everybody from gamblers, to politicians, to bad cops. As Kenny "Kenji" Gallo, a mobster turned informant, said during an interview with the author after Herbie was shot, "No one saw anything? C'mon. They had Herbie under surveillance and they had him bugged. The feds saw and heard everything."

Ironically, at the same time, casino mogul Ted Binion had a hit on his head, put there by the very same thugs. When agents learned from both the bugs and informants of the contracts, they contacted Las Vegas police. Homicide detectives went to Ted's house and warned him he might be a target of a hit and that his life could be in danger. A few months later, a drive-by gunman, in a shooting reminiscent of Chicago in the reckless days of the 1920s, sprayed Ted Binion's home with bullets. After the drive-by happened, law enforcement advised Harry Claiborne, Ted's attorney, that Binion needed to get out of town until things cooled down. But later, federal agents, by their own admission, had not extended the same courtesy to Herbie Blitzstein.

By the time Las Vegas police arrived at the scene of the crime at Herbie's townhouse on Mt. Vernon Avenue, Blitzstein had been dead fourteen hours. Yellow police tape was placed around the house, cordoning it off to keep onlookers from walking on the scene. Lieutenant Wayne Petersen, who headed the homicide unit at the time, lifted the tape, walked under it, and headed to the front door of Blitzstein's home.

When a homicide lieutenant shows up at a scene, it is usually an indication of either an officer-involved shooting or a prominent Las Vegan dying a violent death. Petersen walked into the living room and saw a bullet hole in the back of the dead man's head. Herbie had fallen face-first onto his black leather easy chair. His arms draped the recliner, his pants pockets were turned inside out, and a spent shell casing rested next to his body. The safe on the floor of his bedroom closet was unlocked and empty.

Herbert Blitzstein's death came on the heels of a report two days earlier that the 207 homicides in the Las Vegas Valley in 1996 were up 38 percent from the year before. It was a bad killing streak.

At face value, Blitzstein's slaying appeared to be a clean whack job, a burglary interrupted. But this turned out to be no ordinary murder. It was an unauthorized Mafia contract. In other words, Louis Caruso, the capo with the Los Angeles–based Mickey Mouse Mafia, had not approved the hit. It was a gangland killing, to be sure, but not a sanctioned one, despite the feds later painting a picture of an approved rub out over a gangster turf war.

The execution-style murder stood out from other such killings in another way: FBI agents had not only been tipped off that Blitzstein was about to be killed; G-men had been in Herbie's subdivision—because they had his home under surveillance—at the time of his murder. No evidence has been revealed that they did anything to try to stop the murder, which goes against the FBI's sacred oath that saving a life is paramount over an investigation. "They had an obligation to tell Herbie there was a problem," said John Momot, another attorney for Herbie and a longtime friend, after he learned of the FBI's inaction.

The agency later publicly admitted the lapse after an inquiry was launched at the Department of Justice in Washington, DC. As a result, involved agents were either demoted or moved to other bureaus.

Louis Palazzo, Stephen Cino's defense attorney, questioned in open court the FBI's inaction. "Herbert Blitzstein was killed while FBI agents were basically outside his home surveiling his home, and the killing went on right underneath their noses and they did nothing to stop it."

Palazzo, during Cino's trial while cross-examining FBI special agent Charles Maurer, who'd worked undercover during Operation Thin Crust, reminded Maurer that FBI informant Anthony Angioletti had called the FBI the day Blitzstein was to be killed, expressing concern about Blitzstein's safety.

"What did the FBI do on January sixth to intervene, based on this notification from Mr. Angioletti?" Palazzo asked Maurer.

"We felt that nothing would happen [to Blitzstein]," Maurer answered.

As the record now stands, no one officially killed Herbert Blitzstein. Of the seven Mafia-connected men federal prosecutors claimed were involved in the plot to take down Blitzstein, four pleaded guilty in exchange for reduced sentences, one died in prison awaiting trial, and two went to trial and were acquitted. It was hardly a successful outcome for the prosecution.

With Herbert Blitzstein's murder, the last remaining link to the notorious Mob era in Sin City ended on January 6, 1997. "It's the end of an era for this town," John Momot told the author the day after Herbie's body was found. "Herbie was a gambler by trade. He was a gentleman, a very personable individual. We talked every day. You don't represent someone for almost twenty years and not have a close association.

"The best days," Momot continued, "were when they would all come into the office, Tony [Spilotro] and everybody. Tony would go and see [then Mob attorney] Oscar Goodman downstairs. Herbie would come in and see me. Then we'd all sit down together have a cup of coffee, and talk about the impending indictments. About that time, someone would pick up the phone and get some betting scores.

"Those were the good ol' days, in the late seventies and early eighties. That's when everything was happening."

ABOUT THE AUTHOR

CATHY SCOTT is a true-crime author and journalist who blogs for Forbes.com and writes for *Best Friends* magazine. Her work has appeared in *New York Times Magazine*, *New York Post*, *George*, *Christian Science Monitor*, *Los Angeles Times*, and Reuters news service, among others. Best known for penning *The Killing of Tupac Shakur* and *The Murder of Biggie Smalls*, Scott taught journalism at the University of Nevada–Las Vegas until she left to report on the largest animal rescue in US history in the aftermath of Hurricane Katrina. Her most recent television appearances include shows on Investigation Discovery, VH1 and A&E.

REFERENCE

Quotations used by the author were obtained through direct interviews with those quoted.

Chapter 17

DEADLY UNION

by Patricia Springer

"**D**enton 911, what is your emergency?"

"Yeah, it's Lozano. I need an emergency ambulance please."

The Denton, Texas, Police Department 911 operator immediately recognized Detective Bobby Lozano's voice.

"Okay, what's going on there?" She didn't know Bobby was on duty, but obviously he had run into something serious.

"3800 La Mancha, please hurry."

The address registered in the operator's mind. It was Bobby's home. A home he shared with his wife, son, and mother-in-law in an affluent section of the southern partition of the city.

"Okay, I've got it. What's the problem there?"

"Oh, God . . . my wife has a gun shot," Lozano said.

"She, she's been shot?" The operator stammered in disbelief. Bobby was one of their own. What could possibly have happened to his wife?

"Yes. Hurry," Lozano told her.

"Is she conscious?"

"3800 La Mancha," Lozano repeated without answering her question.

"They're getting on their way, but you need to tell me, is she conscious?"

"No. I don't think so," Lozano responded.

"Is she breathing?"

"I don't . . . let me go check."

"Okay, go check and come back to the phone."

Hearing the sound of the phone receiver being placed on a hard surface, the operator turned her attention to someone in the room with her.

"It's Bobby," she said. "Bobby Lozano's wife's been shot."

"I don't think so," Lozano told the operator when he returned.

"Okay, Bobby, hold on. I'm talking to the ambulance. Okay, they're coming."

"God, please hurry," Lozano urged. "I'm going to leave the phone. I'm going to go check on my baby."

"Okay, go check on the baby and come back."

Moments later, Lozano was back on the phone. "Hello."

"Is the baby okay?"

"He's fine."

"What happened?" The operated asked.

"I don't know. I don't know."

"Okay. The ambulance and police are on the way."

"God Almighty," Lozano said.

"Was it accidental, or what?"

"I'm going to leave the front door open, okay?"

"Okay. Did you just come home and find her?"

"I just came home," Lozano said.

"Okay. Is she breathing?"

"No."

"Okay."

"I'm going to get off the phone."

"Okay, go check on her and come back," the operator instructed.

"I don't think she's conscious," Lozano reported.

"Okay, is she breathing?"

"No, I don't believe so."

"Okay, can you get the phone in there where she is?"

"I am here with the phone."

"Okay, do you want me to tell you how to do CPR?"

"I'm going to do it right now," Lozano said. "I'm just going to set my baby down, okay?"

"Okay," The operator replied.

"Bye."

"Do you need me to tell you how or do you know?"

". . . the ambulance?"

"They're almost there. They're on the way. I don't know exactly where they are. Let me find out for you, hold on."

"Bobby?" The operator said.

The line was dead.

●

Detective Robert "Bobby" Cruz Lozano was a veteran of the Denton Police Department. He had been commended on his work and in the mid-1990s was one of the officers instrumental in taking down a large auto theft ring.

Lozano stood out from his fellow officers, as his desk was always orderly and his paperwork meticulously neat. Also uncharacteristic of other officers, Lozano often talked about clothing and articles on dressing he had read in magazines or seen on television, and he never arrived on duty without polished shoes and expensive clothing.

It was a joke around the station that one time, while chasing a stolen vehicle, Lozano had jumped from his car and run through mud to apprehend the suspect. Seeing Lozano in ankle-deep mud, the other officers teased him about ruining his $400 loafers.

It was also well known that Lozano was a ladies' man and that he considered himself a Latin lover. More than one female police department employee had been warned about his roving eye and the unlikelihood he would ever leave his wife.

Lozano and Victoria "Viki" Kaye Farish met when they both attended Denton High School. Lozano was small in stature but had big dreams.

Viki was Lozano's image of an ideal woman. Her blonde hair, gray eyes, and pale skin were a complementary contrast to his dark hair, darker eyes, and tanned complexion. Viki's father was a professor at the University of North Texas, and her mother, an accomplished pianist, taught music in their home. Lozano came from a working-class family of Mexican Americans.

Viki had suffered from depression while at Denton High and left to live with her grandparents in Arkansas and completed school there.

After returning to Denton, she and a friend stopped at a gas station to fill up when she saw Bobby Lozano. He had certainly changed since high school. He was muscular and buff.

"What have you been doing to yourself?" Viki asked.

"I've been working out at the gym."

"I'd like to work out; will you help me get started?"

And so began Viki's quest to lose weight and win Bobby Lozano.

After college, Viki began teaching at Hodge Elementary in Denton.

At Bobby's insistence, Viki was vigilant about her weight and disciplined about working out. "Bobby doesn't want me to get fat," she told fellow teachers.

He would even take his wife's lunch to school to make sure she ate a low-calorie meal. At one school function, coworkers had been appalled when Bobby had instructed Viki on just how many potato chips she could eat from her plate. He kept a constant eye on her weight.

Viki loved teaching, and the students loved her, but more than anything she wanted a child of her own. That didn't seem likely, since her husband was adamantly against having children.

"He doesn't want me to get fat," Viki told friends.

Although Bobby wasn't very happy to learn the news that, after fifteen years of marriage, they were going to be parents, Viki was ecstatic. Even with all Bobby's control over her and the constant rumors of his infidelity, Viki seemed more determined than ever to make the marriage work after the birth of their son, Monty.

●

Paramedics arrived at the Lozano house at 9:09 p.m. the night of July 6, 2002. From the audibly upset 911 operator, they knew a police officer's wife had been shot.

"CPR is in progress," the operator had told them.

Lozano met Brandon Galbreath, one of the first paramedics on the scene, at the front door while holding his child in his arms.

"Have you done CPR?" Galbreath asked.

"She's over there," Lozano replied without answering the question.

Galbreath made his way through the living room to the bedroom where Lozano indicated his wife was. As soon as he entered the bedroom, he saw Viki Lozano sprawled across the king-sized bed, blood covering her chest, and a gun by her side.

He immediately looked for signs of life: breathing, gurgling noises, but there were none. The lifeless form on the bed was stark white, her eyes eerily half-open.

He studied the body and concluded no CPR had been performed. There was a hole in her pajama top, but no blood was escaping. Galbreath carefully lifted Viki's body to look for the exit wound on her back. Lividity—a discoloration of the skin caused by the gravitation of blood—was present. The tissue appeared blue/red. Galbreath's eyes moved to the victim's right foot, which hung off the bed. Again, lividity could be seen.

Galbreath concluded that she had been dead for more than an hour. Blood had settled in her back and foot, so it hadn't been circulating for at least an hour.

"Are you going to do CPR?" Lozano asked.

"No, she's dead," Galbreath replied.

"Aren't you going to do CPR?" Lozano asked again.

By this time, La Mancha Street was crowded with ambulances and police cars. The flashing blue-and-red lights and the accompanying clamor of frantic voices had brought many of Lozano's neighbors out of their houses to see what was disturbing their normally quiet community.

Richard Godoy, Denton's police social worker, had received a text at his home from dispatch, telling him to go to 3800 La Mancha. He recognized the address instantly. When told there was a dead female on the scene, Godoy wondered if it was Viki or her mother.

Although a certified police officer, Godoy didn't serve in the normal capacity. As a trained counselor and the police department's family-services coordinator, he was routinely called out to crime scenes for the victims.

Godoy and Lozano had been friends since their years at the police academy. Lozano had even been Godoy's best man at his wedding.

As soon as he arrived, Godoy met with Sergeant Kramer and was briefed on the situation. He then asked the uniformed officer at the door where he could find Bobby.

"Bobby, what happened?" Godoy asked his old friend.

"I was gone for thirty minutes. When I came home I called out Viki's name, but there was no answer. I went to the bedroom and found her. I tried to revive her, but she was already dead."

Godoy studied his friend. Lozano seemed as polished as ever. No blood on his clothes. No sign of frantic distress. Perhaps he was in shock.

"What was your weekend like?" Godoy asked.

"We celebrated our wedding anniversary last night. Today we took Monty to the park. I took my gun out to clean it later, and then I went to tan," Lozano said.

Lozano's statement didn't seem odd to Godoy. Everyone in the department knew Bobby frequented the tanning salon and privately laughed about why he would do so when his skin was already a natural light-brown shade.

"Viki's always is tinkering with things. Maybe she was going to clean the gun while I was gone," Lozano said.

Godoy began calling Lozano's family, informing them there had been an accident. Within an hour, Lozano's relatives began to arrive. They appeared devastated by the news of Viki's death, cried, and asked what had happened.

It was a few hours after the initial 911 call when Viki's brother, David, showed up at the house. A pilot for Delta Airlines, he had to be located through the airline to inform him of the situation.

David and Viki's mother, Anna, was inconsolable as she wailed with grief.

"Bobby, what happened?" Anna asked after arriving at the house following dinner with friends.

"A gun shot. Viki's deceased."

"No! Not my Viki!" Anna sobbed. "How did it happen?"

"I'm sorry," Bobby replied. "It must have been an accident. The dogs must have jumped on the bed and set the gun off."

Since the first paramedic arrived on the scene until Anna Farish entered the house, Bobby Lozano had never mentioned their dogs.

Paramedics had to be summoned to look after Anna, and Lozano called Steve Plunket to minister to Anna's spiritual needs.

As Plunket handed Lozano a packet of information on local funeral homes, Lozano informed him that Viki wanted to be cremated and asked how to go about it.

For hours as crime-scene investigators gathered evidence, Viki Lozano's body lay on the bed she had shared with her husband. Finally, Viki's body, concealed in a body bag with a red blanket covering it, was placed on a gurney and rolled to a waiting vehicle.

"I want to see her," Lozano said.

"You can see her, but you can't touch her," the medical examiner said as he unzipped the bag to reveal Viki Lozano's face.

Lozano bent forward and in not more than a whisper said, "Take care," before walking away.

Godoy, standing close by, thought it was an odd thing to say. He again studied Lozano's behavior. As an officer and a counselor, Godoy knew police officers were trained to remain stoic at death scenes, but he considered Lozano's solemn show of grief to be forced rather than controlled.

Detective Lee Howell of the Denton Police Department arrived at the Lozano house and called in the Texas Rangers. It was standard procedure in an officer-related incident. Howell watched Lozano go in and out of the bedroom and found his demeanor to be more nervous than upset. Having known Lozano since the 1980s, and having seen him crying and upset when his father was hospitalized, he found Lozano's behavior during this incident inconsistent.

With Officer Rachael Fleming guarding the crime scene, Howell made note of the position of the body, a newspaper, a brown box with gun-cleaning tools, and a Glock® resting on the bed. He also noticed lividity in Viki's right foot.

Even before the body was removed, the crime scene unit was in to photograph, collect, and bag evidence. The first thing they had to do was find the spent shell casing. A casing can travel up to fifteen feet from the point of ejection. The team looked under the bed and on every inch of the bedroom floor, yet no casing was found.

Frustrated, they began removing items from the bed, layer by layer. The gun, drenched in oil, was picked up and checked to make certain it was safe before dropping it into an evidence bag.

The newspaper that had been spread on the bedcover—presumably to catch any oil from transferring onto the cover—was carefully lifted. Several kernels of popcorn were found on the bedding. Popcorn had also been found in Viki's mouth and on her pajamas before her body was taken away.

More questions came to mind. Why would someone be eating popcorn and cleaning a gun at the same time? It didn't make sense. Salt, corn kernels, and butter could be transferred to the weapon. There wasn't a popcorn bowl or sack on the bed or on the floor. Where was it?

The covers beneath the newspaper were wrinkled. With precision, the bedspread and sheet were slowly raised. There, under the covers, was a shiny object. The shell casing. Not on the floor. Not on top of the bed but under two layers of paper and cloth.

The crime scene just didn't add up. It was inconsistent with the way Lozano had described it.

Even with the inconsistencies in the crime scene and Lozano's uncharacteristic behavior, the police department made every effort to make things easy for their fellow officer and his family. They were allowed to stay in the house, and Lozano was allowed to go in and out of the bedroom.

Procedure would dictate that a gun-residue test be performed at the scene on both Viki and Bobby Lozano, but the only kit available at the scene was out of date. Rather than go to the station to secure another, police elected to forego the standard practice. After all, this was Detective Bobby Lozano, and his wife was dead in their bedroom. Why add to his agony?

Lozano didn't hesitate when he was asked to give a statement of the events leading up to the time he found his wife shot.

Lozano began with a long description of their July 5 anniversary dinner at a Dallas restaurant, complete with special wine for each of the four courses.

He continued by relating family events on the morning and afternoon of July 6. Lozano gave a detailed, almost flowery description of what he described as beautiful moments between him, his son, and his wife.

Lozano said that just after 7:00 p.m., he decided to play a computer game. After playing the game for an hour, he decided to clean his Glock 9-mm handgun.

"Viki and I had made plans to shoot my gun at the Denton PD firing range the following day. I had actually gone to shoot the weekend prior to this and had purchased several boxes of ammunition. Since I had several rounds left over from that particular purchase, I wanted to go out and shoot again," Lozano said.

"I went to the kitchen and grabbed a section of the day's newspaper. I unfolded the paper and laid it on the bed opposite where Viki was lying. I placed my gun cleaning box on the paper and then I removed my gun from my duty shoulder holster. I removed the fully loaded magazine from the gun and placed it atop the paper. I then removed the live round from the gun's chamber. I left the gun with its slide locked open.

"I asked Viki if she would mind if after I cleaned the gun I could go to tan. She offered to clean my gun while I went to tan so that we would have a little more time together when I returned. I told her not to worry about it, since it would take only a few moments to clean the gun. She again offered to do it for me and I told her to relax and watch whatever it was she was watching on TV."

Lozano claimed he left the house at about 8:30 that night, tanned for twenty minutes, then, as he was leaving, asked the attendant how his Fourth of July celebration had gone.

"When I returned home, which was approximately 9:00 p.m., I noticed Viki was lying somewhat awkwardly on the bed. She was facedown and slightly to the left of her left hip. I asked her if she was feeling ill and I received no response," Lozano said.

He stated that he asked her at least three times if she was okay, but she never answered. Lozano said he then noticed that the newspaper and the cleaning box had been moved from where he had left them.

"I raised her up and, as if it were in slow motion, her body fell backward onto the pillow nearest the metal headboard. I saw her tongue hanging from her mouth, and the color of her face was extremely pale. I looked down where she had been lying and noticed a lot of blood on the sheets. I grabbed her by her shoulders and screamed for her to respond. She remained completely lifeless as I repeatedly shook her hoping she would regain consciousness. When I saw the hole in the middle chest portion of her nightgown, I knew that she had been shot.

"I then thought only to run to the bedroom telephone to call 911. I screamed for an ambulance and shouted our home address, even during her attempt to verify what had happened. I begged her to have ambulance personnel come quickly," Lozano stated.

Lozano said he then ran to the bedroom to check on his son.

"When the dispatcher told me to begin CPR until the paramedics arrived, I ran back to Viki's side of the bed. I started to cross my left leg over her body for better leverage when massaging her chest and then began blowing in her mouth. Although I didn't straddle her body, I did begin CPR procedures from her side of the bed. I know I was failing to do it properly, because I was over-come with emotion. I begged her not to die and leave me alone."

As Lozano continued, he stated that when paramedics arrived, he asked them why they weren't working to revive his wife. He said when Officer Binkert offered his condolences and informed him that he would need a state-ment about what happened, he was in complete disbelief. He claimed Binkert later apologized, again offered his condolences, and pulled him to his chest and allowed him to cry.

"I asked only to see Viki once more before she was taken away on the gurney. When her face was revealed, I promised to always raise Monty how she would have wanted me to."

On page four of the single-spaced, typed statement, Lozano stated he believed Viki's untimely death was purely accidental, that she had been so happy and found great joy in the life of their child.

"She lived for him. Viki was not suicidal. She had no reason to be."

Lozano claimed Viki had suffered from depression after the death of her father from cancer. He said she was also ill the last several years of the marriage, suffering from long days of fatigue, listlessness, and an arthritic condition. Through it all, Monty remained the light of her life.

"She had everything to live for," Lozano concluded.

After reviewing Lozano's statement and comparing it to evidence at the scene, authorities found a number of discrepancies.

Lozano said he was gone from the home for thirty minutes, yet, due to the lividity on the body, which takes at least twenty to thirty minutes to appear, Viki had obviously been dead much longer.

Lozano had described his wife being facedown when he found her, but if she had been facedown, lividity would have been on her face, yet none was present.

Lozano claimed to have performed CPR on his wife, yet no blood was present on his clothes.

His fellow officers knew Lozano to be a person who was meticulous about his appearance. During a softball tournament, when the team had played six or eight games, he would go to the motel to shower and change while his teammates remained at the field in their dirty uniforms between games. To his coworkers, the idea of Lozano cleaning his service revolver on the bed didn't match up with the behavior of the Bobby Lozano they knew.

The more they delved into Viki's death, the more questions they had. The biggest question was: What was Lozano's motive? Then they talked to Cindy Waters.

Cindy Waters, an attractive blonde, was a police officer for the Denton Police Department along with Lozano.

Cindy had been warned by other officers that Lozano was a ladies' man, a regular Don Juan, they said. She was advised to stay away from him, that he would be nothing but trouble, but Cindy willingly entered into a relationship with Lozano, one that wasn't a secret from fellow officers.

"We worked out together," Cindy told detectives. "We became close. He told me both he and Viki had had affairs. He told me I'd changed him. I was different from the rest and he wanted to be with me. Bobby said he was getting a divorce."

Lozano knew Cindy's marriage was in trouble and her self-esteem low; he had offered to help her work out, lose weight, and gain back her self-confidence. He paid to have her hair colored his favorite honey blonde. He bought her a diamond and amethyst ring. He used Cindy's vulnerability to his advantage.

Cindy produced a number of love letters written to her by Lozano. The detectives rolled their eyes as they read the words on one of the computer-generated pages. A page that could have been easily adapted for any woman Lozano was seeing.

Cindy,

I came to the office this morning to be alone with my thoughts. Perhaps to reminisce about the few precious moments that you and I have recently shared. I have desperately attempted to define these emotions which have served to envelope my every awakened hour. And yet, even in slumber, have you consumed my dreams. What is it that you possess that has captured my mind, mesmerized my heart, and enraptured my soul? Few have caused my intoxication to such degree. I have prayed for strength to maintain the posture of fortitude. To exemplify decorous intentions . . . and suddenly, you appear before me. Breathless. Nervous. Impervious to my distractions. All of these do I become in the instant of a blink.

Desiring to slink behind you and wrap my arms around your waist. Pull you firmly against my torso as I gently kiss the back of your neck. And during the caress of a twirl, your eyes now facing mine, deduce the fibers of my entire being.

You've asked why the kiss has been so paramount. Through your own confession, it is the beginning of the end. An act sealing the embodiment of fate itself rendering you subservient to emotional peril. For me, it is peaceful sojourn. The banishment of all fears. A requiem for all of my dreams.

When the detective finished reading the letter, he stared at Cindy.

"He was going to leave Viki. We were going to be married," Cindy said softly.

She admitted that she had pressured Lozano to set a date to leave his wife. Lozano had told her he had been to an attorney and was ready to file, but she learned it was a lie. Each date Cindy had set for him to leave home had come and gone. Each ultimatum ignored. Finally, she told Lozano the affair was over.

"When was the last time you saw Bobby?" Detective Howell asked.

"The night before Viki died. He came over around 11:00 p.m. and stayed for about an hour. I knew he had taken Viki out for their anniversary and I told him it was over between us," Cindy said.

"When did you hear about Viki's death?"

"On the night she was shot. I received several text messages from fellow officers breaking the news," Cindy said.

Detective Howell thought about it. Lozano took his wife out to celebrate their anniversary, then left to go see his mistress. The next night, the wife's dead. Suspicion that had crept into the minds of detectives quickly spread over the police department like a fog in the wetlands.

Suddenly, Cindy Waters's affair with Lozano gave them both motive to see Viki dead.

On July 8, five days after Viki's death and three days after his initial statement to the Texas Rangers and Detective Bateman, Lozano asked to make a supplemental statement to clear up some things.

Concerning the night before the tragic incident at his home, Lozano said, "I indicated that my wife and I retired to our bedroom and soon fell asleep. That was incorrect. I did not mention that I had left the house later that morning, shortly after midnight. I had explained to Viki that I needed to return to my office to do some catch-up work. Although she was concerned that the hour was extremely late, I explained that it was better to do it then as opposed to later that same weekend. She requested that I not work too long since we had plans to take Monty to the park the following morning after he finished his breakfast. After I left, I drove to Cindy Waters' home. I stayed there for approximately two hours. Afterward, I returned directly home. I remained home until the following morning when Monty awoke. I did not include this detail in the original written statement, unwilling to reveal details of an affair which I had been having with her [Cindy]."

The seeds of doubt blossomed. Not only did Lozano's explanation of what happened at his house on July 6 not add up; he also admittedly lied to authorities about his whereabouts. What else had Bobby Lozano lied about?

During the investigation, police learned of other Lozano affairs, including one with a woman Lozano had met at the police station who had been accused of a crime. During Lozano's interview with her, the talk quickly and effortlessly turned to sex. Lozano threatened that he wouldn't have the charges dropped against her unless she had sex with him. She consented and spent five hours at the house he shared with his wife.

Two weeks later, Lozano told her he couldn't see her again because she was a convict and he was a detective. Lozano told her his wife had money and he would lose everything if he got divorced. He promised again to have the case dismissed if she never told anyone of their encounter. The case was never dismissed.

Another girlfriend of Lozano's was a rape victim he met at the police department. They began an affair, and she became pregnant but lost the child. She believed the affair ended because she had gained weight.

The third known affair authorities learned of involved a college student who clerked at a local hotel. She met Lozano when he was investigating a credit-card abuse case at the hotel, and they soon became sexually involved. She, too, became pregnant and agreed to abort. She miscarried before the procedure could be performed.

This young woman had been an education major at the local university, and Lozano had arranged for her to observe his wife's elementary class as part of her degree requirement. She was amazed at how different Viki was from the way Lozano had described her. As soon as she graduated, she left town to put distance between her and Lozano.

The last known affair Lozano had before connecting with Cindy Waters was with a temporary employee at the police department.

"He told me about numerous sexual encounters he had," the woman wrote in her statement to police. "He told me that he had cheated on his wife the day before they got married, and the day after they got married. He told me that there were times that he would rent a hotel room and he would have as many as three girls meet him there, one after another. He said he did it because he would get bored with relationships."

Like all the women he had been with, Lozano had written her poems and letters expressing his love for her. He told her his wife had leukemia and only had six months to live.

She, like the others, had gotten pregnant during the relationship. And, again, she was told she would have to abort the pregnancy.

"He would lay his head on my stomach and talk to the baby. He did this up to and on the night before we went to terminate the pregnancy," she told police.

Lozano had developed an ugly pattern. He preyed on vulnerable women, using his charm and authority to lure them in, and then threw them away as though they were nothing more than a disposable bottle.

Detectives Lee Howell and Jim Wawro and the two Texas Rangers called in on the case met with members of the Tarrant County medical examiner's office on July 24, eighteen days after Viki's death. They learned the gun had been six inches away from the midline of her chest when fired. They learned the bullet entered the chest at a forty-five-degree angle, right to left, with an exit wound low on her left side. A self-inflicted wound was possible, but it would have been an awkward shooting position, with the elbow pointing toward the ceiling. Viki's heart, left lung, stomach, liver, and spleen had been damaged.

There appeared to be fresh bruises on her nose, right arm, base of her thumb, lower right leg, and left thigh. A bruise on her forehead matched the slide of the gun.

Howell met with Viki's mother on August 1.

"Viki had never been happier than in the months since she had the baby. She knew how to clean the gun better than Lozano did and I believe she was cleaning the gun when one of the dogs jumped on the bed and caused the gun to go off," Anna Farish said.

Viki's mother expressed her concern for the ugly rumors she had been hearing about her son-in-law's possible arrest, and she blamed the department for starting them. Mrs. Farish stood steadfastly by Bobby Lozano.

Six months after the fatal shooting, Bobby Lozano, who had resigned from the Denton Police Department, was arrested and charged with the murder of his wife. A Denton County grand jury indicted the former police officer on evidence present by then district attorney Bruce Isaacks.

In a surprise move, a year and a half after the murder indictment, Isaacks asked the judge to dismiss the charges against Bobby Lozano, stating that two medical examiners determined that Viki Lozano had committed suicide.

Bobby Lozano had his life back. He continued to live with his mother-in-law and his son, Monty, in the expensive home on La Mancha, and he had a new love in his life. Lozano was seeing Monty's teacher, Renee Whitehead. He had begun a successful real-estate business and appeared to be back on top.

But tides turn and things change.

Bruce Isaacks was defeated in the next election by Denton attorney Paul Johnson, and a huge shift in procedure and personnel took place within the district attorney's office.

Denton police detectives continued to believe that Bobby Lozano had gotten away with murder, as did local newspaper reporter Donna Fielder.

Utilizing the Freedom of Information Act, Fielder gained access to investigative reports on the Lozano case and published an account of the incident in the *Denton Record-Chronicle*. Public opinion began to sway in favor of Lozano's guilt.

Detectives on the case were energized by the election of a new prosecutor and the pubic account of Viki Lozano's death. As they prepared the case a second time, they learned that both medical examiners cited by former DA Bruce Isaacks as determining Viki's death a suicide had denied those findings in sworn statements.

They presented their case against Lozano to DA Paul Johnson and his first assistant, Jamie Beck. They agreed to refile the case and take it before a grand jury. Police were happy to learn Lozano was indicted for murder a second time.

In July 2009, seven years after Viki Lozano's death, her husband was on trial for her murder. Two of the top assistant prosecutors on Johnson's staff had been assigned the case. Cary Piel, family-violence prosecutor, and his wife, Susan, head of misdemeanor prosecutions, were teamed to take on the task.

On the first day of his trial, Lozano walked into court looking as carefully put together as ever. The padding in the shoulders of his well-made suit jacket enhanced his five-foot-ten frame and average build. His naturally tanned skin caused members of the gallery to ask why he would have been tanning in the first place.

Seated to his right was his attorney, Rick Hagen, equally sharply dressed. Hagen, a former Professional Rodeo Cowboys Association bareback rider, was known to take the same competitive spirit he had in the arena into the courtroom and had been named one of the top Texas attorneys by *Texas Monthly* magazine.

Seated just behind Lozano was his new wife, Renee. The petite teacher had been sharing the house on La Mancha with Lozano for some time, but with the fast-approaching trial, they had made the union legal three months earlier.

Courthouse employees, local attorneys, Lozano's family, and a crew from *Dateline NBC* filled the courtroom, anxious for the testimony to begin.

The first witness called by Cary Piel was Cindy Waters. She explained her relationship with Lozano, the broken promises, the ultimatums. She told of the ostracizing she had received from fellow officers and the detriment her decision to be involved with Lozano had been to her career.

Another of Lozano's girlfriends followed Cindy, then a paramedic who had arrived at the house the night of the shooting, the police social worker Richard Godoy, and police officers who worked the scene.

Detective Lee Howell testified that the room where Viki's body was found looked staged. "There were spots of blood on her finger tips and on the sleeves of her pajamas, no gloves were found around the bed, yet no gunshot residue or oil had been detected on her hands. The way the covers were lying and the presence of transfer blood on the covers, all indicated staging," Howell said. "It just didn't make sense the way the newspaper was under the covers. She died quickly. Someone else had to have done it."

Cary Piel approached Howell and asked the detective what he thought of the statement Lozano had made at the police department.

"The time frame said he was gone for thirty minutes, travel time and tan time. That didn't fit the crime scene. Lividity takes longer. I believed he was present when she was shot."

The detective continued. "He described her as being face down and slightly on her left side and pale. If she was face down, you would expect lividity in the face, yet none was present. There was no blood on his clothes, none on the baby's clothes. Blood would have been present if he had performed CPR. And if he did do CPR, it was for a very short time, if compared to the 911 call.

"He said he put everything on the bed to clean the gun. He was always clean and pristine. Sometimes he didn't carry his holstered weapon because he wouldn't want to get anything on his clothes. Even during TAC ops [tactical operations] he was neat.

"After we got his statement we talked to Cindy. He had left his meeting with Cindy the night before Viki's death out of his initial statement. That concerned me. That was significant. That could show motive for homicide. It was a stressful situation, with a number of emotional responses," Howell concluded.

During the testimony of Dwight Crawford, an investigator with the medical examiner's office, Rick Hagen and Cary Piel played verbal volleyball concerning a report by Dr. Donahue of Cook County, Illinois, in which Dr. Donahue ruled Viki's death a suicide. Piel claimed there was no such report, and Hagen insisted there was.

Piel then asked Crawford, "Are you aware that Doctor Gary Sisler rendered the cause of death undetermined? And are you aware Doctor Periwani, the Tarrant County medical examiner, ruled the manner of death undetermined?"

"Yes."

"Has that changed?" Piel asked.

"No."

Rick Hagen asked if the victim's body being rolled by paramedics, if one or two legs were off the bed, or if dogs had been on the bed licking the body would change his opinion on the manner of death.

"Not necessarily," Crawford said.

The team of Piel and Piel were making headway.

Jim Willingham, a forensic computer analyst, was called to testify about Lozano's claim that he had played a computer game for about an hour before heading to the tanning salon.

Willingham stated there was no evidence on Lozano's home computer that he was playing a game between 7:00 p.m. and 8:00 p.m. on the night of his wife's death. In fact, the computer hadn't been used for any purpose during those hours.

Much of the testimony that followed pertained to the way in which the scene was processed, standard procedures for cleaning a weapon, and the impact of the bullet on the victim's body.

The jury learned the bullet hadn't penetrated the back of Viki's pajamas, which indicated that she had been lying down at the time the bullet penetrated her heart. Piel concluded that Viki had to have been lying down on the mattress at the time she was shot, not sitting up and cleaning the weapon, as her husband suggested.

A grapefruit can was introduced into evidence—a can that had been found next to Viki's left arm. The can contained blood transfer and had a human fingerprint on its bottom. Although the print couldn't be identified,

Piel stressed that someone would have had to move the can, since it was highly unlikely Viki would have been able to move it herself.

Texas Ranger Tracy Murphree testified that 99 percent of suicide firearm wounds are contact wounds, no more than three to six inches from the body, and usually up against the skin. In Viki Lozano's case, the gunshot was not a contact wound.

"The slide of the gun must be pulled back with some force," Murphree said. "If the gun fully cycled, a round would have been seeded properly and ready to fire again. If the victim was holding the gun at an angle, it would be difficult for the second round to get into the chamber. It would be hard on the wrist and could cause a malfunction of the next round. Also, if you're going to kill yourself, it's not consistent that you would clean the gun first," Murphree said.

"If the defendant was gone for thirty minutes and she didn't clean the gun until he was gone, in my opinion that doesn't match up with the lividity found on her foot," Murphree added.

Defense attorney Rick Hagen focused on the shell casing found in the bed. He insisted that in no report and in no photographs was it evident that the casing was found under the gun kit.

Cary Piel, a former Army Ranger and an expert in firearms, took the gun for demonstration purposes. "There was a round in the chamber when the gun was found. If there's a round in the chamber, can you stick in brushes?" Piel asked Murphree on redirect.

"No, it would hit the bullet. You would be able to tell if something was in the barrel," Murphree said.

"But no brushes were found around her," Piel said.

"The striker is separate from the firing pen and separate from the bullet. The Glock is a hammerless weapon with a plastic handle. The balance is different if a bullet is in the magazine. It has weight. The weight would feel different from an empty weapon," Murphree said.

Piel pointed out that Dr. DeMayo, a well-known medical examiner in San Antonio, claimed in his research that he had never seen a gun-cleaning accident that was truly an accident.

"If the scene was staged, what's wrong with the scene if it was made to look like a suicide?" Piel asked.

"The lack of a contact wound, the casing under the gun cleaning kit, and the newspaper on top of the blanket, on top of the blood," Murphree answered.

Hagen countered the argument, insisting that no one can really say what someone thinks before he or she takes his or her life.

"On a Glock, if a round is in the chamber and it is ejected first and then the magazine is released, it will fire, right?" Hagen asked.

"Yes."

The problem with Hagen's argument was that the magazine was found in the Glock on the bed beside Viki Lozano's body.

Dr. Gary Sisler, a Tarrant County medical examiner, took the stand to tell the court he had performed the autopsy on Viki Lozano's body. He noted there was no grease or oil found on the victim's hands, yet it had been reported that the gun was soaked in oil. Powder and tattooing were visible, which meant the weapon had been fired three to six inches away from the body. Sisler explained that that evidence indicated that the shot was not a contact wound, that the gun had not made contact with the skin.

Sisler also testified that lividity begins twenty to thirty minutes to two hours after death. The blood, in a fluid state, had leaked into Viki Lozano's soft tissue. He added that the contusions found on the body indicated that something had hit the skin; there were no cuts or skin perforations. Sisler insisted he had always been convinced the manner of death was undetermined. He had never suspected suicide.

The prosecution team called a number of witnesses to shore up their case. One was Patricia Eddings, a Tarrant County medical examiner's trace evidence examiner.

Eddings told jurors she examined Viki's body in the morgue as if it were a crime scene, photographing the body prior to autopsy. "There was a lot of blood on her body. I constantly had to change gloves. It appeared as if she had on make-up, but there were no tear tracks present," Eddings said.

The statement left many in the courtroom to speculate that if Viki had been depressed and contemplating suicide, wouldn't she have been crying?

The state called a number of teachers who knew Viki well. Each told of their friend's controlling husband and her deep love for her son.

The fifth day of trial was shaping up to be the most dramatic. The courtroom was filled to capacity. As soon as the bed frame and mattress were brought into court, it was evident it was Viki Lozano's actual deathbed. The foul odor of dried blood permeated the courtroom, and a number of jurors covered their mouths and noses in an attempt to block out the offensive smell.

The defense began by calling their expert medical investigator, Lawrence Renner. His testimony was intended to cast doubt on the prosecution's theory of the staging of the crime scene and the ability of someone to move after being shot.

Hagen asked Renner to step down from the witness stand and take evidence from a black plastic bag. After putting on latex gloves, Renner pulled a bloody sheet and mattress pad from the bag. Jurors wrinkled their noses as the offensive items were spread across the bed, and one young female juror sat farther back in her chair in an attempt to distance herself from the blood-stained material.

The jury was asked to step down from the jury box and make a semicircle at the end of the bed.

"I see lots of hairs," Renner stated, leaning over the bed. "Could be animal hair, some could be human."

Renner made the same remark as each bed linen was presented. The sheet, blanket, comforter, and pillow all contained both human and dog hair.

When one juror indicated she felt nauseous from the smell, Hagen sprayed air freshener in an attempt to block out the odor.

When asked about the collection of the shell casing, Renner stated he would have used a metal detector to help locate the spent shell casing, rather than remove items completely from the scene.

In a dramatic fashion, Hagen removed his suit coat, tucked his yellow tie into his white shirt, and lay across the bed. He rolled from one side to the other in an attempt to demonstrate how Viki's body could have been positioned by paramedics in the manner in which it was found. He claimed the brain keeps working after the shot and demonstrated by trying to get up after a fake shot to his heart.

"Her leg could have moved," Hagen said.

"The potential for homicide just isn't there. Their best physical evidence doesn't support it. There's no physical evidence Bobby was in that room," Renner said.

"If she was shot before he left he would have been in the room, right?" Piel asked sarcastically on indirect questioning.

Juror number four smiled and nodded.

Cary Piel climbed on the bed. "We agree. To be working on some object she would be sitting up."

"Unless on her elbow," Renner replied.

Piel began to demonstrate the position both the victim and the gun had to be in for the bullet to have entered her chest in the manner described in autopsy. He twisted his arm so that his elbow pointed to the ceiling and the barrel of the gun pointed toward his heart. An awkward position, to say the least, but his demonstration was clear. For Viki Lozano to have killed herself, she would have had to maneuver into a difficult position.

Piel then demonstrated the recoil of the weapon, had she held it in the position described.

Tracy Murphree was called in to assist Piel in his demonstration. Murphree stood over the bed and held the gun pointed at Piel.

"Is it consistent with the physical evidence that I have both hands up?" Piel asked.

"Possible."

"Yes or no, is it possible?"

"Yes."

Piel hoped the jury understood that if Viki Lozano's hands were up, it could explain the blood on her sleeves and the position of the body. And it would mean someone else had pulled the trigger.

On redirect, Hagen asked if muscle movement after the shot would have been possible.

"Muscle movement continues. You wouldn't expect them to do the minute waltz, but they can move," Renner said.

The final witness for the defense was Anna Farish, Viki's mother. She continued to live in the house she once shared with her daughter and son-in-law now shared with Bobby and Renee.

From the beginning, Anna Farish had supported Bobby Lozano and his assertion that he did not kill Viki. She claimed Viki and Bobby were extremely happy at the time of Viki's death and that their son was their greatest joy.

Anna testified that Viki had suffered from depression for years, even attempting to take her life at some point. Anna Farish discussed her daughter's weight problem since childhood and cast a most negative shadow on her daughter.

At that point, Sarah Roland, Hagen's associate, slipped a video into the player and pushed the play button for the tape to begin for the jury.

Bobby is seen bathing Monty as a small baby.

"Why's his belly so big?" Bobby asked someone offscreen. "He has a body like he's from Ethiopia. Look at that belly. We need to go jogging. Big ole' belly."

Members of the jury and gallery frowned. They had been hearing for days about Lozano's obsession with his wife's weight, as well as his girlfriend's weight. Now they saw it in relation to his son.

After a short time, jurors heard Lozano's voice on the tape again.

"Three months and seven days old, baby boy. Daddy. That is the only word you ever have to remember." The words hung in the air like a cold northern had swept through the courtroom. Was it some sort of sign that Monty's mother wouldn't be around forever?

Anna Farish stood beside the jury box but never looked at the video. The pain she felt was evident on her face, but those in the gallery wondered how she could continue to support the man many were convinced killed her daughter.

Bobby Lozano stood at the opposite end of the jury box. He remained expressionless as he watched his wife and son on the video.

Susan Piel questioned Farish for the state. She asked if she knew that Lozano was having an affair, if she knew he had rented an apartment and promised his mistress he was moving out, if she believed her son-in-law had taken the life of her daughter. To each of these questions Farish replied, "No."

Both the defense and the prosecution rested their cases. In closing arguments, Rick Hagen told the jury that the evidence was inconclusive and circumstantial. He reminded them the state's job was to prove guilt beyond a reasonable doubt.

"Not could be, probably be, but they had to prove his guilt beyond a reasonable doubt," Hagen said. "Despite how vile he is, the way he treated her for sixteen years, you are required to say innocent if they haven't proved their case beyond a reasonable doubt."

In contrast to the soft-spoken defense attorney, Cary Piel presented his closing arguments with passion.

"Do you realize how ludicrous it is to think that girl killed herself in that position? He shot her and murdered her. There's no reason to believe a dog made her shoot herself. He should have had blood all over him. He should have held that girl! He couldn't because he killed her.

"Maybe she'd had enough. Maybe she was on her way out. He would lose everything. The fancy home, the BMW® he bought after her death. He loves himself more than anything or anyone.

"My officers say it was staged and you know they're right. It's time for justice for Viki and for Monty," Piel concluded.

The case was now in the hands of the jury. After seven years of waiting, the case would finally be settled.

Upon reaching their verdict, the members of the jury filed in quietly, not looking at the defendant as they took their seats.

Bobby Lozano stood and listened as the judge read the verdict. Guilty. Lozano showed no emotion as the verdict was read. His wife appeared shocked. Before the former police officer was handcuffed and escorted from the courtroom, he leaned toward Renee and said, "Take care of Monty."

On August 3, 2009, Bobby Lozano stood before Judge Bruce McFarland and awaited sentencing. He was expressionless, as he had been throughout the trial, and remained so when Judge McFarland read the sentence handed down by the jury.

"Forty-five years."

Bobby Lozano is currently serving his sentence in the Daniel Unit of the Texas Department of Criminal Justice.

ABOUT THE AUTHOR

PATRICIA SPRINGER is the author of nine true-crime books. She has covered cases in Texas, Michigan, and Tennessee. She has appeared on numerous television broadcasts, including *Deadly Women*, *Forensic Files*, *Cold Case Files*, and *Geraldo*.

Patricia is the editor and reporter of a small newspaper in the north Texas area. She resides with her teacup poodle, Louie.

REFERENCES

Beck, Jamie. 2009. Personal interview with the author, August 6.

Bobby Lozano's statements to police provided by Susan Piel, August 17, 2009.

Bobby Lozano's love letters provided by Susan Piel, August 17, 2009.

Bond information obtained from sheriff records search.

Grossman, James. 2008. Personal interview with the author, August 17.

911 call transcript provided by Susan Piel, August 17, 2009.

Notes from author's attendance of Bobby Lozano's trial, Denton, Texas, July 24, 2009–August 3, 2009.

Piel, Cory, and Susan Piel. 2009. Personal interviews with the author, August 17.

ABOUT THE EDITOR

R. Barri Flowers is an independent literary criminologist and crime writer, with a bachelor of arts degree and a master of science degree in criminal justice from Michigan State University's renowned School of Criminal Justice. He is the author of more than sixty books, including the bestselling true-crime tale *The Sex Slave Murders: The True Story of Serial Killers Gerald and Charlene Gallego, Prostitution in the Digital Age: Selling Sex from the Suite to the Street*, and *Mass Murder in the Sky: The Bombing of Flight 629*.